THE LOCI COMMUNES OF
PHILIP MELANCHTHON

The inquiry of truth, which is the love-making or wooing of it; the knowledge of truth, which is the presence of it; and the belief in truth, which is the enjoying of it—is the sovereign good of human nature.
Bacon.

At Deum immortalem! Quod inventionis acumen! Quæ sermonis puritas et elegantia! Quanta reconditarum rerum memoria! Quam varia lectio! Quam verecundiæ regiæque prorsus indolis festivitas!
Erasmus about Melanchthon.

THE LOCI COMMUNES OF PHILIP MELANCHTHON

WITH A CRITICAL INTRODUCTION BY THE TRANSLATOR

CHARLES LEANDER HILL, S.T.M., Ph.D.

An ordained Elder of the A. M. E. Church,
Pastor of Bethel A. M. E. Church
Columbia, South Carolina

AND A SPECIAL INTRODUCTION BY
DEAN E. E. FLACK, S.T.M., Th.D., D.D.
Hamma Divinity School

Wipf & Stock
PUBLISHERS
Eugene, Oregon

Wipf and Stock Publishers
199 W 8th Ave, Suite 3
Eugene, OR 97401

The Loci Communes of Philip Melanchthon
with a critical introduction by the translator
By Melanchthon, Philip
ISBN 13: 978-1-55635-445-8
ISBN 10: 1-55635-445-2
Publication date 5/1/2007
Previously published by Meador, 1944

Hunc Librum
Suis Parentibus Obitis
Auctoribus Omnes res quascumque
Perfecit
Carolus Leander Hill
Dedicavit

PREFACE

I take great pleasure in introducing to English speaking people, and even in warmly recommending to them, this priceless piece of Reformation writing by way of translation. If such a task could fairly be construed into a subscribing to all of its sentiments, or a blind admiration for its author, I should have shrunk from such an attempt, regarding it as a piece of presumption and gross vanity. But the being exposed to such imputations would not have deterred me from this undertaking. For I have the interest of my fellowmen at heart, and sincerely hope that this book may contribute to extend the circulation of a work which discusses the most important themes with rare ability, and whose author is not adequately known, due to the fact that the Latin tongue in which his works lie buried, far removed from the eye of the average individual, presents an insurmountable difficulty to many persons who otherwise might be vitally interested in things Melanchthonian.

The topics which the "Loci Communes" of Melanchthon discusses are at once the sublimest and purest reflections of divine science, and matters of vital importance to human salvation. If for no other reason than this, the translation needs no apology. But in addition to this, the sources for the Reformer's theological thought are, as has been stated, couched in the Latin tongue. Few men, other than theologians, have either the desire or the sufficient discipline and training in philology requisite for a true and proper understanding of such source materials. It is therefore, as a matter of justice to the author, greatly to be desired that

Melanchthon should be known in the English tongue, by some of his own works, which are not only scripturally constraining but also awakening, sublime, stately and informative.

Moreover the very eminence of Philip Melanchthon raises another claim which justifies a translation of one of his works. The neglect of the Latin tongue is a matter which is greatly to be lamented. Especially is this true with respect to the writings of Melanchthon. On this score Luther has fared better than Melanchthon, for the literary productions of the former have found their way into the English language. But with respect to the latter, aside from the usual notices in textbooks on Church History and the History of Doctrines, and one or two Biographies, the works of Melanchthon are for the most part unknown in English circles, and where known, are greatly misunderstood. Perhaps this is due primarily to the fact that interdictions and tabus have been placed upon Melanchthon because of his so-called divergences from the "Pure Lutheran Wing."

Few men within the Lutheran Church have been found who dared to disregard the tabu and ventured to do anything constructively along the lines of Melanchthon theology. Among the German scholars a few have espoused the cause of Melanchthon, but American Lutheranism has stood too far aloof from this great Reformer. As far as I am concerned, what I teach may be called a "Philippismus Redivivus"; for in Melanchthonianism I see what seems to me to be the true Evangelical tradition of the gospel.

It is indeed refreshing to know that amidst the vain and empty disquisitions of the Roman theologians, in perhaps the darkest period of the history of the Church, when the vagaries of Rome had carried men's spirits off into a theological slough of despond; at a time when the darkness of scholasticism had bequeathed to the sixteenth century its offspring of mental chaos and spiritual night in the forms of papal indulgences, traditionalism, legalistic work-righteousness and general obscuration of the New Testament principles, some were found nestled in the bosom of the true church who held the truth which is according to godliness and the godliness which is according to that truth. Of such was Melanchthon. We meet in him a sweetness, a pureness, a ray of spiritual light unheard of before in the whole of doctrinal theology. And the greatest monument to this pureness and sweetness of thought is to be found in the "Loci Communes."

At a time when Protestant theological thought is in a state of flux and when Protestantism is feverishly rethinking the nature and function of the church in the world, with a view to making on constructive contribution to the establishment of a new social order which must follow the disintegration of the old, it is most fitting that the voice of the Universal Standard Bearer of the Protestant Revolt should be heard, in this the first work on doctrinal theology ever written by a Protestant theologian.

The translation has been done on the basis of Kolde's last edition of Plitt's monumental text. This text has been diligently collated with that contained in Corpus Reformatorum. In addition to this, George Spalatin's German translation has thrown some light on the dubious meaning of several passages in the Latin text.

Moreover all of these texts and codices have been compared over against the original manuscript located in the Ducal Library of Gotha. Several weeks were spent in intensive research at the Luther House in Wittenberg, Germany. And now after fourteen years of study and several thousand miles of travel, I have come to the place where I feel that this little work can be promulgated with a certain sense of authority.

It is indeed a difficult thing, that any translation of this work should be faithful and precise to the matter of the author, and at the same time preserve the characteristics of his manner. How well this has been done is for others to judge. I have attempted to give as true a rendering of the text as possible without being cumbersome in the English idiom. The fact remains, however, that any translation is, by and large, an interpretation. Since this is true, the task of the translator is a laborious and a difficult one. For how often must he attempt to render the idioms of one language into the peculiarities of another by periphrasis! It is my sincere hope that I have not read into the Loci ideas which are not already contained therein, nor omitted any sublime ideas which are definitely and surely there.

I desire to express my thanks to the preceding illustrious line of Melanchthon scholars, to whose scholarly works on Melanchthonianism in general I am so deeply indebted, although frequently I have made bold to gainsay several of their conclusions. My thanks are due in an especial and extraordinary manner to Professor John O. Evjen (deceased), who, during my student days at Hamma Divinity School, as my Professor for Church History, first introduced me to Studia Melanchthoniana and encouraged me to put the hand to Melanchthon's Loci. I desire to express my profound gratitude to Professor John Frederick Krueger (deceased), my former professor for New Testament and Missions in Hamma Divinity School, for securing for me a research fellowship to the University of Berlin (1931–1932) on the

American-German Student Exchange system, where the majority of the research for this work was carried on. My sincere thanks are due also to my former colleague, Professor Vernie C. Clinch of the English Department at Morris Brown College, for correcting the manuscript and offering several suggestions which greatly improved the translation. I wish to thank Professor A. H. Jones of Turner Seminary who, with cheerful alacrity, has read the proof. I acknowledge my great debt to Mrs. Warren J. Jenkins, secretary to the President of Morris Brown College, for prepaing the manuscript for the press. My thanks are due also to Dean E. E. Flack of Hamma Divinity School who has read the manuscript and offered constructive criticisms, and has written a special introduction to this work. Finally, I desire to thank my wife whose encouragement, during the dark days of research and investigation necessary to bring this work to completion, did much to lighten the burdens of the translator.

May the reader find this little book not altogether unprofitable! And may God Most Great, Most Good, be pleased to grant to the "Loci" of Melanchthon a greater sphere of influence than it has enjoyed hitherto by means of this translation, in the propagation of the Gospel of the Son of God, and therefore in the shaping of human characters!

CHARLES LEANDER HILL

Scribebam e Murrisensis Brunensis Collegio
Atlantæ in Georgiæ Civitate
Mense Martio MCMXLIV

INTRODUCTION
By Dean E. E. Flack, S.T.M., Th.D., D.D.

In Melanchthon's back yard in old Wittenberg, Germany, there flows a spring which the professor himself dug. The oldest well in Wittenberg, it has given forth its sparkling waters continuously since Reformation times. Near the spring stands a tree, under whose very branches the Reformation is said to have been born. For it was in this garden that Luther and Melanchthon and their friends on the faculty of the University frequently assembled on quiet summer evenings to discuss the principles which under God changed the course of subsequent history.

These two witnesses, the tree and the well, are living symbols of the links which we have with Luther and Melanchthon. Everything else which the visitor sees in Wittenberg seems to be in the form of some memorial. Melanchthon's house is a museum, exhibiting mementoes of that remarkable man. Within a stone's throw stands the old Augustinian monastery which Luther occupied. It is likewise a museum, now known as Luther Hall, housing the world's largest collection of Luther material. But the evangelical doctrines which Luther and Melanchthon promulgated are not antiquarian. Like the tree and the spring, they are living expressions of that fertile age. Though at times forgotten and neglected, they have provided perennial refreshment to Protestant people in every province of the world.

Now and then there arises some new soul with the

mind to sit in meditation under Melanchthon's tree of learning, to drink deeply from his overflowing spring of evangelical truth, and then to make a fresh contribution toward a better understanding of Reformation life and thought.

Such a contribution one finds in this volume. Strangely enough, it had its inception in the new Wittenberg in America. Although the author and translator of Melanchthon's original work belongs to another race and communion, the African Methodist Episcopal Church, he began his higher education in a Lutheran school, Wittenberg College, Springfield, O., where he specialized in the classics. An ardent student, he came to be recognized by the professor of Latin as one of his ablest pupils in half a century. Following his four years of college work, he continued on the campus three more years attending Hamma Divinity School, from which institution he graduated with honors. Receiving a scholarship to study abroad, he went to the University of Berlin for graduate research. Later he returned to his Alma Mater for his master's degree in theology and then completed the requirements for the doctorate at Ohio State University, as his record indicates.

Through all these years of graduate study Doctor Hill's mind turned more and more toward Philip Melanchthon, whom he, like Luther, came to know affectionately as his "dear Philip." It is not so strange, therefore, that he should desire to prepare a work which no one before him had undertaken, namely, to translate *Melanchthon's Loci Communes of 1521* into exquisite English. That he has performed his task in a very scholarly and admirable manner the intelligent reader will readily recognize.

Not every reader, however, will be able to follow him in his interpretation and appreciation of Melanchthon. Most historians regard Luther as "the greatest spirit of the age" and Melanchthon as "the second leader of the German Reformation." The latter became the collaborator and the complement of the former. Providence entrusted them with a great mission together. Luther was bold and boisterous, the fiery champion of evangelical truth; Melanchthon, quiet, kind, and conciliatory, a man of peace. The one as with dynamite shattered the stumps of mediæval superstition; the other, with tender hand watered and nurtured the trees of the new planting. The one with courage and conviction called forth great councils for the consideration of pointed issues; the other, with great scholarship and moderation wrote the primary symbol of Protestantism. Neither one could have accomplished what he did without the other. In the earlier years they were of one mind and spirit. Melanchthon set forth in his *Loci of 1521* the evangelical principles which Luther also caught and which were recognized as basic. So enthusiastic was Luther regarding this document that he actually declared it worthy of a place in the Canon. Later, however, the two grew somewhat apart in their thinking. Luther continued to maintain his uncompromising position, while Melanchthon came to be somewhat vacillating. He modified his position in his writings, altered the Augsburg Confession, and toned down the distinctive doctrines to such an extent that a very definite reaction set in against him, demanding adherence to the unaltered form of the Confession and the repudiation of his compromising position.

So vigorous was this opposition that by the middle of the seventeenth century no great theologian any longer appealed to his authority. For more than a century after this his name was still held in disfavor.

But when in 1760 the anniversary of his death was first commemorated, a new appreciation of the man began to crystallize. The observance of the three hundredth anniversary of his passing a century later, in 1860, evoked a much greater response. While the Melanchthonianism which he fostered has failed to outgrow its opprobrium, Melanchthon himself is held in high regard, particularly because of the positive contribution which he made in his earlier years.

In his researches on Melanchthon and his translation of his original *Loci Communes,* Dr. Hill has caught something of his scholarly spirit, his evangelical outlook, his sympathetic understanding of men, and his desire for the unity and tranquility of the Church. Having drawn deeply from the perennial spring of Reformation truth, his spirit overflows with gratitude and enthusiasm. His creative criticisms should compel many a reader to re-examine the sources.

E. E. FLACK

Hamma Divinity School,
Springfield, Ohio

TABLE OF CONTENTS

Part I. Prolegomena

Chapter		Page
I.	Biographical Sketch of Melanchthon	19
II.	Critical Estimate of the Character and Influence of Melanchthon and of His Contributions to the History of Thought	29
III.	History of the Formation and Character of the "Loci Communes" Up to 1521	50

Part II. English Translation

Section		
1.	Dedicatory Epistle	63
2.	Common Topics or Theological Outlines	66
3.	On the Powers of Man, Especially Free Will	69
4.	On Sin	81
5.	The Power and Fruit of Sin	85
6.	On Law	110
7.	On Divine Laws	117
8.	On Counsels	122
9.	On Monkish Vows	126
10.	On Judicial and Ceremonial Laws	129
11.	On Human Laws	130
12.	On the Gospel	143
13.	On the Meaning of the Gospel	145

CONTENTS

14. On the Power of the Law 154
15. On the Power of the Gospel 165
16. On Grace 169
17. On Justification and Faith 171
18. On the Efficacy of Faith 202
19. On Love and Hope 204
20. Summation: Law, Gospel, Faith 215
21. On the Old and the New Man 234
22. On Mortal and Daily Sin 236
23. On Signs 238
24. On Baptism 243
25. On Penitence 249
26. On Private Confessions 255
27. On Participation in the Table of the Lord 258
28. On Love 260
29. On Magistrates 262
30. On Offense 265
31. Bibliography 268

The Loci Communes of Philip Melanchthon

CHAPTER ONE

Brief Biographical Sketch

Philip Melanchthon, the Co-reformer of Martin Luther, was born in the small town of Bretten in Baden on February 16, 1497, and died in Wittenberg, April 19, 1560. The city of Bretten was situated on the trade route to the lower Rhine from Italy, and though very small, was nevertheless often frequented by commercial people and travelers.

The populace was mostly agricultural and hence, very conservative. The citizens had a wide reputation for stern piety and intense zeal for the church. As an indication of the degree of their zeal one need only turn to the Chronicles for the year 1504 wherein the records show that five persons were burned at the stake for witchcraft. But neither a stern piety nor an intense zeal for the cause of religion, nor the burning of witches affords Bretten with a bid to immortal fame. It will be remembered in history primarily as the birthplace of Philip Melanchthon, the "feminine principle of the Reformation," the humanistic genius, the Præceptor Germaniæ, and the greatest spirit of the age.

Philip's father was George Schwarzerd, famed armorer and engineer in the services of the Emperor

Maximilian. George Schwarzerd died in 1507, leaving besides Philip, another son, George, and three small daughters. The care of these charges was left to his very pious and faithful widow, Barbara. But while he lived, George Schwarzerd was vitally interested in the education and training of his children. Realizing that the very nature of his profession thwarted paternal supervision due to his frequent absences, he had entrusted the education of his children to their grandfather.

Philip and his younger brother, George, were put in the town school where they learned the rudiments of education and made rapid strides in the acquisition of knowledge. Philip especially early in life manifested extraordinary talents for study and learning. So precocious was he, that he has won a place in the list of Enfans Celebres of Baillet. As a child he was afflicted with stammering, but through consistent practice and effort, he succeeded in overcoming this defect.

During the French Plague, the boys were taken out of the town school and the grandfather sought counsel of John Reuchlin, their grand-uncle, who sent John Unger of Pforzheim to become their private tutor.[1] It was from Unger that Melanchthon received his first training in linguistics. The poems of Batista Mantuanus served as the textbook, and later in life, Melanchthon speaks in glowing terms of praise of Unger, because of his strict discipline and linguistic ability.[2]

---

[1]Camerarius: *Vita Melanchthonis:* p. 6 Leipzig, 1556.

[2]Concerning Unger, Melanchthon writes in Explicat., Evangel. Dom. p. 804, p. III, these words: "Ego habui præceptorem, qui fuit excellens grammaticus. Ille adegit me ad grammaticiam, et ita adegit, ut constructiones facerem: Cogebar reddere regulas constructionis per versus Mantuani 20 aut 30. Nihil patiebatur me omittere: quotiens errabam dabat plagas mihi, et tamen ea moderatione, quæ erat comemiens. Ita me fecit grammaticum. Erat vir optimus, dilexit me ut filium, et ego ut patrem." Cf. C.R. 25:448.

After the death of the grandfather, the burden of
the boys' education fell upon their grandmother, Elizabeth Reuter, the sister of Reuchlin. This Reuchlin is
the celebrated Greek and Hebrew scholar. The grandmother removed to Pforzheim and thus Reuchlin became a frequent visitor in the home.

The school in Pforzheim was a celebrated one, with
such scholars as Hiltebrant and Helvetius on its faculty.
It was here that Melanchthon was introduced to Classicism and consequently it was here that he began to
lay that linguistic foundation which fitted him to' become one of the greatest forces of the Reformation age.

Reuchlin's influence over Melanchthon from the very
first was great. He presented Melanchthon with a
Greek grammar and praised him highly. On one occasion, he challenged him to write some Latin verses to
be presented upon his (Reuchlin's) return. Meantime
several of the boys of the school practiced a school
comedy written by Reuchlin and presented it for his
entertainment upon'his return. It evoked such praise
from Reuchlin that he gave Melanchthon a new name,
saying that such a brilliant spirit should not have the
lowly name of Schwarzerd, but should carry the
Greek equivalent, Melanchthon (μέλαν † χθών, black
earth). From 1531 on he wrote it, Melanthon, no
doubt to facilitate its pronunciation, but his friends
persisted in writing it, Melanchthon.[3]

Persuaded by Reuchlin, Melanchthon left Pforzheim
to matriculate in Heidelberg in 1509.[4] He began the
study of philosophy, but did not highly regard his

---

[3] C. R. 28 4 in: Annales Vitæ.
[4] C. R. 1: 146. The register for the year 1509 reads as follows: "In Rectoratu II Mag. Johannis Wysers de Oberspach, Jurium Licentiati, Intitulatus est d. XIII. Oct. 1509 Philippus Schwarzerd de Bretten."

studies here, calling them "Garrula Dialectices" and "Particula Physices."[5] He supplemented the course of study by reading privately the classics, philosophy and literature. Geiler's sermons were making a marked impression upon him.

After careful study he took his Bachelor's degree in 1511 under Leonhard Dietrich. The following year was spent in the study of Scholasticism, at the end of which, he presented himself for the Master's degree but was refused by the board of directors on the ground of "his youth and boyish appearance."[6]

This greatly enraged Melanchthon and he decided to go to Tuebingen, where he zealously applied himself to philosophy, humanistic culture, law, medicine and astronomy. Representatives of the old and the new schools were to be found here. He heard Heinrich Bebel lecture on poetry and eloquence. He met again Hiltebrand and Simler, the latter directing him to Aristotle. He took dialectic from Franz Kirchner, heard Stoeffler read astronomy and astrology, and took theology from Lemp.[7] Œculampadius gave him private lessons in Greek, and he began to read Cicero, Demosthenes and Quintilian for rhetoric. He devoted some time to the study of Pliny and read the three books of Rudolf Agricola on dialectic. It was this last work that opened his eyes to scholastic logic and dialectic.

In 1514 he won the Master's degree. He became a privatdocent and lectured to the students of his burse on ancient languages. He began with Virgil and Ter-

---

[5] C. R. 4: 715.
[6] C. R. 1,146.
[7] Jacob Lemp was a professor of theology at this time lecturing on scholasticism. Melanchthon writes of him: "The old Doctor of Theology, who pictured transubstantiation on the blackboard." C. R. 4: 718, cf. C. R. 28: 4, in Annales Vitæ.

ence, later adding Livy and Cicero. He did much to revive the classics at Tuebingen. While here he edited editions of Terence (1516) and a Greek grammar (1518). He was engaged by Thomas Anshelm as proof-reader in his establishment.

He received calls from the universities of Ingoldstadt and Leipzig but refused them upon the advice of Reuchlin, who had recommended him for the chair of Greek in the new university opened in 1502 by Frederick at Wittenberg. It was here that he became acquainted with Martin Luther, professor of theology.

He proceeded to Wittenberg and arrived on August 25, 1519. He delivered his inaugural address from the subject "De Corrigendis Adolescentiæ Studiis", in which he looked forward to a reformation of the church through the assistance of humanism. His intimate association with Luther led him to a deeper knowledge of the Scripture and he decided to place the languages in the service of the gospel. This latter becomes Melanchthon's orientation. His program for the acquisition of education is the study of the fine arts. He is not content with the trivium of the scholastics; he enlarges it to include all the arts. His ideal of education becomes "eloquentia" or as he often called it in the German equivalent "Beredsamkeit". While busily engaged in professional duties, he critically reflected upon all the implications of true education and arrived at its inner conception.

By now his fame was spreading abroad, and it is said that he had as high as two thousand students who packed the lecture rooms to hear this great scholar expound Homer and the New Testament. He devoted much of his time to literary work, assisting Luther in his translation of the Bible and publishing his own commentaries on the New Testament.

He was induced by his friends to marry Katherine Krapp, daughter of the town mayor, which he did in 1520.[8] It was against his will that he did so, but upon the urgent pleas of his friends he finally yielded, that he might have someone as Luther put it "to care for his weak body." The nuptials were performed November 25, 1520.[9]

He began to espouse the cause of Luther more and more. He assisted Luther in the Leipzig disputation, and otherwise helped him under the name of Didymus Faventinus.[10] In 1521 he published his "Loci communes rerum theologicarum seu Hypotyposes theologicæ," the first Protestant work on dogmatic theology. In 1524 he went south for his health, where he met the legate Campegius who tried to persuade him to recant. But he refused and issued his "Summa doctrinæ Lutheri."[11] He took part in the visitation of churches and schools in 1527. In 1529 he attended the Diet of Spires and the Marburg Colloquy. n 1530, the epochal year of the Reformation, he released to the

---

[8] C. R. I, 150. In a letter dated August 15, 1520, to Langus, Melanchthon says: "Secutus sum Amicorum Consilium." cf. C. R. I, p. 212.

[9] He posted the following announcement to his students: "A studiis hodie facit otia grata Philippus, nec vobis Pauli dogmata sacra leget." Of Katherine Krapp Camerarius speaks thus, in his Vita Melanchthonis (p. 38): "Cum ea vixit in matrimonio castissimo annos XXXVII, et utriusque sexus liberos suscepit quaternos, filios duos et totidem filias. Desiit autem parere illa anno conjugii duodecimo. Fuit fœmina hæc religiosissima et viri amantissima, materfamilias assidua studiosa, ut et dando sive discrimine, et deprecando pro illis, et conciliando quibis aliquid posset commodi, non modo suarum rerum facultatumque minus rationem habere, sed interpellatione et compellatione pro his ad alios uti soleret nonnunquam intempestiva. Summa vitæ morumque integritate, inque perpetua cura religiosæ pietatis honestatisque et victus et cultus negligens. Neque hoc Philippus Melanchthon offendebatur, qui nullis deliciarum blanditiis caperetur, et voluptatum omnes illecebras fugeret."

[10] In an "Oratio adversus Thoman Placentinum pro Luttero" delivered February 20, 1521.

[11] C. R. I, 154.

public the "Confessio Augustana" the "magna charta" of Lutheranism.

For several years after the Diet of Augsburg, he spent his time in retirement. In 1532 he published his great commentary on Romans. After his meeting with Bucer at Cassel where the two discussed the Lord's Supper in 1534, he departed more and more from the dominance of the thought-forms of Luther, and began to build up his own system of religious ideas. In 1536 was the great battle with Cordatus who attacked Melanchthon's views of Justification, and in 1535 the second edition of the Loci was published in which he is accused (but wrongly so) of going over to synergism.

Theological battles were raging in Wittenberg in the years from 1536 to 1538. These coupled with the infamous bigamy of Philip of Hesse began to work upon Melanchthon's sensitive conscience, the result being prostration upon a sick bed in 1540. He tells us he was restored to health by the will and prayers of Luther.[12]

Hardly was he restored to health when Luther took him to an assembly in Eisenach in July 1540. In spite of his weak condition, Melanchthon continued his literary activities and research, and in the same year, wrote epigrams and prefaces for various books written by his intimate friends. He participated in the Diet of Worms, taking a leading part as official representative and spokesman for the Protestant theologians and church. He responded to speeches which had been delivered by the Catholic Campegius, Papal Legate to the Diet, and by Granvell, Legate of the Emperor. Amidst the hectic days of the religious controversies

---

[12]cf. C. R. I, p. XCIII No. 13, a letter of Ratzeberger. Melanchthon later also discussed this sickness in a letter to Camerarius dated March 23, 1543.

of 1541, there occurred one thing to relieve the strain from the mind of the Reformer: his stipend as a Professor on the faculty of the University of Wittenberg was appreciably increased.[13] Now for the first time in his professional life, he could pursue his duties unhampered by financial worries.

In December of 1541 Melanchthon saw the appearance of the Basel edition of his letters. In 1542 Melanchthon released a German redaction of his famous theological works, the *Loci Theologici*. In the preface he warns the reader of slight changes of opinions which had been made because of increased familiarity with the ancients and the scholastic philosophers.

The Reformer's heart was made heavy by the death of both his sister and sister-in-law during this same year. These he bore with Christian faith and steadfastness.

In 1543 Melanchthon published a commentary on the book of Daniel, wrote prefaces to textbooks on various subjects, dispatched several important letters, published books on dialectic, ethic, and catechetics. The commentary on Daniel shows a facile use of the Hebrew scriptures and also the Greek text.

Luther's death in 1546 had profound influence upon Melanchthon. From now on to his own death, he became the leading light of the Protestant revolt, shaping its policies and directing its course. For all eyes turned toward him as the logical successor of Luther. Luther's funeral oration was delivered by Melanchthon on February 22, 1546. It ranks as a classic, and for elegance of style, it has few, if any, superiors. Melanchthon in this oration very clearly fixes upon the historical significance and contribution of Luther to

---
[13]De Wette: "Luther's Letters," T. V., p. 387.

the Christian Church. It is at once a eulogy and a character analysis of a great historical personality.

In 1547 Melanchthon was occupied with the Leipzig Interim and his heart was vexed by the Adiaphoristic Controversy. In 1549 a theologian named Osiander (the same man who wrote the preface to Copernicus' revolutionary work) attacked Melanchthon's doctrine of Justification, while contemporary with these discussions, was the controversy over the Lord's Supper. He was accused by the so-called Gnesio-Lutherans (persons who would be more Lutheran than Luther himself) of apostasy from pure Lutheran dogma.

In 1553 Melanchthon was busy with the Stancarian Controversy and also with a refutation of Osiander. The last years of his life were spent in deep sorrow and gross misunderstanding.

Consequently Melanchthon began to grow tired. For in January 1560 he wrote to a friend: "Ego patriæ cœlestis desiderio afficior, et si diutius in his ærumnis vivendum est, longius abesse me ab barbarie optarim."[14] He even prayed for death as a release "a rabie theologorum." The trying and turbulent days of the Reformation were beginning to tell on him. The bitter and sarcastic opprobrium heaped upon him by the Flacian party and their charges of Calvinising and falsification of Luther's doctrines, had now touched him deeply. In a letter to a friend he writes that he is "cruelly tortured by many hostile enemies." But this torture was not to last much longer. For upon returning from Leipzig whither he had gone to examine the Elector's Stipendaries, he contracted a severe cold that was followed by intermittent fever. He lectured, wrote letters, revised manuscripts for the press unto the last.

---
[14] C. R. 28 142.

As his weakness increased and the end drew nigh, Peucer his friend asked him if he wished anything else. His answer was: "Nothing but heaven." The pastor prayed and in the evening pronounced a blessing on him while Professor Winsheim read from the Psalter. At 6:45 p. m. on the evening of April 29, 1560, Philip Melanchthon, the soldier of God, fell on sleep, aged 63 years, 2 months and 3 days.

The body was placed in a tin coffin, and this in a wooden one with a Latin inscription which recounts the chief details of his life. Doctor Paul Eber, pastor of the Parish Church of Wittenberg, delivered a German sermon on The Hope of Immortality. The remains were then taken to the Castle Church where Doctor Veit Winsheim, professor of Greek, pronounced a Latin funeral oration. Melanchthon was laid to rest by the side of Luther—"lovely and pleasant in their lives, and in their death were not divided."

In Wittenberg, Germany, is still standing the house where our philosopher-theologian lived and died. A tablet high up on the front bears this inscription:

"Hier wohnte, lehrte und starb Philipp Melanchthon."

On the second story of this building is Melanchthon's study and also the place where he breathed his last, as is indicated by the following inscriptions:

"Ad Boream versis oculis hac sede Philippus Melanchthon scripta dedit, quæ nunc præcipua orbis habet." "Siste Viator.

Ad hunc parietem stetit lectulus in quo pie et placide expiravit vir reverendus Philippus Melanchthon. Die XIX. April. dodrante horæ ante VII. anno. MDLX."

---

[15]The following chapter is the concluding chapter of my doctoral dissertation titled: "An Exposition and A Critical Estimate of the Philosophy of Philip Melanchthon." Ohio State University Library, 1938.

CHAPTER TWO

Critical Estimate of the Character and Influence of Melanchthon and of His Contributions to the History of Thought

The task is set before me to give a critical estimate of the character and influence of Melanchthon, and of his contribution to the history of thought.

Melanchthon was a man of mildness and moderation of temper and of conscientious prudence. He was above all a lover of peace. He possessed a keen intellect which could make penetrating observations upon the most abstruse matters. He was by nature cool and sedate. Perhaps this was due to his vast humanistic culture and to his innate love of peace. He hated crude and rough contentions and his gentle spirit was tortured by the strife and dissension of the age in which he lived. This inherent love of peace and tranquillity accounts also for the irenic tone of his writings. It led him to undertake conciliatory measures whenever conditions warranted such behavior. His mild nature made him of the churchly disposition.

Compared with the rather rough, boisterous and crude character of Luther, Melanchthon may seem to many to lack courage. His moderation and caution in matters have been explained by some as fear and cowardice. If he does seem too moderate and cautious, his caution was exercised, not in his own behalf, but in the interest of the Protestant revolt and church.

Although in the natural temperament of his mind, there was a softness, tenderness and suave timidity, nevertheless when dangers seemed to impend, or when the cause of religion and the Protestant reformation was in jeopardy, he feared nothing and was always at hand, to champion and to defend what he thought to be right. Luther himself has given us the index to his real nature when he says: "I am rough, boisterous, stormy and belligerent. I am born to fight against innumerable monsters and devils. I must remove stumps and stones, cut away thistles and thorns, and clear wild forests; but Master Philip comes along softly and gently, sowing and watering with joy, according to the gifts which God has abundantly bestowed upon him."[1]

Melanchthon was by far the most outstanding scholar of his age. His enemies confessed that much: "All know, and even his enemies confess that few men of any age can be compared with him, whether for learning and knowledge of both human and divine things, or for his richness, suavity, and facility of genius, or for industry as a cholar."[2] The powers of his mind were astounding. He possessed an extraordinary ability to comprehend and to express in simple language the most abstract, abstruse, and metaphysical subjects. Lovgren has paid a glowing tribute to the genius of Melanchthon's learning when he says: "For learning Melanchthon was no doubt the greatest genius of his day, and his systematic comprehension and presentation of the new doctrine gave it from the beginning a high degree of clearness and solidity."[3] Likewise Rudolf Sohm has pointed this out in no uncertain terms: "Luther was the first herald of the Reformation; but he was not the only man who determined the character of its progress. Side by side with him stood

---
[1] Preface to Melanchthon's Commentary on Colossians.
[2] Mosheim: "Ecc. History," Vol. 3, pp. 25-26.
[3] Lovgren: "Church History," p. 173.

Melanchthon, the refined scholar and theologian whose humanism went far to compensate for much of Luther's hardness, and who became the creator of the Protestant system of education and Protestant scientific theology."[4]

When he turned such learning and ability to the cause of the Christian Church, it can be safely said that this man, by his genius and erudition, has done much for the cause of religion. His writings show that he thought out everything he said. The clarity of his thinking is reflected in the clearness of his style of writing. Such learning as he possessed, and such finesse in expressing his thoughts could not but widely influence the culture of his time and win for their owner the title of "Præceptor Germaniæ", or teacher of Germany. McGiffert in his fine work on Luther confesses this very thing: "One of the greatest scholars and teachers of the century, Melanchthon immensely enhanced the fame of the university, and his class-room was thronged with students of many nationalities. His title, Præceptor Germaniæ, was fairly won, for he did more than any other man to reform the educational system of the country."[5]

The influence of Melanchthon has been felt as a theologian, moral philosopher, biblical exegete, homiletician, philologist, and pedagog. As a theologian, Melanchthon occupies one of the foremost places in the Reformation age. He is more than a Co-reformer. He is, in the language of Dr. Landerer, "the leader of the German Reformation"[6] or as Hase calls him "das allgemeine Panier der Reformation."[7]

As a moral philosopher Melanchthon's three chief

---
[4]Sohm, R.: Outlines of Church History," p. 175.
[5]McGiffert: "Martin Luther: The Man and His Work," New York, p. 109, 1911.
[6]Landerer: "Realencyklopädie," art. on Melanchthon.
[7]Hase: "Kirchengeschichte," 10. aufl. S. 422, 1856.

works on ethics are classical; while in the science of homiletics he has been regarded as the author of the methodical syle of preaching which follows a subject. His works on rhetoric greatly influenced later writers in the field.

His influence and activity in philology and pedagogy have been the chief things which earned for him the title of Præceptor Germaniæ. For he is the founder of the higher schools in Germany. It has been said that Melanchthon accomplished for the liberal arts and the schools what Luther did for theology. "He freed them from the corruptions they had contracted, restored them, and gave them their currency in Germany."[8]

We have to do then, with no ordinary man in Philip Melanchthon, and so far as I am concerned, he ought to be honored as one of the greatest religious geniuses in the history of the Christian Church since the days of St. Augustine.

Nor has Protestantism alone profited from his labors. All Germany, Protestant and Catholic, reaped the immediate benefits of his endeavors, as Hartfelder so ably contends.[9] Catholic historians have idealized the virtues of Melanchthon. Doellinger is loud in the praise of Melanchthon's achievements in the field of thought: "The most brilliant phenomenon which proceeded from the Erasmian school, equal to his master, Erasmus, in many respects, superior to him in others. Riches of knowledge, the choicest classical culture, facility of expression, versatility of composition, rhetorical fullness and improvisation, united to untiring industry—this rare combination of excellences fitted him

---

[8] Mosheim: "Ecc. History." p. 26, Vol. 3, 5th edition.
[9] Hartfelder: "Melanchthon als Praeceptor Germaniæ", in the introduction, Berlin, 1889.

above all others for the literary leadership of the mighty movement."[10]

Concerning his vast and profound learning, Carl Bretschneider has this to say: "nemo autem omnium doctorum sec. XVI ejusmodi cura dignior videtur, quam Philippus Melanthon, græcarum litterarum simulque theologiæ in academia Vitebergensi doctor, Reuchlini discipulus felicissimus illustrissimusque. Non solum enim in iis fuit, qui de restaurandis litteris, imprimis græcis, optime meriti sunt, sed etiam in philosophia, historia, astronomia, litteris, elegantioribus et fere in omnibus quæ ad subtiliorem doctrinam spectant, tum ipse satis eruditus fuit, tum vero alios feliciter instituit eorum studia juvit. Præ cæteris autem præstitit in theologia, in qua Lutherum si non superavit, certe æquavit."[11]

In my judgment, the importance of the Melanchthonian system for the history of Protestant theology, and for all of that for the history of doctrine in general, has been greatly underestimated. This unfortunate situation has been created partly, by the devotion of Lutheran dogmaticians to the so-called "Pure Lutheran Tradition", and partly by a total misunderstanding and a false interpretation of particular writings of Melanchthon.

The traditional approach to Melanchthonianism has served to cast dark shadows of suspicion upon the whole system. For all the way from the Flacian controversy up to the latest dogmatician of the church, the system of Philip Melanchthon has come in for more than its share of unjust criticism. I have long thought that Modern Protestantism could be greatly enriched by the religious and intellectual heritage found

---
[10]Doellinger: "Die Reformation", Bd. 1, S. 349, Regensburg, 1846.
[11]Bretschneider: Præmonenda in Corpus Reformatorium, 1, p. 25 f.

in Melanchthonianism. For Melanchthon has a much needed message for present-day Protestant thought.

Ritschl in his work "Reconciliation" has most inconsistently censured Melanchthon. But the manifold attention which Ritschl devotes to Melanchthon, and the so-called "fatal scholastic deformity of Protestant theology" which Ritschl charges to his account, are both evident testimony as to what a significant factor in the historical and doctrinal development of Protestantism our Reformer has really been. And even those scholars within the church who have manifested a degree of sympathy and understanding for Melanchthonian thought have given us by no means as full a development of Melanchthon's system as is desirable. True it is that Baur[12] views Melanchthonianism as an equally significant system along side of Lutheranism and Calvanism in the Reformation age. Likewise true it is that Heppe finds the original construction of Protestant dogma and church in Melanchthonian thought.[13] Notwithstanding, both Baur and Heppe fail utterly to define and differentiate clearly Melanchthonianism as over against Luther's views on the one hand, and Reformed principles on the other.

Present day scholars in viewing the system of Melanchthon, seem to be unable to see that his is a completed system of thought entirely his own. They think that Melanchthon has significance for the history of thought only in the traditional relation which he has sustained to Luther. It is my conclusion that we have a perfect right to speak about a Melanchthonian system of theology and philosophy; and that too, in the

---

[12]Baur: "Abhandlung ueber das Prinzip des Protestantismus," in "Theologischen Jahrbuechern," Tuebingen 1855, S. 1 ff.

[13]Heppe: "Geschichte des deutschen Protestantismus," Gotha, 1857, cf. also: "Philip Melanchthon der Lehrer Deutschlands," Marburg, 1860.

sense of a clearly and logically developed system, in which are to be found very pronounced and vital contributions to the theological and philosophical speculations of the Reformation age. Incidentally there is contained in this system, a message of deep significance for the effete and completely watered down Protestant thinking of our own age.

Consequently I can no longer share the view of Klotsche[14] for instance, who holds that Melanchthon's significance for the history of doctrine lies in the fact that he collected and systematized Luther's doctrinal views. This assertion is the result of a hasty generalization and a great unfamiliarity with the independent system of Melanchthon. It is certainly not at all borne out by the evident and clear facts of the case. For me Melanchthon's significance for the history of thought lies in the fact that he made a conscious and definite contribution to Protestant doctrine; that he devised both a system of theology and of philosophy decidedly his own; that he shaped the course of the Reformation in no small degree. Melanchthon was no "mere voice" uttering words dictated by another. He spoke in his own right. And as such, the system of Melanchthon must be regarded in its proper place and light namely, in the productive period of Protestant theology, and as the major part of the cultural development of the entire Reformation age. And to what extent his system has influenced Lutheran dogma can be easily seen.

Rothe[15] thinks that the very framework of the Reformation age in the fields of exegesis, dogmatics, and the history of doctrine, was the product of Melanchthon's work: "was in der Reformationszeit fuer den

---

[14]Klotsche: "An Outline of the History of Doctrines," p. 97.
[15]Rothe: "Heidelberger Festschrift" of 1860.

Aufbau einer evangelischen Theologie in Deutschland geschehen ist, auf dem Feld der Exegese, der Dogmatik, ja auch schon der Dogmengeschichte, war sein Werk. Der eigentliche Begruender einer deutsch-evangelischen Theologie war Melanchthon." And concerning the widespread influence of the man in his own age, we have the words of a contemporary: "Et in tota Germania omnes Cathedræ, scholæ et pulpita scripta ejus sonant: hæc omnium manibus, tam puerorum quam adultorum teruntur."[16]

Added to these witnesses, is the testimony of the Lutheran confessional literature. Everywhere it bears his stamp and character. In several doctrines of the Lutheran Church, one can readily see that they were formulated and developed on the basis of the point of view of Melanchthon.[17] Particularly is this true with the Formula of Concord where it treats of the doctrines of grace, freedom, and human salvation. No less a dogmatician than Dorner confesses that in this respect, the Formula of Concord adheres to Melanchthon's fundamental tendency: "The later expounders of the Formula of Concord, notwithstanding their aspersions of Melanchthon, have simply adopted this conception of the way of salvation in order to save their own "ordo salutis" at its most critical point from the inconsistence and absurdity of pure accident."[18] "The fundamental tendency" referred to above is the characteristic doctrine of human freedom of the will developed by Melanchthon in his own philosophical ethics away from the "servum arbitrium" of Luther. And following Melanchthon on this locus of free will and pre-

---
[16]C. R. Vol. XX, p. 301.
[17]Herrlinger: "Die Theologie Melanchthons," S. 464 Gotha 1879.
[18]Dorner: "History of Prot. Theol.," I, 218.

destinarian determinism, are such able Lutheran theologians as Thomasius, Kahnis, and Luthardt.

But indeed the system of Melanchthon is important for the history of thought for several other reasons. In the first place, it furthered the cause of rationalism. I have marked out as the signal contribution of Melanchthon to Protestant dogma, his insistence upon the rights of speculative reason in matters pertaining to religious doctrine. He strove to give a rational foundation to the dogma. In so doing, he broke down the Medieval distinction between the sacred and the secular, between the authority of the church and its temporal power and the rights of the individual conscience to decide the problems of faith and morality according to the faculty of reason. Thus our Reformer fostered the spirit of critical reflection and independent thinking. In this respect, he represents the spirit of the modern era, that is, rationalism.

Moreover in his appeal from ecclesiastical authority and churchly tradition to the human conscience, Melanchthon was giving impetus to the spirit of individualism. By shifting from the elaborate system of works and cultus worship of the church to an inner ethical and personal religion, he liberated human personality from its bondage to the Medieval synthesis. The individual has meaning in his own right and not merely as a member of an order, guild, town or corporate society.

Furthermore when the new church felt the need of rationalizing its faith, it was to Melanchthon that the task of creating a Protestant system fell. He went about this task with critical discernment and acumen, and gave to the Protestant revolution a clarity which it could never have had without his keen, penetrating, and philosophically orientated mind. Although he has not been given due credit by the Lutheran Church as I have said, nevertheless on several fundamental loci of Lutheran dogmatics, these doctrines are developed by some of the most learned and judicious dogmaticians within that branch of Christianity, away from Luther and solely on the basis of the views of Melanchthon. He is the formulator of the confessional literature and the philosopher-theologian of Lutheranism.

By no means unfruitful were his labors in behalf of the cause of education in Germany. He advocated and fostered universal education in Germany, and because of this aspect of his system, he rightly deserves the title "Teacher of Germany." His literary activity along the lines of text-books, grammars, and editions of the classical writers, in a word, his humanistic proclivities gave to German education that depth and gravity and reach of universal culture, which have been ever since its most distinctive features. Melanchthon's humanism is the prototype of German humanism in general. But when Nitzsch remarks that Melanchthon "ein Zweiter Erasmus geworden oder geblieben wære," I must rejoin that he did not remain an Erasmian humanist, for his is a humanism which is tempered and restrained by the gospel.

Melanchthon is a "man of the school." This fact cannot be denied. Some scholars have seriously upbraided him for "turning the church itself" into a school. Especially has the German scholar, Schenkel,[19] raised the criticism that Melanchthon, by confounding the concepts of the divine word and churchly confession respecting theological doctrine, has changed the church into a school. It is clear that Melanchthon does compare the church to a school, but it is equally clear

---

[19]Schenkel: "Wesen des Protestantismus" III, S. 183.

in what sense he does this. His language is purely metaphorical as can be seen from his "Postilla"[20] and elsewhere. It is remarkable that he regards the church as a moral life community. It is a "worship-community," having a transcendental ground in the divine decrees and is thus distinguished and distinguishable from the state, and all other sociological magnitudes.[21] If Melanchthon calls the church a "schola" it is only to say that the evangelical church should be and is constituted out of an inner working power of religious proof and instruction as opposed to the outer legal principle of authority so characteristic of Roman Catholicism. The church is the elected organ for the declaration of the gospel. Its whole function is to show the "efficaciam verbi divini." But in thus proclaiming the efficacy of the divine word, its ministry must teach as well as preach.

The system of Melanchthon is the last great attempt to reconcile Aristotle and Christian doctrine. He has attempted to do for Protestantism what Averroes did for Islam and what Moses Maimonides did for Judaism and what Thomas did for Catholicism in the Middle Age: to resolve the problem of how a thinking person can harmonize philosophy and science with the beliefs of faith. In addressing himself to this task which busied the scholastic philosophers of the Middle Age, whatever criticism may be made of his method and efforts, whatever inconsistencies may be pointed out, this much is certain that Melanchthon has caught the spirit of Aristotle in a manner that provokes great admiration for his powers of discernment and understanding as an interpreter of "the philosopher." For in his hand, Aristotelianism becomes quick, warm and en-

---
[20]C. R. 25: 26. 21: 825. 826. 25: 165. 586. 24: 126.
[21]C. R. 21: 955. 12: 520. Cf. Third draft of the Loci passim.

ergizing; free from the hair-splitting and subtile distinctions to which it had been reduced by the scholastic system.

Another fundamental aspect of his system deserves attention. It is the contribution which he made to the science of jurisprudence and political philosophy. In his substitution of the doctrine of the Bible for Canonical law, he emancipated jurists from a superstitious reverence for the latter. This emancipation permitted law to walk its own way and to develop itself unhampered. It also made Melanchthon a coöperator in bringing about the evolution of a philosophy of law which was developed later on by the anti-ecclesiastical political philosophy of Machiavelli, Bodin, Gentilis and Grotius. With the same blow Melanchthon broke the ice for the naturalistic political philosophy of Thomas Hobbes.

The doctrine most significant for the ethics of Melanchthon was his notion of the "natural light." As I have said, this doctrine is a reproduction of Cicero and St. Paul. It became the basis of Melanchthon's conception of natural law which so greatly influenced subsequent writers. Beneath all argumentation and underlying the first principles of every science are certain ideas, innate in all men, implanted by God: noticiæ nobiscum *nascentes, divinitus sparsæ in mentibus nostris.* This doctrine is developed by our Reformer in the Liber de Anima and the Erotemata Dialectices, as is shown by an examination of Melanchthon's psychology and theory of dialectic. His final conclusion is that the ten commandments of the revealed law and the natural moral law are identical. Natural law is thus given a natural, independent, and rational foundation of its own. It is thus possible for human life to be ordered, according to rational laws. This thought was the wedge to open up the possibility for civil life to develop independently, according to purely humane principle. How far reaching and important this notion was may be seen when we remind ourselves that the same idea is picked up by the Dane Hemmingsen and made the point of departure for his great work *De lege naturæ apodictica methodus of 1562*. This work, inspired by Melanchthon's theory of natural law, is the first scientific exposition of natural law in the Rennaissance and Reformation age. Natural law is now emancipated forever from theology and all so-called supernatural authority.

Moreover when Melanchthon rejected the temporal authority of the church and made various observations on magistrates, kings, governments, and their powers, he was in reality calling attention to an aspect of political philosophy which was fully developed in Jean Bodin's *La Republique of 1577*. For in this work, Bodin, in a clear and methodical way, developed that concept of sovereignty already discussed (however superficially) by Melanchthon. In addition, the antithesis between the inner and outer man, which was a characteristic doctrine of Melanchthon, was pressed all the way to the notion of political freedom by John Althusius in his famous work, *Politica methodice digesta atque exemplis sacris et profanis illustrata of 1603*. And there is much in Hugo Grotius' *De jure belli ac pacis of 1625* that reminds one of reflections contained in Melanchthon's writings, particularly the Loci Communes of 1521 and 1535. Thus Melanchthon's views were of no small importance for political philosophy.

Moreover, the system of Melanchthon was all inclusive in the sense that it embraced the sum total of all the sciences and learning of his day. He neglected none of the branches of the "orbis litterarum." For this was his pedagogical program: through knowledge to piety. The Latin and Greek Chrestomathies of 1524 and 1525 indicate the wide range of his interests. In this respect, he approaches the ideal of modern philosophy as a "universitas scientiarum." To Melanchthon, philosophpy was criticism; criticism of the concepts of all the arts and sciences of his day. I need not stay to remark that this conception of philosophy as criticism of concepts is one that is held by many outstanding contemporary philosophers.

In my judgment, the most signal and decisive contribution of Melanchthon to Protestant thought is his formulation of the idea of God. The whole scheme of Protestant theology hangs on the concept of Deity. If protestant theology stumbles here at this locus, it stumbles at the very threshold of the Christian faith. And who is it that will not confess that present day Protestant theology has been cut loose from its moorings, and is afloat on the wild and stormy ocean of speculation about the idea of God. Without a clear-eyed conception of God, Protestant scientific theology walks its way today shorn of its inner strength and beauty, and deprived of its historical connection with primitive apostolic thought and the traditions of the Reformers. There is little wonder then that the camp of theology is speaking much of a "theology of crisis." For the inner degeneration and dissolution and complete decay of theology begins with the falsification of the idea of God.

That there has been such a falsification may be clearly seen when one examines various contemporary theological treatises. It will not be saying too much when one remarks that modern theology in America has become philosophy of religion. Following this tendency, until recently, the attitudes toward the nature of God in Protestant circles have become in turn, God as mere idea, God as abstract principle, and God as a cosmic process. Such notions constitute a rejection of the New Testament conception of God. For the distinctive feature of the New Testament conception of God is, and always has been, to regard God as a cosmic person with cosmological significance. On this point Melanchthon has a message for modern Protestant thought. The Reformer holds fast to the doctrine of the immanence of God.

For Melanchthon, the immediate presence and activity of God in creation constitutes the very essence of the notion of God. This formulation is made on the basis of Augustine's idea of "creatio continua." In one of his exegetical works Melanchthon in almost the identical words of Augustine says: "genus humanum non posset manere unum diem, nisi filius die protegeret."[22] In another place he rejects a second extreme: God is not to be likened unto a house-builder who turns the completed edifice over into the hands of its owner: "non enim intelligi debet deus deservisse res a se conditas, sicut faber domum ædificatam relinquit et commendat hero."[23] Again: "Gott ist nicht von seinem werck weg gegangen, wie ein Zimmermann vom Schiff, das er gebawet hat, weg gehet, und lesst es darnach, andere regieren end flicken. Sondern er bleibet bey sienen creaturen, bey Himmel und Erden, Engeln und Menschen, und macht die Erden jerlick fruchtbar, gibet allen gewechsen, Thieren und Menschen Krafft und Leben."[24] In addition: "Firmissime statuendum est etsi deus est alia res distincta a creaturis, tamen adesse eum

---
[22] C. R. 14, p. 1040: "Annotationes in Matthæum," of 1558.
[23] Comm. ad Rom. of 1532.
[24] Ord. Ex. of 1554, p. 16.

universæ creaturæ, et omnium creaturarum substantias, quæ servantur et quatenus servantur, sustentari a deo."[25]

Melanchthon develops this doctrine of the immanence of God in a manner strikingly similar to the way Kant later on formulated his famous doctrine of the moral law. The guarantee for the reality and objectivity of the Christian knowledge of God, the Reformer finds in the immanence of the eternal moral law of God.[26]

Such a view of God which Melanchthon voices, steers clear of the deterministic predestination of Luther and the rigid Stoicism of Calvin. Such a mediating view as Melanchthon has constructed, is, in my judgment, both superior to any other Reformation world-view, and at the same time, more closely akin to the traditional Christian doctrine of God formulated on the basis of the Old and New Testaments and Greek philosophy.

It is on the locus of God that we see most clearly the Reformer's speculative interest. For here, as in no other place, does he unite philosophy and scripture, reason and revelation. Melanchthon felt, as no other Reformer of his age, the need of a rational foundation for the concept Deity in his theological world-view. Consequently as far as I am concerned, Ferdinand Christian Baur has stated what holds good only for one period of Melanchthon's development (and that too a very early one) when he says of Melanchthon: "Alles menschliche Wissen von Gott, von seinem Dasein und Wesen, seinen Eigenschafften . . . beruht auf der goettlichen Offenbarung."[27] For beginning with Me-

---

[25]C. R. 12, p. 405, p. 402, p. 639. 23, p. 8. 21, p. 1077.
[26]Expl. S. Nic. of 1557, C. R. 23: p. 386.
[27]Baur, F. Chr.: "Vorlesungen ueber die Christliche Dogmengeschichte," IV, S. 72, Leipzig 1867.

lanchthon's Commentarius ad Epistolam Sancti Pauli ad Romanos of 1532, he manifests a decided fondness for the doctrine of "natural law" which is construed as "inborn," after Paul.[28]

In the Commentary on Romans of 1540,[29] is the first appearance of his nine-fold proof for the existence of God. As further proof of the speculative interest of Melanchthon on the locus of God, one need only turn to his critique of Plato's definition of God. Plato's definition of God is not necessarily wrong. It includes all that lex naturalis can see "De Deo sine patefactione divina." Natural light reveals to sinful man, the fact of God's existence, and that this God is all powerful, all-wise, and omnipresent in the world which he has created. But the churchly definition of God is "illustrior" in that it reveals the true character of God and his holy will. There is a comparative relation between the pagan or philosophic and the Christian definition of God; that is, the Christian definition is richer, has a plus sign over against the other.[30] This addition follows directly from the evident coördination of both norms of certainty: reason and revelation. From such an epistemological interlacing of reason and revelation, natural and revealed theology, Protestant thought of today may learn a much needed lesson.

The influence of Melanchthonian philosophy upon subsequent thought is clearly seen in his doctrine of the freedom of the human will. I have already pointed out the general outlines of the development of this theory. It will suffice now to call attention to the in-

---

[28]Romans 1. cf. Haussleiter: "Aus der Schule Melanchthons." S. 99, Th. 24, 405, Greifswald 1897.
[29]C. R. XV, 566 f.
[30]Init. doctr. phys.: C. R. 13, 199.

fluence of it upon the history of Protestant theology and philosophy.

As was pointed out, in the earliest period of Melanchthon's theological views, he was decidedly under the dominance of Luther's theory of the Bound Will. In fact, his deterministic predestinarianism was more acute than that of Luther himself. But under the influence of Erasmian humanism and idealism, he departed from Luther's notion of the Bound Will and fixed upon the theory of human freedom. The historical occasion for this change of view was undoubtedly the appearance of Erasmus' work on the freedom of the will. Now when Melanchthon went over to Erasmian humanism and idealism, he began a development within Protestant thought that has been cultivated in various directions up to the present day. For under the influence of Melanchthon's view on this score, there grew up and developed a line of idealistic thinkers beginning with such contemporaries of our philosopher-theologians as George Major, Johann Strigel, and Pfeffinger, and continuing through the Aufklærung in the philosophic writings of Kant (Critique of Practical Reason,) Ritschl (various works on Dogmatic Theology, especially "Reconciliation,") and finally Schleiermacher, whose "Christliche Glaube" and "Reden" betray a decided influence of Melanchthon's formulation of the locus of the freedom of the human will.

The chief contention of Melanchthon on the locus of freedom was this: In connection with Luther's contention of the ethico-religious slavery of the will, what becomes of the question of the individual guilt and moral responsibility of man? Melanchthon would say that in any theory of the Bound Will, morality becomes superfluous, and a science of ethics is impossible of construction. The sense of responsibility, the experience of guilt, actually demands human freedom in the very nature of the case. Given no freedom then man is not responsible for his actions. One cannot choose the good nor do the good who does not have power of free choice. Melanchthon's argument on this point is essentially the same as that formulated by Kant later on to wit: Du sollest denn du kannst. We might well say that a fundamental assertion of Melanchthon on the locus of freedom is: *Ultra posse nemo obligatur.*

With Melanchthon the present day puzzle of the conflict between the descriptive and normative sciences would be resolved by a purely practical interest: If determinism is the only alternative, then our whole philosophy of life would be meaningless. Law and ethics would be destroyed; all our social and political activities would be blighted. Thus for our philosopher there was only one thing to be done, and this he did: to reject totally Luther's Determinism or the so-called "servum arbitrium" in the interest of the clear facts of personal responsibility and the sense of guilt. Thus he could have said what Kant did: "Two things fill me with awe; the starry heavens above me and *the moral law within me.*"

In Melanchthon is to be found that interest which has been such an earnest one in all subsequent humanism and idealism which are in close relationship with Erasmus: the problem of responsibility and personal guilt. Melanchthon's theory of human freedom raises man above the level of animality, above an automaton relentlessly driven by biological and instinctive urges or drives, and vouchsafes unto him full rational personality capable of developing endlessly in the path of freedom, not merely a psychological one as with Luther, but also in matters pertaining to religion and ethics.

In spite of the many progressive thoughts which one meets in Melanchthon, thoughts which are in many respects, far in advance of his own age, there is a counter-current: the endency to lag back, to remain in the quaint Aristotelio-Medieval world. Herein is shown the spirit of conservatism: Melanchthon's continued belief in the astrological speculations and superstitions of his age, and his utter rejection of the Copernican revolution. It is indeed a thing surprising that such a man as Melanchthon, whose mind was so open, so critical, so investigating, and so intellectually curious, could upbraid so seriously a youthful contemporary, Joachim Rheticus, disciple of Copernicus at the University of Wittenberg, for advocating the Copernican scheme. Melanchthon briefly refers to it in his *Initia doctrinæ physicæ,* and regards Rheticus, his colleague, as "greatly unsettled" in his views.

But such behavior on the part of our Reformer is well understood when we learn that he regarded the implications of the Copernician theory as conflicting with the revealed truth contained in the Bible. This alone is sufficient to account for his rejection of it. Yet there is another reason why he parted the way with Copernicus and held fast to the Aristotelio-Ptolemaic universe: the superiority of the latter view is seen in the fact that such a world-scheme presented a framework which corresponded with the teaching of sensuous perception. And for the naïve Melanchthon *videre est credere.* For in his lectures on physics, Melanchthon combines Aristotelian physics and Ptolemaic astronomy with certain Biblical imagery: a combination quite easy to make, since the whole world-scheme was based on immediate sense data.

We do not have then in Melanchthon a complete *novus homo*—a man of the modern age. His is a spirit progressive and modern in some respects, reactionary, conservative, and medieval in other respects. He may be best described, I think, by the term which I have ascribed to him: *a twilight man.*

In fine: Whoever reads the writings of Melanchthon will be rewarded by the refreshing waters of this fountain of Evangelical truth and pious learning. The coloring which Melanchthon's system has given to Lutheran dogmatic theology; the natural superiority of his system over Zwingli's world-view; its possession of an originality so greatly missed in Calvin's system of thought; the absence of the wearisome thetical-anti-thetical divisions of Peter Lombard's works; its freedom from the subtle and hairsplitting distinctions so characteristic of Thomistic Peripateticism; its wholesome practical aim and exceptional interest in personality-culture; and its scriptural bases and frequent use of the rationalistic process are some of the factors which serve to elevate the system of Melanchthon above most of the other systems which have come down to us from Medieval and Reformation times.

I close this discussion of the life and system of a man of universal culture, refined tastes, diversified gifts, gentle and dignified bearings and Christian piety, with the words that appear on a painting of Melanchthon by Albrecht Duerer:

"Viventis potuit Durerius Ora Philippi mentem non potuit pingere docta manus."

And also with the words of Erasmus concerning our philosopher-theologian: "At Deum immortalem! Quod inventionis acumen! Quæ sermonis puritas et elegantia! Quanta reconditarum rerum memoria! Quam varia lectio! Quam verecundiæ regiæque prorsus indolis festivitas!"[34]

---

[a]Erasmus' Commentary on Thessalonians of 1515.

CHAPTER THREE

History of the Formation and Character of the Loci Up to 1521

The Loci Communes of Philip Melanchthon has passed through a very interesting development. It is necessary to follow minutely this development in order to have a proper understanding of the nature and genius of the Loci of 1521.

Since tihe time of George Theodore Strobel,[1] the historical development of the Loci has been distributed over seven periods. They are as follows:

Period I, The first adumbration of the Loci not published by the author himself.

Period II, The editions of the years 1521–1528 which embraces the first redaction edited by Melanchthon himself.

Period III, The editions of the so-called "second age" of the Loci, embracing the years 1535–1541.

Period IV, The editions of the "third age" of the Loci embracing the years 1542–1559.

Period V, The German translation of the Loci.

Period VI, The several other translations of it.

Period VII, Embracing the books pertaining to this work.

Our immediate interest in this connection confines us to an examination of the various literary phenomena up to, and including, the Loci of 1521.

---
[1]Strobel: Versuch einer litterar Geschichte von Philipp Melanchthons Locis theologicis als dem ersten Evangelischen Lehrbuche, Altdorf und Nurnberg, 1776. 8.

OF PHILIP MELANCHTHON 51

A. The First Adumbration

In 1518 when Melanchthon was called by Frederick the Wise to the chair of Greek in the newly founded Academy of Wittenberg, he spent the major part of his first year teaching sacred literature, especially the Gospel of Matthew and the Epistles of Paul to the Romans and to Titus.

His observations on Romans fell into the hands of his students who published them. To these observations Melanchthon had given the name "Lucubratiuncula", as he himself informs us already in the Loci of 1521.

The original draft of the Lucubratiuncula has been lost. But fortunately Roediger discovered in the Ducal Library of Gotha a history containing three very important documents. Codex 973 as it is called, contains three writings: I. Melanchthon's annotations of the Epistle to the Romans. II. The Wittenberg edition of the Loci of 1521. III. The Lucubratiuncula embracing the most common topics of theological science.

The character of the Lucubratiuncula[2] is best described as the rather extended outline of the lectures of a professor.

B.

In addition to the Lucubratiuncula, another little work titled Theological Institute of Melanchthon upon the Epistle of Paul to the Romans, deserves at least passing notice.

---

[2] For a fuller discussion of this work, Cf: Johann Christian August: Philip Melanchthons Loci theologici illustrati, Leip. 1821. Strobel: Historisch-Litterarische Nachricht von Philip Melanchthons Verdiensten um die Heilige Schrift, Altdorf 1773. 8 p. 96-119. Seckendorf: Commentarius de Lutheranismo, Ed. 2 Leip. 1694.

Kohl,[3] a professor in Hamburg first published this work in 1752, purporting to contain the autograph of Melanchthon.

This work is not to be identified with the Lucubratiuncula as some scholars have done. That it is a distinct work is borne out by the fact that the text of it which is extant, differs widely from the Lucubratiuncula. Because of such a great difference, I believe that Strobel and Friedmann who follow Kohl are in error when they call the Institute, the first adumbration of the Loci Communes.[4] The Institute is but another set of lecture notes which served as a sort of "Obeliscos" for Melanchthon during his lectures.

C. *The First Complete Edition of the Loci of 1521*

The Lucubratiuncula were prepared as a guide for the Lectures on Romans. However, as we have seen, they were published in 1520 without the knowledge or the consent of the author, by some of his students. After unsuccessful attempts to suppress the circulation of it, Melanchthon decided to revise the Lucubratiuncula. This he did. In the process of revision, he no doubt made use of the work titled "Institute on the Epistle to the Romans." This composite and revised work appeared in 1521 at Wittenberg under the following superscription:

"Loci communes rerum theologicarum, seu Hypotyposes Theologicæ. Auctore Philippo Melanchthone, Wittembergæ. an. MDXXI."

Three editions made their appearance in Wittenberg

---
[3]Kohl: Gesammelter Briefwechsel der Gelehrten auf das Jahr MDCCLI, Hamburg MDCCLI.
[4]Strobel: Neue Beytræge zur Litt. Ges. des XVI Jahrh. Vol. V, 2. p. 323-344. Cf. Friedmann: Philipi Melanthonis prima adumbratio locorum theologicorum. Wittembergæ, 1823.

during the year 1521. These editions were published under the personal care of Melanchthon. Between the years 1521–1525 fourteen editions appeared in Basil, Strassbourg, and Hagenau, but not under the personal supervision of Melanchthon.

Although primarily we are not interested in the succeeding editions of the Loci after 1525, yet we should note that several changes took place in the development.

Between the edition of 1525 and the first edition of the second age, Melanchthon published his Enchiridion Locorum.

Being a lover of truth, and knowing that the human mind errs, and the only way to banish error is by further thinking, Melanchthon decided that his previous Loci needed revision and amplification. He therefore proposed to make changes as can be observed already from his Commentary on the Epistle of Paul to the Colossians, 1527.[5] Thus as early as 1527 he had conceived the idea of revision and had observed imperfections in his work.

But he was so taken up with various projects, such as, The Saxon Visitation, public Colloquies, the Augsburg Assemblies, and added to these, the problem of examination of the writings of his enemies Eck, Cochlæus, Campanus, Carlstadt, and Schwenkfeld, he did not get around to it at once. Hence scholars[6] disagree when this was sent to the press.

---

[5] C. R. Vol. II p. 456, sqq.
[6] Fried, Myconius in his Historia Reformationis, p. 95, refers it to 1531. Some: Huttler in his Loci, p. 10, Mayer in his Dissertatio de Locis Theol. Philip Melanchthon, p. 12; Sontag and Wendler in Diss. de præcipuis quibundam Sec. XVI et XVII Theologis, p. 83; Durrer in Isag. ad Lile. Norm. Nurmba, p. 96; Baumgarten in Erlæuterungen der S. Schr. p. 255, and likewise Walsh, Budde, Brucker, refer it to year 1533. Cf. Melanchthon's own words which seem to favor 1533: Epist. ad Camerarium data Martio 1544 in C. R. V. p. 332, also: Epist. ad Brentium data Julio 1533 in C. R. II p. 666 sq. On the other hand Pezel in his Epist. dedicat. Locorum Theol. Vict. Strigelii,

Several doctrinal changes[7] are to bbe noted in the successive drafts of the Loci after 1521. The many changes in the subsequent redactions of the Loci are due to the author's continuous research and study, to the criticism of his opponents, to contact with Reformed and Catholic theologians, but especially to the growing independence of his own humanistic mind.

The Loci appeared under various titles during its development. They were successively known as:
1. Loci communes rerum theologicarum seu Hypotyposes theologicæ.
2. Loci communes theologici.
3. Loci theologici.
4. Loci præcipui theologici.

In the Loci of 1521 Melanchthon refers frequently to the works of Luther and praises them highly. The works of Luther to which he refers are: *The Antilatome, Freedom of the Christian Man, Babylonish Captivity, On Vows, on Spirit and Letter.*

How moving this little book was is attested by the words of Nicolaus Gerbel in 1521 who, writing to Joh. Schwebel on December 20, said: "Methodus Philippi adeo me commovit, ut dies et noctes nihil aliud somniem, nihil agam aliud, quam Wittenbergam."

Cochelæus,[8] who wrote a confutation against one Didymus Faventinus[9] (Philip Melanchthon) likened it unto a new Koran and called it a pest. The book

---

refers it to 1536. It is my own personal opinion that the weight of evidence is on the side of 1535.

[7]For following the theological development of the Melanchthonian doctrines throughout the various periods of the Loci the best works are: Galle: Charakteristik Melanchthons, Halle 1840; Herrlinger: Theologie Melanchthons.

[8]Cochlæi confutatio abbreviata adversus Didy. Faven. Philip Melanchthonis olim scripta, nunc primum edita in admonitionem fidelem Catholicorum apud exteros, Lipsiæ, apud Mich. Blem, 1531.

[9]For the assumption of this name by Melanchthon, vide C. R. Vol. I, p. 286. sqq.

was also severely attacked by John Eck in his Enchiridion Docorum communium adversus Lutheranos, Landishutæ 1525. Eck also published another work from Ingolstadt in 1530 against the Loci of 1521 in which he submits 404 articles for disputation. Moreover John Campanus wrote a book against it titled: Goettlicher und Heiliger Schrift-Restitution und Besserung.

On the other hand, Luther praised the work very highly, deeming it worthy of being placed into the new Testament Canon.[10]

In regard to the arrangement of the Loci of 1521, a marked influence of John of Damascus is readily seen.[11] For it was through the advent of the writings of John of Damascus into the West, that the topical method of writing became known to the occidental theologians.

The Loci opens with a brief but pointed consideration of the trinity, but in keeping with its practical aim quickly passes over the metaphysical doctrines of Christian theology and descends to a consideration of what the author judges to be the fundamental doctrines of faith and piety. It discusses such noble themes as Man, Sin, Law, Gospel, Grace, Faith and Justification, Sacraments, the Magistracy, Church Government, and such other doctrines as are deemed essential to a knowledge of saving faith.

The Loci is a clear and forceful statement of the Protestant position, and forthwith rejects many Roman Catholic teachings. It is highly polemical in tendency; so much so that on this score, it has been severely criticized by many. It is further objected that the work

---

[10]Cf. Jacob Heerbrand; Oratio Funebris: C. R. 10, 303. 293-313. 305.
[11]Migne, J. P.: Patrologiæ: Patrum Græcorum Traditio Catholica, Vol. 94: cf. the "Fons Scientiæ" of John of Damascus.

lacks something of the didactic nature of a handbook of theology.

It is an evident fact that the Loci is a child of its age, and as such partakes of the qualities of its age. The whole period was one of strife, contention, war, and bitter struggle. Moreover, while the author was preparing this little book, he no doubt had in mind, the crude roughness of Rhadinus as well as the subtle Aristotelian pratings of the theologians at Cologne, Louvain, and Paris. I am of the opinion that its highly polemical nature was absolutely indispensible at this time. For in the incipiency of the Protestant revolt, it would have been a tremendous mistake to have been purely didactic. It was as necessary to reject much of the dialectical nonsense emanating from the scholastic faculties under the name of "theology", and that too in a polemical fashion, as it was to establish and proclaim in a scientific and didactic manner, the system of Evangelical truth.

At any rate, the Loci of 1521 is something new and unheard of before in theological science, a system of doctrinal positions built upon and drawn solely from the word of God. The Loci is more than a mere textbook of Protestant dogmatics. It is at once a living, dynamic and motivating principle. Because of its practical aim and nature, and due to its scriptural basis, the work marks an epoch in theology, as Professor Schaff has so well said: "The book marks an epoch in the history of theology. It grew out of the exegetical lectures on the Epistle to the Romans, the Magna Charta of the evangelical system. It is an exposition of the leading doctrines of sin and grace, repentance and salvation. It is clean, fresh, thoroughly Biblical and practical. Its main object is to show that man cannot be saved by works of the law, or by his own merits, but only by the free grace of God in Christ as revealed in the gospel. It presents the living soul of divinity in contrast to the dry bones of degenerate scholasticism, with its endless thesis, anti-thesis, definitions, divisions, and subdivisions."[12]

After Melanchthon's death the Loci continued to be published and various commentaries were written on it. For fifty years it was the textbook of theology in the universities of Germany. However, Hutter wrote a Loci in 1610 which put Melanchthon's Loci in the shade during the 17th century.

One may say that the theological positions laid down by Melanchthon in the Loci of 1521, are merely a restatement of Luther's theological reflections up to this time. Melanchthon carefully sets forth in a systematic manner his master's teachings. And perhaps the case was inevitably so, for Melanchthon, the humanist, was indebted to Luther for his whole theology, for his religious interests during this period of his life. The stormy, blustery nature of Luther completely dominated the passive and reserved humanistic scholar when first he came to Wittenberg as a Professor of Greek in 1519. To a marked degree, then, Melanchthon is, in this period at least, shackled to the thought-forms and religious concepts of Luther.

Consequently, the Loci of 1521 becomes merely a scientifically arranged compend of the pure "Lutheran tradition." By this statement I do not mean to say that the views contained therein are not "Melanchthonian." But the association of these two Reformers was so intimate, the relationship so personal, the spirits so kindred, that what Luther thought, Melanch-

---

[12]Schaff: History of the Christian Church. Vol. 6. p. 369.

thon also entertained. The Loci thus becomes what both the Reformers held in common. Hence whoever seeks the so-called "Melanchthon tendency" must look beyond the first edition of the Loci of 1521. For in it, is not to be found that "independent spirit" which is a "Charakteristik" of his later works.

A brief glance at the implications of the Loci of 1521 may serve to cast light on the nature of this first Protestant work on dogmatics and also may serve to illustrate the position which Melanchthon sustained to Luther during this early period of his theological development.

Throughout the Loci of 1521 Melanchthon put far into the background the more abstract doctrines of the Christian religion, in the interest of more practical considerations. To his practical mind, there were certain dogmas which were incomprehensible. To quibble over the doctrines of the Trinity and to discuss the mode of the Incarnation, is just so much time uselessly spent. For: "mysteria divinitatis rectius adoraverimus, quam vestigaverimus."[13] To attempt to fathom the depths of such dogmas is but to degenerate into scholastic jokes and heresies.

In fact, Melanchthon entertained the same dislike for scholastic theology and philosophy as did Luther at this time.[14] Philosophy is disparaged and belittled by both of the Reformers. Both Reformers rule out philosophy and human reason as wholly unable to throw any light on the metaphysical doctrines of Christian faith. Again and again the reader confronts this same disparagement of the rationalistic process throughout the Loci of 1521. Divine revelation is the sole method

---

[13] C. R. 21, 84.
[14] C. R. I, 404: Melanchthon's "Defense of Luther against the Sorbonne Theologians."

by which the Christian is to approach an understanding of the doctrine of the Trinity or that of the Incarnation. The "foolishness of preaching" is superior to any scholastic syllogism or metaphysical reasoning.

The contribution of Melanchthon to the field of theology which won for him the honor of being styled an originator, was his view of Scripture and its relation to the science of dogmatic theology. In seeking to give his Loci a purely Christian theological foundation, he seized upon the notion that the very "forma christianismi" is contained in the Holy Scriptures. Thus he can say "Faillitur quisquis aliunde christianismi formam petit, quam e scriptura sacra." Dogmatics is to be a general reflection upon the whole of Scripture, not a dialectical or churchly development.

Scripture itself is to be the sole source for dogmatics. All else is mere hallucination. Commentaries are treacherous things and lack the purity of Canonical Scripture. As a rule they are more confusing than they are helpful. The only way to rightly understand scripture is to study it as first hand: "Multa enim docebit scripturarum usu spiritus, seu Johannes ait (I. 2, 27,) unctio, quæ quantavis humani ingenii industria non queat assequi."[15] Such views account for the copious reference to Scripture and direct quotations from it, which appear on almost every page of the Loci of 1521.

In the section dealing specifically with psychology or better, anthropology, it is easy to see that the author shares the Augustinian view. He follows Augustine to the ultimate conclusion of deterministic predestination. The will of man has no freedom. And why? Simply because the Scriptures say so. Then, too, in-

---

[15] K. P. 58.

dividual experience shows that this is the case: "Experientia enim usuque comperimus, non posse voluntatem sua sponte ponere amorem, odium aut similes affectus, sed affectus affectu vincitur."[16] Thus the Loci of 1521 teaches that the human will is unfree in both external and internal affections. Melanchthon is careful to make clear that he views deterministic predestination from the infralapsarian standpoint.[17]

One may remark that Melanchthon did not abide by such views as presented in the Loci of 1521 concerning, for example, the Trinity and the human will. For early as 1523 in his Commentary on John, we find a philosophic attempt to lay a theological foundation for the Trinity in which there is much speculation; and after the controversy between Luther and Erasmus on the freedom of the human will, Melanchthon forsook his former Augustinian view and espoused the cause of human freedom.

It is most gratifying for one who holds the evangelical view, to learn that Melanchthon would not share the lax views of sin as taught by some of the modern schools. In the Loci of 1521, sin is not a mere contingent antagonism (cf. Kant's view of sin as a spontaneous declension from the moral law), nor a quiescent predisposition or natural tendency alone, but is a full and living realization. Hence sin for Melanchthon was something more than the Thomistic notion of the loss of original righteousness; it is more than "vulneratio naturæ," or "defectus," or "languor." Nor was Melanchthon contented with Duns' conception of sin as a "rebellion from original righteousness," or a loss of the "donum superadditum." Sin for Melanchthon is "true impiety," "contempt of spiritual things," "true

---
[16] K. P. 71.
[17] K. P. 81.

flesh." As a result of sin, man is in darkness, error, blindness; man is dead: "cum absit vita, nihil esse in nobis nisi peccatum et mortem.[18]

In the sections dealing with law, Melanchthon voices already in this early period, two ideas which have become special features of his completed world of thought namely: the doctrine of the "lex naturæ" and the Stoic principle of κοιναὶ ἔννοιαι.

In his treatment of justification, the forensic notion is not voiced in the Loci of 1521. In fact this theory of justification did not come into definite form until very late in the doctrinal writings of the Lutheran church. It was not formulated until 1549 or the date of the appearance of the third edition of the Loci. Both Reformers, it would seem, were solely occupied with merely defining justifying faith and not with what justification in its deepest sense really was. Their sole interest lay in salvaging the doctrine of faith from the Roman Catholic wreckage. Melanchthon's thesis is the characteristic Protestant formula "sola fides." In his treatment of it, he drives a cleavage with Pelagian work-righteousness.

In the section dealing with the sacraments, Melanchthon energetically expresses the sufficiency and absoluteness of the principle of faith. Forthwith he rejects the Thomistic notion that the sacraments work "ex opere operato." The presence of faith in the hearts of believers is an absolute necessity. The particular sacraments during the period which includes the Loci of 1521, retain only symbolic meaning. The author gives a brief but pointed critique of the Catholic sacraments.

The Loci of 1521 is a very important work in the

---
[18] K. P. 95.

history of Protestant theology. This is true not merely because it is the first Protestant work on dogmatic theology, and, as such, has its historical importance, but also because it affords us with a glimpse at the very fundamental principles which form the basis for an independent system of theology, with its own interests and problem, and attempts at a solution of those problems.

Even when one acknowledges that the Loci does lack the didactic nature of our modern handbooks of theology, nevertheless, the reader will be richly rewarded for his diligent and patient study of it, by the keen, practical aim of the author, which is the priceless virtue by which he has commended the glorious message of the New Testament, in its purest and most unmingled simplicity, not only to the people of his own day, but to the men of every age.

PART TWO

Translation of Loci Communes

DEDICATORY EPISTLE

"To the equally Pious and Learned man, Dr. Tileman Plettner:[19] Greetings from Philip Melanchthon."

Last year, while expounding the Epistle of Paul to the Romans, I arranged in a methodical manner so to speak, the most common topics of theological science. In addition, I set in order the medley of the epistle itself. This laborious study, though prepared for the sole purpose of indicating to those whom I privately taught the nature of the argument of the Pauline disputation and its manner of refutation (καὶ ἔλεγχον) in as fruitful a way as it possibly could be done, was nevertheless circulated by some unknown persons. In a word, whoever published it, I approve their zeal more than their judgment. Especially is this the case, since I had written it in such a way that, without the Epistle of Paul it could not have been properly understood, what theme I had followed throughout the entire work.

Now because it is not within my power to suppress a book made almost for common use, it seems best to revise and re-arrange it. For indeed, many things contained therein wanted a more accurate argument, and

---

[19]Tileman Plettner, "Magister et Plebanus in Stolberg" had studied in Leipsic and Erfurt and matriculated in Wittenberg in 1520. Upon the elevation of Wolfgang to the Rectorship of the university in 1521, Plettner was made vice-rector. He subsequently became a licentiate and on Oct. 14, 1521, received the Doctor of Theology degree. More can be learned of this interesting character by consulting E. Pfiitzner: "Tilemann Plettner," Stolberg, O. J. (1883) cf. C. R. 1. 459f.

likewise many things, revision. Moreover, because it concerns the whole argument, the principal topics of Christian discipline are indicated in order that youths may understand both what things are to be sought out in the Scriptures, as well as learn under what base hallucinations they labor everywhere in theological science, who have handed down to us the subtle pratings of Aristotle, instead of the doctrine of Christ.

I am indeed treating everything sparingly and briefly, due to the fact that I am discharging the duty of an Index rather than a commentary. Hence, I am only stating the nomenclature of the topics, to which that person roaming through the Divine Scriptures may be directed. I am not doing this to lead the studious away from the Scriptures to some obscure and intricate arguments of my own; but if possible, to incite them to the Scriptures.

For on the whole, I am not quite equal to the commentaries, not even to those of the Ancients. So far from that am I, that I would not by any longer writings of mine, restrain[20] anyone from the study of the Canonical Scripture. On the contrary, I would desire nothing quite so much if it were possible, as that all Christians be thoroughly conversant with divine letters alone, and be wholly transformed into their nature. For since the Godhead has expressed its most complete image in them, it cannot from any other source be more

---

[20] The same sentiment was expressed by both Luther and Calvin. In a letter to Melanchthon, Luther said: "Sola scriptura, inquis, legenda est citra commentaria. Recte de Hieronymo et Origene et Thoma hisque similibus dicis. Commentaria scripserunt in quibus sua potius, quam Paulina aut Christiana tradiderunt: tuas annotationes nemo commentarium appellet, sed indicem duntaxat legendæ scripturæ et cognoscendi Christi, idquod nullus hactenus præstitit commentariorum, qui saltem extet." "Luther's Letters": DeWette 11, 239. For similar views expressed by Calvin see: C. R. 29, 257. cf. Stæhelin. "John Calvin" 1, 58.

surely or correctly known. He is mistaken who seeks the form of Christianity in any other source than Canonical Scripture. For indeed how much do the Commentaries lack the purity of Canonical Scripture? In Canonical Scripture, one will find nothing but what is worthy of honor, while in the Commentaries how many things depend upon the valuation of human reason! Things I say, which diametrically oppose spiritual judgment! The authors did not impair the natural (τό ψυχικόν) so as to hope for nothing save spiritual things. If you take away from Origen his absurd allegories and his forest of philosophical sentences, how little will be left! And yet, the Greeks with great unanimity follow him, as do certain of the Latin writers like Ambrosius and Jerome, men who seem to be pillars. And after these, almost every author, the more recent he is, the more adulterated.

In short, Christian discipline has degenerated into Scholastic jests, concerning the which, one may doubt whether they are more impious than foolish. Finally, it cannot be but that human writings often entangle even the cautious reader. But if at all, prophecy is a certain afflatus of the Divine Spirit, the knowledge of things divine, why then do we not embrace this kind of letters, through which the Spirit will flow? Does God accomplish all things by means of his word? For the Spirit will teach many things by the use of the Scriptures, or as John says (I, 2:2) the unction, which the activity of human nature be it ever so great, cannot comprehend. I have nothing in view but to assist in one way or another, the studies of those who wish to be conversant with the Scriptures. If this little work will not seem to fulfill this task, may it certainly perish; to be sure though, I in no way propose to retract my words, whatever the public opinion of the public work will be.

COMMON TOPICS OR THEOLOGICAL OUTLINES[21]

In the individual sciences certain topics or places are wont to be sought, whereby the whole of each science is comprehended.[22] These topics are to be considered a goal to which all our studies may be directed. Now in theology, we see that the ancient authors aimed at this indeed cautiously and prudently. Of more recent authors, John of Damascus and Peter Lombard both foolishly did so. For John of Damascus plays the philosopher too much, while Peter Lombard chose to heap up the opinions of man rather than to present the judgment of Scriptures. And although I do not wish the studious to tarry in one place, as I said before, nevertheless, I am giving this almost necessary classification by Particulars, in order to indicate at least, on what topics the whole scheme hangs, and to the end that they may understand whither they must direct their studies.

Moreover, these are for the most part, the principal heads[23] of theological science:

God	The fruit of grace
Unity	Faith
Trinity	Hope
Creation	Charity
Man, the strength of man	Predestination

---

[21]Hypotyposis: So used by Aristotle: "Ethic. Nicom: 1, 7: is then an "Adumbratio et institutio brevis," or as Melanchthon says: "Simplex et certa forma doctrinæ," as opposed to the "dissimiles et ambigui modi loquendi." C. R. 23, 116.

[22]This and the following sentences are expanded into a discussion of "methods of the sciences" in the preface of the edition of 1535. In it one can see the influence of "scholastic dialectic" which is somewhat depreciated in the edition of the Loci of 1521.

Sin	Sacramental tokens
The fruit of sin, vices	The estates of men
Punishments	Civil offices
Law	Bishops
Promises	Condemnation
Renewal through Christ	Blessedness
Grace	

As certain of these are straightway incomprehensible, so on the contrary, there are some that Christ has willed the entire company of Christians to know fully. The mysteries of divinity we have the more rightly adored than investigated. On the other hand, they cannot be put to test without danger, because not rarely holy men indeed have attempted to do so. And too, the most High God clothed his Son with flesh, in order to incite us from the contemplation of his majesty,[24] to the contemplation of the flesh and indeed our own frailty.

Thus Paul writes in I Cor. 1:21, that God wills to be known without doubt by a new method, through the method of the "foolishness of preaching," since he could not be known in his wisdom through wisdom. Accordingly, then, there is no reason why we should put much labor on the greatest topics such as, God, on

---

[23]"Capita": This shows a decided influence exerted over Melanchthon by Rudolf Agricola. The themes are almost identical in both writers. In the background may be seen John of Damascus, who introduced the thetical-antithetical method into the Western Church. His Fountain of Knowledge is a striking example of his use of this method.

[24]Contemplationem invitaret: Melanchthon's position in the field of philosophy was that of nominalism. The phrase reflects his attempt to distinguish sharply the sphere and sources of philosophy and theology. The point of departure for all Christian theology he learned from Luther. This is essentially the same view as Luther expressed to Spalatin in a letter: "Luther's Letters" DeWette 1, 226. As Didymus Faventinus, Melanchthon used sharper words. C. R. 1, 305.

the Unity and Trinity of God, on the great mystery of Creation, and on the mode of Incarnation. I ask you, what did the Scholastic theologians gain so many years ago, when they busied themselves with these topics alone? Did they not, as Paul says, become vain in their disquisitions,[25] while trifling a whole lifetime about universals, formalities, connotations and I know not what other meaningless words? And moreover, their folly might have gone unnoticed had not their foolish disputations for a time obscured to us the Gospel and the Benefits of Christ.

Now if I should like to be a clever person in a matter that is unnecessary, I could easily tear down whatever arguments for the dogmas of faith they have produced.[26] And how many of them would seem to make for sure heresies more rightly than for Catholic dogmas!

I do not see how I can call that man a Christian who is ignorant of the remaining topics such as the power of sin, the law and grace. For by them is Christ properly known, if indeed this is to know Christ, to wit, to know his benefits and not as they teach, to perceive his natures and the mode of his incarnation. Unless one knows why Christ took upon himself human flesh and was crucified, what advantage would accrue from having learned his life's history? Or on the other hand, is it of no consequence for a physician to have become acquainted with the kinds, colors and properties of plants, in order to know their native power? Ac-

---

[25]"In disceptationibus suis": Melanchthon has in mind the passage in Roms. 1, 21, where the Vulgate reads: "evanuerunt in cogitationibus suis."

[26]In the draft of the Loci of 1522, known as C, the author inserts "e philosophia." The phrase would then read: "Whatever arguments for the dogmas of faith they have produced from philosophy." He had by this time become acquainted with the false philosophical foundation of scholasticism, and this accounts for the insertion of these words.

cordingly it behooves us to become acquainted with Christ who has been given as a remedy for us, or to use the language of Scripture, "for our salvation," in some other way than that exhibited by the Scholastics.

Precisely this is Christian knowledge, to know what the law demands, whence you may seek the power to discharge the injunctions of the law, whence you may seek pardon for sin, how you may arouse a wavering mind against the Devil, the flesh and the world, and finally how you may console a dejected conscience. Of course the Scholastics teach such things, do they not? In the Epistle to the Romans, when he drew up a compendium of Christian doctrine, did Paul the author philosophize about the mysteries of the Trinity, the mode of the Incarnation or about "creation active and passive?" On the contrary, what does Paul do? He reasons most certainly about the Law, Sin, and Grace. Topics, I say, on which alone the knowledge of Christ depends. How frequently Paul testifies to the faithful that he wishes for the rich knowledge of Christ! For he foresaw it would come to pass that with respect to the remaining salutary topics, we would turn our minds from Christ unto the frigid disputations of others. And accordingly I shall delineate another plan of these topics in order to commend Christ to you, to confirm your conscience and to arouse your mind against Satan. Many seek the topics of virtues and vices only in the Scriptures, but this observation is more philosophic than Christian. Why I put it thus, you will indeed understand somewhat later.

ON THE POWERS OF MAN, ESPECIALLY FREE WILL

Augustine and Bernard wrote on Free Will but the former, indeed, retracted his writings in many ways in the later works which he wrote against the Pelagians. Bernard is not consistent. There are some works on this subject even among the Greek authors, but they are rare. Since I shall not follow human opinions, I shall set forth the subject with simplicity and clarity, a thing which authors both ancient and modern have almost obscured. And they have done so because they interpreted the Scripture in such a way as to wish to satisfy simultaneously the judgment of human reason. It seemed not civil enough to teach that man by necessity sins; and it seemed too cruel to blame the will for being unable to turn itself from vice to virtue. Therefore they attributed to human powers more than was proper, and too, they strangely wavered when they saw that everywhere the Scriptures opposed rational judgment.

Within this topic, although Christian doctrine differs from philosophy and human reason, philosophy has gradually crept into Christianity, and the impious dogma of Free Will has been received and the beneficence of Christ has been obscured by that profane and natural wisdom of human reason. The word "free will" has come into usage[27] from divine letters, and is most incongruous with the sense and judgment of spirit, by which things we see that holy men have been offended quite frequently. That which is designated "reason" has been taken over from Platonism, and is especially pernicious. For just as in these latter times the church has embraced Aristotle in preference to Christ, so immediately after the inception of the church, Christian doctrine was weakened through the fusion of Platonic philosophy. And so it happens that besides the Canonical Scriptures, there are no pure

---

[27]Usurpata: Spalatin in his German translation renders this phrase as follows: "ist in Gebrauch Kommen."

letters in the church. In general, whatever has been handed down by way of commentaries, smells of philosophy.

In the first place then, in giving a description of the nature of man, I shall have no need of the many divisions employed by the philosophers, but shall use only a few. In fact, man is divided into two parts only.[28] For in man are the faculty of cognition (vis cognoscendi) and the faculty by which he either follows up or shuns those things which he has learned. The faculty of cognition is that by which we perceive or understand; by which we reason and mutually compare things and deduce conclusions, one after the other. The second part, or the faculty from which the affections take origin, is that by which we either resist or follow after the things known. This faculty is sometimes denominated will (voluntas), sometimes affection (affectum), sometimes appetite (appetitum). I do not see that any great importance is to be attached to the separation of the senses (sensus) from the intellect (intellectus) as they say; or the sensuous from the higher as being not only that in which are contained hunger, thirst, and the like passions of brute beasts, but also as being that in which are to be found love, hate, hope, fear, sorrow, wrath and those passions which originate from these. This they call the will (voluntas). Cognition serves the will, and accordingly the will (voluntas) joined with cognition or deliberation of the intellect they call by the new term "free will" (liberum arbitrium). For just as a tyrant is in a republic, so also is the will in man. And as a senate is obnoxious

---

[28] In order to get a full understanding of this and what follows, it is necessary to compare this section with the author's remarks contained in a little work called "Lucubratiuncula" which is really the original out of which the Loci of 1521 grew. cf. C. R. XXI, 14.

to a tyrant, just so is cognition obnoxious to the will; so that although cognition may advise good, nevertheless, the will rejects it and is carried away of its own desire, as I shall more fully explain later on. Again, the intellect joined with the will (intellectum cum voluntate conjunctum) they call "reason" (ratio). I shall employ neither "reason" (ratio) nor "free will" (liberum arbitrium); but I shall denominate the parts of man simply as the faculty of cognition and the faculty which is subject to the affections, that is, to love, hate, hope, fear and the like. This ought to teach how that hereafter, the distinction between law and grace can be more easily shown. And too, how it can the more certainly be known whether there is freedom within the power of man.

In this matter, it is wonderful how laboriously both ancient and modern authors have engaged themselves. If anyone shall misrepresent these things I shall freely and bravely protect my statements. For I have desired to delineate man in as full a manner as possible, and it appears to me that I have spoken of the parts of man as much as is necessary.

Moreover, the law pertains to the faculty of cognition, that is, the knowledge of things which should be done; while virtue and sin pertain to the faculty of the affections. Freedom (libertas) is not rightly said to belong to the "knowing part" (in partem cognoscentem) but conforming to the will, it is torn hither and thither. On the other hand, this is freedom, to be able to do or not to do, to be able to do thus or otherwise. And so it is to be investigated whether and to what extent the will is free.

REPLY

Seeing that all things that happen, happen necessarily according to divine predestination, there is no freedom of the human will. Paul in Roms. 11:36 says: "For of him and through him," etc.; and in Eph. 1:1, "Who worketh all things according to the counsel of his own will." Matt. 10:29: "Are not two sparrows sold for a farthing? And one of them shall not fall to the ground without your Father?" I prithee, what statement could be clearer than this sentence? Prov. 16:4: "The Lord hath made all things for himself, even the wicked for the day of evil." And again, Prov. 20:24: "Man's goings are directed by the Lord. How then can a man understand his own way?" Moreover, Prov. 16:9 reads: "A man's heart deviseth his own way, but the Lord directeth his steps." And even the divine histories teach the same things. Gen. 15:16: "The iniquity of the Amorites is not yet full." I Sam. 2:25: "They heeded not the voice of their father, for the Lord would kill them." What is more like fortuitous chance than the fact that, Saul going off to seek asses, is annointed by Samuel, thus inaugurating the kingdom? Again, I Sam. 10:26: "There went away with Saul a part of the band of men whose hearts God had touched." I Kings 12:15: "The King hearkened not unto the people, for the cause was from the Lord, that he might perform his sayings which he spake unto Jeroboam the son of Nebat, by the hand of the Shilonite." And what else does Paul do but refer to divine purpose, all things which are made? Roms. 9:11. Carnal judgment or that of human reason shrinks from this thought, whereas on the contrary, spiritual judgment embraces it. Nor may one learn with more certainty from any other source, either the fear of God or trust in him, than when the mind is imbued with this thought of predestination. Does not Solomon teach this everywhere in Proverbs, so as to instruct sometimes in the fear of God, sometimes in faith? Does he not inculcate the same in the book of Ecclesiastes? For indeed, it is of great importance for both the restraint and condemnation of the wisdom and prudence of human reason, to believe firmly that God created all things. Does not Christ in Luke 12:7 console his disciples in an effectual manner with the words: "All the hairs of your head are numbered?"

"What then," to use the term of some (the Schoolmen), "is there no contingency[29] in things, no chance, no fortune?" The Scriptures teach that all things happen by necessity. Such is the case; and it may seem to you that there is contingency in human affairs but in this idea, rational judgment must be overruled. Solomon occupied with the notion of predestination says: "And I beheld that for all the works of God that are done under the sun, man cannot find out the reason." Ecc. 8:17. But I may seem foolish to discuss in the very outset of this work, a topic so difficult as that of predestination, and yet, what consequence in saving will there be, whether I treat in the first or last topic, a matter which falls into every department of my disputation? And since freedom of the will must be treated in the first topic, how could I dissemble the opinion of Scripture when it destroys freedom of the will by the very necessity of predestination? Nevertheless I do not think it at all profitable forthwith to imbue the minds of youths with this opinion that all things come to pass not by the plans and attempts of mankind, but according to the will of God. Does Solomon in that book written expressly for youths at

---

[29]Contingentia: The opposite of "necessitas." This is aimed at Thomas who taught that: "Effectus habet contingentiam vel necessitatem." Summa 1, 25, 3, and 4. cf. also Duns Scotus: "Voco contingenter evenire, evitabiliter evenire." Sent. II dist. 25, qu. 1, 22.

once point out this fact? No! And moreover, the fact that scriptural belief in predestination seems too harsh to the mass of people, is attributable to the fact that the impious theology of the Sophists has so inculcated us with the doctrines of the contingency of things and free will that, as a result, our delicate ears shrink from the truth of Scripture.

Hence, in order to be considerate of those persons who regard what I have said about predestination as too harsh, I shall more minutely investigate the very nature of the human will itself, to the end that the studious may discover that the Sophists are wrong, not only in theological science but even in natural judgment. Moreover I shall speak about the subject of predestination a little later in its proper place, and shall in as brief a manner as will be permissible endeavor to refute all those things which the Sophists have written on the subject. Eccius says that Valla, because of his refutation of the opinion of the Schools on free will, wished to know more than he had learned to know. That is to say, Valla was an exceedingly witty jester. Now if these sirens should likewise bring the charge against me that a man who is a professor of languages is engaged in the science of theology, what else would I object but that they should not estimate a work by its author. Now it makes no great difference what we may teach, but whether those things are true which we teach. Nor should we consider any other thing than the teaching of sacred things, unless of course we are not Christians, seeing indeed that Christian Doctrine ought to be common to all.

1. If you estimate the power of the human will as touches its natural capacities according to human reason, it cannot be denied that there is in it a certain kind of liberty in things external. These are matters

which you yourself might experience to be within your power, such as: to greet or not to greet a man; to put on certain attire or not to put it on; to eat meat or not to eat it as you will. Upon this contingency of external works those philosophers who attributed freedom to the will, have fastened their eyes. In truth, however, because God does not look upon external works but upon the inner motions of the heart, Scripture has recorded nothing about such freedom. Those who do fashion their character by an external and affected affability teach this sort of freedom, especially the philosophers and the more recent theologians.

2. On the other hand, internal affections are not within our power. For by experience and practice we have found out that the will of its own accord cannot assume love, hate or the like affections; but that one affection is conquered by another. So much so that for an instance, because you were offended by one whom you one time loved, you now cease to love him. For you love yourself more ardently than you love anyone else. Nor may I agree with the Sophists in their denial of the fact that the human affections such as love, hate, joy, sorrow, envy, ambition and the like, pertain to the will. For now, nothing is said about hunger or thirst. But what is the will if not the fountain of the affections? And why do we not use the word "heart" instead of the "will" since Scripture calls the heart the most powerful portion of man, and that in which the affections take origin? Moreover, the Schools are mistaken in their imagination that the will by its very nature is opposed to the affections, or that it can assume an affection as often as the intellect advises or warns it.

3. Why is it that we men often choose that which is opposite to an affection? In the first place, because in external works we sometimes select a thing other

than that which the heart, or for that matter, the will, desires, it can happen that one affection is conquered by another. Thus it cannot be denied that although Alexander of Macedon may be a lover of pleasure, nevertheless because he is more eager for glory, he chooses labor and spurns pleasure. He does this not because he does not love the latter, but because he more strongly loves the former. To be true we see that in other characters, other affections rule, and that each man is influenced by his own desire. In stingy individuals the desire for possessions dominates; while in those who are more liberal, according to human judgment, the desire for fame and popular thanks rule supreme.

4. Then too perhaps it may be that something is chosen exactly contrary to all affections. When this is done, it is done out of simulation; so that when someone treats kindly, courteously and affably, a man whom he hates from the bottom of his heart, and to whom he truly wishes some evil, there is perhaps no certain cause. Such a man as this, although not perceiving it, is conquered by some other affection—for there are some characters so blind that they flatter even those whom they hate—such a man, I say, feigns affability in an external work in which there may seem some kind of liberty. Now this is that will which the foolish Scholastics have fashioned for us when they teach their fictitious penitences to wit, such a power which, no matter how you may be affected, can temper and moderate the affections. Just according as you are affected, they think that there is a faculty of the will for bringing forth, as they say, "good acts."[80]

---

[80]"Elicere actus bonas": In the Lucubratiuncula Melanchthon expresses himself against the schools teaching "free will" which can assume or put down any affection whatsoever. This is the "Ausgangspunkt" for his argument against "actum elicitum." cf. C. R. 21:

If you hate someone, the will can determine to hate this person no longer. Thus although we are by nature without reverence for God, they teach that the will can elicit that which will in the future love God. I ask you, dear reader, whether you do not think those to be insane who have devised such a will as this for us! Would that the Sophist who misrepresents this were near me, that I might have the opportunity to refute by a true book and a sane disputation, that foolish, impious, and erroneous opinion about the will! For when he who hates does decide to put away his hatred, unless indeed he is overcome by some more vehement affection, it is not the result of an act of the will, but is plainly some false reasoning power of the intellect. If Paris decides to put away the love of Cenone, unless he has been overcome by a more vehement affection, it is a counterfeit and false reasoning of the intellect. It can happen that something differing from the intellect might be enjoined by the heart upon your external members, tongue, hands, eyes, and even the soul may be affected, because by nature we are mendacious. Just such was the case with Joab, when he ordered his tongue and his eyes in such a manner as to seem to approach affably Amasa (II Sam. 20:9 f). But in reality, he could not command his heart to put away the affection which he had already conceived. He does put it

---

16f. Duns Scotus in opposition to Thomas Aquinas has posited the supremacy of the will over the intellect. Duns taught that the will possesses freedom and that too in an absolute sense. It is self-determined and has experienced no actual "vulneratio naturæ" through sin. cf. Scotus in Sent. lib. 11 Dist. 28, Qu. 1. Against such the author inveighs. Perhaps he has in mind Eck's statement at Leipsic: "Intendo probare illud esse conveniens sacræ scripturæ, sanctis patribus fidei Christianæ, liberum arbitrium, voluntatem humanam habere causalitatem activam, vim productivam, elicitivam operis meritorii. cf. Loescher: Reformationsakten 11,294.

away, however, when this affection with which he is seized has been overcome by some stronger desire.

5. The Schools do not deny the affections, but call them a weakness of human nature. They also say that it is enough that the will produces certain diversely "elicited acts." But for my part, I deny that there is in man any faculty at all that can seriously oppose the affections. I am of the opinion that these so-called "elicited acts" are nothing but a false reasoning of the intellect. For since God judges hearts, it must be that the heart together with its affections, constitutes the highest and most powerful part of man. And besides, why would God estimate man by his weaker part and not rather by his better part, if the will is different from the heart and is better and even stronger than the part called affections? What will the Sophists say on this score? But if we use the word "heart" as Scripture does, instead of Aristotle's word "will," we would avoid such crass and stupid errors as these. Aristotle defined the will as that choice in external works. This is indeed false. But what relation do external works have to Christian discipline if the heart is adulterated? Besides, Aristotle himself did not produce those "elicited acts"[81] which Scotus has fabricated. But I am not contending so much to refute them as I am to teach you, Christian reader, what you ought to follow. I confess that in the choice of externals there is some liberty. But of a truth, I forthwith deny that the inner affections are within our power to oppose seriously the affections. These things I speak of the natural man. They who are justified by the Spirit, in them I say, the good and evil affections are at war, as I shall teach below.

---

[81]"Elicitos Actus": A. and B. read "licitus actus." This, however, is a mistake in printing.

6. In addition, of what consequence is it, to discuss freedom in external matters when God requires purity of heart? Whatever foolish and impious men have written about freedom of the will and work righteousness, is an utter Pharisaic tradition. Now when an affection shall have been a little more vehement, it cannot be but that it will sprout forth; or as an ancient proverb reads: "although you may expel nature with a two-pronged fork, yet it will hasten its return with might and main."[32] And now, as many things as we do which seem good as far as external appearance is concerned, and which we ourselves deem to be good because we do not realize that the affection is base, whence, I ask, does the deed take origin? For says Solomon in Prov. 14:12: "There is a way that seemeth right unto a man, but the end of it leads unto death." And Jeremiah (17:9) says: "The heart of man is perverse and inscrutable." And David (in Ps. 18:13): "Who understands his faults?" Also Ps. 24:7: "Remember not my sins of ignorance." An affection carries off blind men into so many things that we simply cannot determine them. Therefore, a Christian mind ought to consider not of what kind a work is in appearance, but what is the nature of the affection in the mind; not what kind of liberty there is in works, but wherein there is liberty in the affections. Pharisaic Scholastics will declare the power of free will, but a Christian will confess that there is nothing less within his power than his own heart. And I would that the foolish Scholastics might see how many thousands of souls have been destroyed by the Pharisaic traditionalism about free will. Moreover, when I treat of the topic of original sin, I shall have more to say about the affections.

---

[32]This is a quotation from one of the "Epistles" of the well known Latin poet, Horatius Flaccus. cf. Epistles of Horace: 10, 24.

Summary

If you refer the human will to predestination, there is liberty neither in external nor internal works, but all things come to pass according to Divine purpose.

If you refer the will to external works there seems to be from natural judgment, some degree of liberty.

If you refer the will to the affections, even from the point of view of natural judgment there is plainly no liberty.

Now when an affection has begun to rage and to burn, it cannot be restrained from bursting forth.

You see, reader, how much more certainly I have written about freedom of the will than either Bernard or for that matter any of the Scholastics? Moreover, the things which I have so far disputed, will become more and more clear in the remaining topics of this compendium.

On Sin

The Sophists exceedingly obscured this topic of theology in their distinctions between actual and original sin and many other things too numerous to mention. For indeed, of what moment is it to relate in a compendium all the dreams of all these Sophists? I shall relate the whole matter in but a few words and shall employ the word "sin" as the Scripture does.

The Nature of Sin

1. Original sin is a native propensity and a certain genial impulse[33] and energy[34] by which we are drawn

---

[33]Concerning the doctrine of free will Melanchthon underwent several changes during the various stages of his theological development.

away into sin. It was propagated upon all posterity by Adam. Just as there is a native force in fire by which it pushes upward, so is there in man a native force to sin; or we may liken it to the force of a magnet which attracts iron unto itself. Scripture does not call the one "original" and the other "actual." For original sin is clearly some actual depraved desire. But the Scripture calls sin "vice," as much original as actual, although it sometimes denominates as the "fruits of sins" what we call actual sins. Paul is wont to do this in the Epistle to the Romans. And what we call "original sin" David sometimes speaks of as "crookedness," sometimes "iniquity." But I shall not dispute over these foolish relations in sin. Sin is a depraved affection, a depraved motion of the heart against the law of God.

Origin of Original Sin

2. When God most Great most Good made man sinless, through His Spirit He was present with man, to incite man to pursue the right. This same Spirit would have controlled all of Adam's posterity had he not fallen. Now subsequent to Adam's fall God opposed man, so that the Spirit of God is not with man to serve as his guide. Thus it happens that the soul

---

But in the midst of these changes he, like Luther, always had an ethico-practical interest in predestination. It was for Melanchthon as later for Calvin a sort of "locus consolatorius." It was that which was certain for him, when all else was not clear. Cf. C. R. I, 538. For this gradual process of development consult the following works: F. Frank: "Die Theologie der Concordienformel" I, 130 ff. Luthardt: Lehre vom freien Willen" 149 ff. Herrlinger: "Die Theologie Melanchthons." 72 ff.

[34]Energia: Sin is no mere passive something but a definite, living, active reality. Hence Melanchthon defines original sin as an "energy." In C (edition of 1522) he writes: energia et genialis impetus carnis ignorantis deum, quærendi carnalia propagatus.

being without celestial light and life is in darkness. As
a result, it most ardently loves itself, seeks its own desires and wishes nothing but carnal things and despises
God. But how can I reach with mere words the depravity of the human heart? It cannot but be true
that a creature whom the love of God has not absorbed,
loves itself in the highest degree. It is impossible for
the flesh to love spiritual things. For in Genesis 6:3
we read: "my spirit will not persevere with man, for
he is flesh." And Paul says (Roms. 8:5) "they that
are after the flesh," that is, they that are without the
spirit of God (for indeed it appears from the passage
in Genesis, that by the flesh is meant human powers
without the spirit of God), "do mind the things of the
flesh"; and again, "The carnal mind is enmity against
God." Thus when the Sophists teach that original sin
is lack of original righteousness, they teach correctly.[35]
But why do they not add that, where original righteousness or the spirit is lacking, there of a truth is the flesh,
true impiety, true contempt for spiritual things? And
so the first and chief affection of human nature is self-love, by which it is drawn away to wish for and desire
only what seems to its nature good, sweet, pleasant and
glorious. It hates and dreads things which appear to
be natural calamities, and is opposed to that one who
keeps it from whatever it desires, or who enjoins it to

---

[35] This sentence and the following ones constitute a sharp polemic against the scholastic doctrine of original sin. The scholastic notion on this locus is somewhat as follows: "Original sin is merely a 'defectus,' a sort of "languor." For Thomas it was something negative, a "vulneratio naturæ," or as elsewhere he called it "quidam habitus corruptus." But all the while, "inclinatio naturalis ad virtutem non amittitur"; it was only weakened by original sin. cf. Thomas: Summa Prima sec. quæst. 85 art. 1–3. Duns Scotus looked upon it as "rebellio" in the natural state of man. Sent. II dist. 30 quæst. 2. Biel expressed it in these words: Rectitudo autem naturalis voluntatis ejus scil. libertas, non corrumpitur per peccatum; illa enim est realiter ipsa voluntas, nec ab ea separabilis" Sent. Lib. II dist. 30 qu. I. Art. III dub. 4.

seek and pursue whatever is displeasing to itself. Alas! how incomprehensible is the misery of man. On the one side there arises in man, hatred of God and the Divine Law; while on the other side, as I shall explain later, God is a consuming fire to man.

3. The Pelagians, whose teachings Augustine has learnedly destroyed in several volumes, appear to have denied that there is any original sin. In this controversy he most of all predominates in such manner that, almost all the rest that he wrote against the Pelagians seems rather cold. I shall submit several topics that witness to the fact of original sin. What can be plainer than Eph. 2:3? "We were by nature children of wrath even as others." But if we are by nature, children of wrath, we were certainly born so. For what else can Paul mean than that all of our faculties are born subject to sin, and that at no time is there any good in any of our faculties? In Roms. 5, Paul has established an argument concerning sin, grace, and the law, wherein he teaches that sin was propagated upon all mankind. How is the sin of one man propagated, if all are not born sinners from one man? Nor can it be truly denied but that Paul is here talking about original sin. Now if he were speaking of each man's sin, he could not say that many died by one man's offense. For this would be a thing which could not possibly be said about what they term "actual sin." Who, with the exception of anyone who wishes to misrepresent the text, does not see this fact?

Now if Adam is not the author of sin, Christ alone will not be the author of righteousness, but Adam also. Likewise, if he is speaking here of each man's sin, why do children die who have as yet not committed what they call "actual sin?" And since death enters not except by sin, children necessarily are guilty of sin, and possess sin. But what kind of sin, I ask? Most assuredly original sin. Moreover Paul is speaking of that sin by which all have been condemned to death. Why not consider the figure of Paul's language? As in Romans so elsewhere in Corinthians (I Cor. 15:22) Paul writes: "For as in Adam all die, so in Christ shall all be made alive." The prophet's exclamation pertains to this theme also: "Behold I was shapen in iniquity, and in sin did my mother conceive me," Ps. 50:7. Now David signified that he was born a sinner. Besides, if "every imagination of the thoughts of man's heart is vain and depraved continually," as Genesis 6:5 records, then we are of necessity born with sin, and if we all are blessed in Christ, then must we all have been cursed in Adam. But what does it mean to be cursed if not that we stand condemned of sin? In the types of the law, both the impurities and the slaughter of the firstborn of Egypt have reference to this. What does it profit us to discuss the subject at great length, when Christ in John 3:6 so plainly asserts that, "what is born of the flesh is flesh?" And if it is flesh as I have above indicated, then it seeks its own, it loves itself. If the first birth is not subject to sin, the why is it of consequence that one be reborn? Nay, more, if the birth of the flesh be good, what importance is to be attached to the rebirth by the Spirit?

The Power and Fruit of Sin

4. The older Pelagians can be rooted out with less difficulty than can the newer Pelagians of modern times. Although the latter do not deny the fact of original sin, yet they do deny that it is the power of original sin that causes all human works and all human attempts to be sins. Therefore my treatment of this

locus on the power and energy of original sin will be rather extended.

Original sin is a certain living energy at no time bearing any fruit save vices. For when is it that the human soul does not burn with evil desire, wherein things most disgraceful and offensive are not even checked? Avarice, hate, ambition, envy, emulation, the flames of lusts, anger! Who is there that does not some time or other feel them? Arrogance, pride, a Pharisaic tumor, contempt of God, distrust of Him, blasphemy, while the chief affections but a few feel.

There are some who in outward appearance live right honorable lives. They have nothing in which to glory, seeing indeed that their souls are subject to those disgraceful and wretched affections which they do not perceive. For what if at any time, say in the hour of death, God opens the eyes of the little saints to behold their vices and diseases.[36] Do they not know that Isaiah 40:6 says: "all the glory of flesh is as the glory of the grass." You see now how deep-seated, nay more, how inscrutable, the malice of the human heart is. And still it does not shame our Sophists to teach work-righteousness, satisfactions, and the philosophic virtues.[37]

Granted that there was some constancy manifested in a Socrates, chastity in a Zenocrates, temperance in a Zeno! Nevertheless because they were in impure minds, nay because they took origin in self-love, and out of desire for praise, these shadows of the virtues should be regarded as vices and not real virtues. Socrates

---

[36]"Suos morbos sanctuli cognoscant: a case of irony. George Spalatin's German translation reads: "die lebendigen hayligen."

[37]Philosophicæ virtutes: The four chief virtues of the Greeks are meant: prudentia, justitia, temperantia, fortitudo. These Thomas and Ambrose considered the cardinal virtues or "virtutes principales," alongside of the three theological comforts: "fides, charitas, et spes."

was tolerant, but a lover of glory or else prided himself for his virtue. Cato was brave, but it was because he loved praise. Moreover God pours out upon the nations the shadows of such virtues, and upon the ungodly and on anyone who does not otherwise have the form, he bestows riches and similar gifts.

Now while the entire human reason marvels at this outer mask and spectre of virtue, our pseudo-theologians deceived by blind natural judgment, have commended unto us philosophic studies, philosophic virtues, and the merits of external works. But what do the philosophers in general teach (if there be any who teach well), but reliance on self and self-love? Take M. T. Cicero in his work *De Finibus* for instance. Now he estimates the whole scheme of virtue by self-love and self-regard (φιλαύτια). And, too, what pride and arrogance are to be found in Plato! To me at least, it seems easily to be the case that, Platonic vanity would be productive of some crime were any person, though he be himself noble and strong, to read it.

The teaching of Aristotle is altogether a certain fancy for dispute, so that it would not even be fitting to number him in the lowest place among the hortatory writers. But of philosophy I shall have somewhat to say, when I treat the topic of "laws."

5. To sum up in a few words: all men according to their natural powers are truly sinners and do always sin. Gen. 6:5 "Every imagination of the thoughts of man's heart was vain and evil continually." The same sentence is repeated in chapter 8:5: "The imagination of man's heart is evil from his youth." When I read "prone to evil" which is not far from the original, nevertheless I preferred to use a kindred reading because it is clearer, simply affirming that man is depraved.[38]

---

[38] Both passages Melanchthon quotes according to the original.

Nor can any Thomist draw me away from Moses with the fact that since proneness or inclination is not an act, therefore it cannot be sin. For thus they philosophize. But Isaiah 9:17 reads: "For all are hypocrites and evildoers, and every mouth speaketh foolishness." Again in chapter 41:29: "Behold they are all vain, and their plans are an empty wind." Again Isaiah 51:6: "all we like sheep have gone astray, each has turned to his own way, and the Lord hath placed on Him the iniquity of us all."

In this passage the prophet, in a dear word of prophecy, has set forth the history of Christ's passion and its results. For he predicted that Christ should suffer such things and that he would seem the most dejected of all men. And through his sufferings he should justify many, seeing indeed that we are all sinners and the only way whereby our justification is possible, is through faith in Christ. In verse 9, he says, "He will take his grave with the wicked and the rich in His death." He says this of those who wish to be justified through their own strength and works, and not through Christ. Verse 12 also pertains to the same: "He shall divide the spoil with the strong." Now the wicked, the rich, and the strong are plainly those who, ignorant of Christ, assert human righteousness, free will, philosophic virtues, and in a word, human strength.

You see in how brief a statement the prophet Isaiah has described the whole power of the gospel. Do Thou O Christ, truly bestow thy Spirit, to open up these things and to explain such mysteries! Now let us hear David who has perceived the same thing and

---

The Vulgate reads Gen. 6:5. "cuncta cogitatio cordis intenta ad malum omni tempore." The Septuagint reads Gen. 8:9 ἔγκειται ἡ διάνοια τοῦ ἀνθρώπου ἐπιμελῶς ἐπὶ τὰ πονηρά. Both of these were used to defend the Scholastic position, cf. Thomas: Prima secund. quest. 85, art, 2 resp.

that, too, in many places. For instance Ps. 115:11: "all men are liars." And the whole of Ps. 13 thunders forth this sentiment, as is seen from the first verse and following: "The fool hath said in his heart, there is no God; corrupt are they and abominable have they made themselves in their works. There is none that doeth good. The Lord looked down from heaven upon the children of Adam, to see if any did understand and seek after God. All have gone off to the side, they are altogether become useless. There is none that doeth good, no not even just one."

Behold David in this passage does not accuse mankind of the simple vices but of crimes the most atrocious: impiety, unbelief, foolishness, hatred of and contempt for God! Of crimes, I say, which none save the Spirit of God can possibly comprehend! What have the theological hypocrites to say on this score? Will you attribute these works of free will and these human powers unto us men? You pretend that you do not deny original sin, yet you teach that man can do good by his own powers. What! Can an evil tree bear good fruit? Can you not see that the prophet has described a tree together with its fruits, when he speaks not only of the heart of the fool, but of all human pursuits, plans, desires, works and attempts as well? Moreover you see what a great difference there is between the judgment of philosophy or human reason about man and that of the scriptures. Philosophy looks only upon the external masks of man, whereas Holy Writ discerns the innermost and incomprehensible affections.

When a man is dominated by these, Holy Writ judges his works according to the affections. For since in all our works we seek our own personal gains, our works are necessarily true sins. Meantime I shall not speak of the crass cupidities of those who outwardly live good lives. Nevertheless is it not a fact that one man is forced into characters of this kind by an aversion for human affairs, another by the fear of fortune, another by ambition, and still another by the love of tranquillity—for these were heretofore the philosophers' causes for an outwardly better life, but now are they the reason of mankind in general—and still another by a certain feigned fear of divine punishment? Others have other reasons for so doing. For who can understand the labyrinth of the human heart? Especially true is this since the diversity of affections is as great as the diversity of individuals. Who of all natural men is it, who does not prefer to be permitted to indulge his appetites? Who does not consider it a severe thing to bear to be forced by law? If you do not so think, it matters not; for there comes a time when you shall know for a certainty, how indignant the soul will be when its own cupidities are coerced by law. Besides John 1:12 says: "as many as received him to them gave he the power to become sons of God, to those who believe on his name, who are born not of bloods, nor of the will of the flesh, nor of the will of man, but of God." You clearly see that the will of man, the will of the flesh, and the blood are all condemned. That is to say, whatever belongs to the nature of mankind is condemned. But sons indeed are born again of God. There are many passages in addition to this one which a studious reader will observe for himself. For example there is the verse in John 15:4: "Even as a branch cannot of itself bear fruit except it abide in the vine, so neither can ye except ye abide in me."

Incidentally it happens that I must refute what those impious Sophists yelp about when they dilate upon such clear sentences as these: that the natural man cannot meritoriously do the good, for thus they speak. And so they invent and devise a two-fold good,[39], one meritorious and the other non-meritorious and that too lest it should be necessary to argue the philosophic virtues of free will, these external shadows of virtues and those of vice. Oh, what impiety! But is this not that "play upon words" (κυβεία) which is spoken of in Ephesians 4:14, to devise a good which, in some respects is meritorious of eternal life, and in other respects is not? You may of a certainty believe, that nothing good or meritorious can be done by mankind through any natural powers of its own. For indeed, the Scriptures say (Gen. 6:5): "Every desire of the imagination of man's heart is vain and depraved." Now the passage does not only say that, "it does not merit eternal life"—for I must use their words—but that it is most assuredly "not good." To this effect David says (Ps. 115:11): "Every man is a liar." And Isa. 9:17: "all are hypocrites and depraved, and every mouth speaketh foolishness." Behold he says it is not only not meritorious but plainly evil. From what I have treated up to now and shall note a little later, each thing itself in every respect will refute their many jokes. For the impious Sophists did not estimate works by the affections of the heart, but after the philosophic custom which, indeed, was the sole reason for their hallucinations.

Now Paul in almost all of his epistles, and especially in Romans and Galatians, teaches in general that all the attempts which he made were but sins and vices. Does he not do this, I ask? For example take Roms.

---

[39]Sic enim loquuntur: Melanchthon refers to the teaching of Thomas Aquinas: Summa II, 1 qu. CIX art. II. Duns Scotus taught a similar view also: "bonum meritorium" and "bonum morale." Cf. Sent. II dist. 28. H. sqq.

3:9: "all are under sin." And this theme he elucidates in a most magnificent and splendid manner, by the testimony of the prophets. In chapter 8, after arguing our inability to do the law, he makes a comparison between the flesh and the Spirit. In this he teaches that the flesh is utterly subject to sin; while moreover the Spirit is life and peace.

Now the Sophists call the flesh the "sensitive appetite,"[40] forgetting all about the phrases and tropes of Scripture. For Scripture in using the word flesh means thereby not only the body, a part of man, but the whole man, soul as well as body. And just as often as it is compared with spirit, it means the best and most outstanding powers of human nature apart from the spirit. And again spirit means the Holy Spirit Himself together with his motions and works within us. Thus John 8:15: "ye judge according to the flesh." Again Gen. 6:3: "My spirit will not always abide with man because he is flesh."

Therefore we should understand that the word flesh means all of man's powers and faculties. Otherwise Paul's argument in the whole epistle to the Romans would fall. For he is wont to deduce such conclusions as this: the flesh could not fulfill the law, therefore the Spirit is needed to fulfill it. If then, in that place, flesh stood for a part of man only, how would Paul's argument stand?[41] For it could be eluded after the follow-

---

[40]Appetitum sensitivum: Against Duns Scotus, sent. 1. II dist. 29 Nr. 4. and especially against Gabriel Biel, who in his investigation concerning the nature of "concupiscentia," finally came to the conclusion that it was "qualitas carnis inordinata, inclivans appetitum sensitivum ad actum deformans et vitiosum in habente judicium rationis."

[41]Enthymema: Used by Aristotle as a conclusion to premises which are generally considered true but as such have not been strongly established. The syllogism would read: "Flesh cannot fulfill the law; all mankind is flesh; therefore the work of the Spirit in the fulfillment of the law is necessary." The second member of the syllogism

ing manner: although the flesh could not do the law, some better part of man could have done it, and hence, it would not have been necessary for the spirit to fulfill the law.

Of a truth, we have forgotten not only the belief of Scripture because of the learned philosophers, but also its language as Esdras 10:2 records: "We have married strange wives and have used their language instead of our own." Therefore I use the word "flesh" to express both the best powers of human nature, and for its most beautiful attempts. The splendid virtue of a Socrates is as much a fruit of the flesh as are the parricides of Cæsar. The most splendid qualities of Paul with which he was endowed before his knowledge of Christ, were as much the fruits of the flesh as were the adulteries of Claudius.

Now that which is here called "flesh," is sometimes wont to be named the "Old man." But this term signifies the same thing: that is to say, whatever pertains to human nature.[42] For the word itself clearly indicates this. He would not seem to be using common sense who wished to describe only a part of man by the term "Old man." For who is there who when hearing the word "man" would only think of the body? Moreover Paul interchangeably uses the following words: Old man, the flesh, and the body of sin. And too, the "outer man," further signifies what the term "Old Man" does, that is not only the exterior part of man, but all of man's natural faculties. Of the various parts within man, I shall have more to say when we come to

---

is viewed as self-evident. Melanchthon points out its necessity however, saying that without it the whole conclusion would be false.

[42] Cf. Luther in his Theses of 1516: "Carnis nomine dicitur homo vetus, non tantum quia sensuali concupiscentia dicitur, sed (etiamsi est castus, sapiens, justus) quia non ex Deo per Spiritum renascitur. Er. ed. opp. V arg. I, 235.

the topic of "grace." May it suffice for the present time to have considered the meaning of the word "flesh." For they are indeed mistaken who think that, in man who has not been renewed and purged by the Holy Spirit, there is something which cannot be called flesh and that too corrupt.

Hence, in order to examine the Pauline view I submit his own words Roms. 8:3: "'The impossibility of the law"[43] (in that it was weak through the flesh), God sending his own Son in the likeness of sinful flesh and for sin condemned sin in the flesh, that the justification of the law might be fulfilled in us, who walk not after the flesh, but after the Spirit." Up to this point, Paul has set forth the sum of the matter, that since it was impossible for us to fulfill the law in that we were carnal, God has sent His Son to satisfy the demands of the law for us who are dead through the flesh, but made alive by the Spirit. I ask just now, what he calls flesh? For since it is plain that what is called "spirit" really means the Holy Spirit and His motions and impulses, it necessarily follows that we may call "flesh," whatever is in us that is alien to the Holy Spirit. Then the Apostle returns to the argument already set forth (V.5ss.): "They are of the flesh who do mind the things of the flesh, and they are of the Spirit who do mind the things of the spirit. For the mind of the flesh is death, but the mind of the spirit is life and peace." Behold! why cannot the law be satisfied by the flesh! Because those who are after the flesh, do mind the things of the flesh, just as though he had said:

---

[43]Impossibilitatem legis: Melanchthon is following the original text and not the Vulgate. The latter reads: "nam quod impossibile erat legi; in quo infirmabatur per carnem." Nor does he follow Erasmus' reading: "Etiam quod lex præstare non poterat, in quo imbecillis erat per carnem." He lets Justificatio stand as the translation of δικαίωμα with Erasmus.

"ye Pharisees and hypocrites, ye think ye can do the law by your own powers! Outwardly ye seem to do well; ye seem to be endued with very beautiful virtues. But they are all but dross. For since ye are flesh, ye seek your own and ye do outwardly well either from the fear of punishment or the love of gain, or else from some other carnal affection. It cannot be but that within you there is no sense of God since ye are flesh. And too, ye cannot therefore desire or pursue the things of God! For who is there, no matter how good he may seem to be in appearance, who loves God to the extent that he would freely endure death and hell itself, if He so willed?"[44] It is impossible to say how many grand things the Apostle has comprehended in such a brief passage. "They who are after the flesh, do mind the things of the flesh." On the other hand, "they who are after the Spirit, do mind the things of the Spirit." That is to say, in those in whom the Holy Spirit is shed abroad, there is a sense of God, a reliance on Him, and a love for Him. Likewise they who are of the flesh, manifest nothing but contempt and hatred for God. That is what the Apostle means when he says in Roms. 8:6: "the mind of the flesh is death, but the mind of the Spirit is life and peace." And verse 7 follows: "The mind of the flesh is enmity toward God, for it is not subject to the law of God, neither indeed can be." Consider I prithee, how that Paul's epilogue to Romans ends with the thought that every impulse of our flesh is hostile to God, nor can it be subject to the law of God. But if it cannot be subject to the law of God, why are we in doubt as to the fruits it bears?

---

[44]"Melanchthon doubtless refers to a passage in Staupitz: "Love of God:" "Dem wir aus Lieb Alles wieder geben sollen—auch uns selbst, zum Tod, Zum Leben, Zum Himmel und Zu der Hoelle." Edited by Knaake: I, 94.

Now he not only says: "it is not subject to the law of God"; but plainly that, "it cannot be subject to that law." And so it follows that human works however laudable in appearance they may be, nevertheless they are evidently corrupt and are sins worthy of death.

To such a degree then, if you please, do the Sophists carry their frivolous little distinctions between flesh and spirit, between good and merit, and whatever is of like nonsense, in order that they might wrest from us the judgment of Paul. For what statement is any clearer than what Paul says, namely, that the justification of the law is not fulfilled except in those who are after the spirit. Therefore those who are not filled with the Holy Spirit, do not satisfy the law. And what is failure to do the law but sin? For indeed it is certain that every motion and impulse of the mind against the law is sin.

Hence when the Sophists teach that there is "original sin," and that it consists in being cut off from the divine favor and in an absence of original righteousness, they should add[45] that since we are without the spirit and benediction of God, we are accursed; since we have no light we possess nothing but darkness, blindness, and error; since we have no life we possess nothing within us but sin and death. Thus Paul in Ephesians 2:3 explains what he calls "children of wrath"; all of us formerly lived in the desires of the flesh, doing the will of the flesh and its imaginations, and were by nature children of wrath." Later on when I shall discuss the topic on the "powers of the law"

---

[45] Debebant addere: The Scholastics were not forced to this conclusion since in their theory, "justitia originalis" did not pertain to the natural state of man, but was a "donum superadditum." The so-called "naturalia hominis" remain though somewhat weakened by sin and hence to such a state of man no actual guilt was attributed by them.

many things can be appropriated to this topic, and therefore I wish to spend no more time on it just now. For just what is the power of sin is not precisely discerned until the law is revealed, and the law argues that all men are sinners. "For the Scripture includes all under sin," as the apostle writes in Gal. 3:22, "that the promise of the faith of Jesus Christ might be given to them that believe." From what I have discussed in this topic one can gather what ought to be thought about the powers of man; and wherein there is any liberty or freedom of the will as the theologians boast, simply because they discern whatever they desire in accord with their own belief, but apart from the Scripture. For what liberty can there be without the Spirit, since sin, that well-known tyrant of ours, is in the flesh, causing trouble even to those who are overflowing with the Spirit? For when has there ever been a saint who has not deplored this servitude, nay more, this very captivity? Paul in Roms. 7:23 says that he sees a law in his members fighting against him and bringing him into captivity. This law in his members, or this tyrant of sin is the ardor and force of sin with which we are born.

From this it likewise follows, as I shall more copiously discuss later on, that these precepts are impossible (to be kept).[46] That passage which I produced from Romans VIII seems sufficient proof of this fact: "The flesh cannot be subject to the law of God." Likewise that passage which reads "It was impossible for the law to justify," meaning of course that the law was unable

---

[46]This sentence is directed against Scotus and his disciples. Duns Scotus proceeds from the premise that the demand to keep the divine law consists for all in this fact: whether they have now lost grace or have never been sharers of it, and on the other hand that God cannot demand the impossible. Therefore he concludes that it is possible for man even in the state of original guilt to fulfill the law. cf. Werner: Scotus: S420.

to show us what we should do, but the Spirit had to be conferred through Christ, to incite us to love the law. Precisely at this point, that impious and foolish idea of moral philosophy and of freedom of the will held by the theologians, and which the Scotists intone with full cheeks falls, namely: that the will is able to conform itself to every precept of true reason; that is, the will can will whatever true reason or true counsel of the intellect will prescribe. On the contrary Paul says it was impossible for the law to justify, meaning thereby that it was not able to prescribe what we ought to do, in that the flesh was weak and aversed to the law. They have fixed their eyes upon this point because they have invented a certain new kind of a will which should possess "elicited acts" and whither it should lead the affections. But if they had observed the language and phraseology of scripture, they would have easily seen that there were falsehoods and vain cogitations of the intellect which they have fabricated about "elicited acts." For the exterior members can never be stimulated to action by any other thing than that by which it led the affections. But when this is done, it is done through simulation and falsehood.

Although I am to discuss much later the strength of the law, yet I cannot restrain myself at this point from incidentally pointing out to the Christian reader the silly, insipid, and impious arguments by which they prove that we can, through our natural powers, love God. For thus they argue: A lesser good can be chosen also.[47]

---

[47]Fundamentally against Gabriel Biel, who in his addition to Scotus in sent. lib. III dist. 27 writes: Et hæc procedunt de cognitione et amore naturali, qua homo ex cognitione et amore sui ascendit ad cognitionem et amorem dei: quia enim naturaliter homo se ipsum diligit amore amicitiæ diligit etiam omne quod sibi bonum est amore concupiscentiæ et ita deum suum summum bonum. Et quoniam ex eo quod cognoscit deum esse bonum suum, cognoscit enum in se bonum, ideo ex amore concupiscentiæ assurgit ad amorem dei amicitiæ." The fal-

Undoubtedly this is the language of Christians which Paul wishes to be seasoned with salt, is it not? Truly this is a humorous and an adulterated Aristotelian comment; a comment worthy of Aristotelian theologians. In the first place it is the nature of love for us to love only those things that seem first good to us, then pleasing, and then useful. Therefore whatever we love, we love with a view to personal gain. You love wealth or money not because money is a good thing in itself, but because money serves the exigencies of life. Likewise you do not love God however good He may be except that for reasons of your own, you think God to be useful unto you. Now indeed if you should love with a view to personal gain, your love is servile and with a depraved and perverted natural affection. Moreover you would clearly sin. But the fact is, you do not love even after this fashion. For no gains are to be experienced from God save as the Holy Spirit has purified the heart and has engraved upon a pure and pious heart, the beneficence of God. How about it, moreover, when conscience shows you an angry God threatening eternal death and that horrifying condition of your expression, just as David says.[48] At this time when it is afflicted with only the thoughts of things evil, undoubtedly the punishments that are inflicted by God, I ask you, can human nature

---

lacy lies in the fact that man loves that which appears good to him, and not necessarily that which is in itself good, so that the judgment about the object to be loved depends on its own moral nature and is purely subjective. Gabriel Biel goes farther in that he defines "dilectio dei super omnia" as the final goal of self-conditioning for the "gratia infusa." Luther already in 1517 very energetically contended against both of these in his Theses 18, 20, 26, cf. Erl. Augs. I, 316 ff. Weim. A. I, 224 f.

[48]Melanchthon undoubtedly refers to Ps. 21:9, 10: "Pones eos ut clibanum ignis in tempore vultus tui," etc.

[49]Annon ille iræ dies: Perhaps a reference to the famous Medieval hymn of Thomas a Celano: "Dies iræ, dies illa," etc.

direct the human mind to love, to suffer kindly even the punishment of hell? And besides, when the conscience has stricken the mind with terror and it is in a manner resisting, it dreads God as though He were a cruel and vindictive hangman. And what is even more atrocious, it dreads God as though He were unjust. Now, Sophists, what will these "elicited acts" of yours, what will that illustrious will of yours which you have devised, what at this score, I ask you, will they accomplish? Will not that day of wrath,[49] that fire, I say, declare that these human judgments of free will are nothing except a deception and mere powder? Will it not declare that all the glory of the flesh is but as the glory of the grass?

When the law was given, did not Israel shudder at the fire and vapors, nay even at the very face of Moses? Did not the earth tremble and shake, and were not the very foundations of the mountains disturbed and troubled because God was angry with them? But about this I hope to say more when I treat of the strength of the law.

And so, reader, you have it, that in the first place we do love only those things which are useful to us. But God does not will to be loved simply with a view to gain. He wills to be freely loved. For he does not love God but himself who loves gain. And how many warnings there are in Scripture against such a depraved love as this is! Another argument is to be advanced not altogether unlike the preceding one: "It ought not seem absurd for them to teach that it is possible for us without the work of the Holy Spirit, to love God more ardently than we love even ourselves, seeing indeed that we often meet death for mere transitory things. In fact, we meet death for our fellowmen, our sweethearts, our children and our wives." Such is the argument. At this point a refutation should be given which must be drawn from the very nature of the affections.

In the first place, no man by nature rejoices to die; and those who endanger their lives for the state or for their families in reality prefer to live. Indeed Curtius would rather live, and so would lucretia. But because human nature truly shuns adversities we prefer to die rather than to live a wretched life, say for an instance, would rather live, and so would Lucretia. But because he thinks the future will be unhappy without Thisbe, he wishes to snatch his life from evil and bury it along with his soul. Saul likewise prefers to live, but out of fear of disgrace and anger and desperation, ended his life just as though he would once for all put an end to adversities by suicide. But why do I go to the trouble of giving so exact an account of the nature of the affections, since rare deaths as these (that of Lucretia and of Saul and the like) are but extraordinary examples of Divine majesty.

Now these things which the Sophists have advanced about harmonious merit namely, that we merit grace by our moral works, that is, by those things which we harmoniously perform by our natural powers,[50] (for that is their language), you yourself know, dear reader, are but blasphemies fabricated to injure the grace of God. Indeed since it is true that our natural powers

---

[50]Thomas Aquinas denies principally any merit of man in his conversion in that he tracks back all to God as the "primum movens:" quod homo convertatur ad deum, hoc non potest esse nisi deo ipsum convertente . . . Sed liberum arbitrium ad deum converti non potest nisi deo ipsum ad se convertente etc. Summa th. II, I qu. 109 art. 6. But in the question respecting the meeting of the "opus meritorium" which merits "vita æterna," he makes a twofold distinction: a "meritum congrui (e congruo, congruum) or "condigno" (e condigno, condignum). "Secundum quod ex gratia spiritus sancti procedit" arrives at the work "condignitas," and is "opus meritorium vitæ æternæ." "Secundum quod ex libero arbitrio procedit" is only a certain "congruitas." Qu. 114 art. 3, 4.

without the afflatus of the Holy Spirit can do nothing but sin, what will we merit by our human efforts but wrath? These "elicited acts" prescribed by the Sophists are simulations and lies. And what they falsely call "good intentions" are fictitious arguments. So far are we from obtaining grace through these, that there is nothing which so opposes grace as these Pharisaic preparations.

Moreover Paul in the whole Roman Epistle (as of course elsewhere) most persistently censures such impiety as this, when he says none other than that grace is not grace if it is bestowed on account of work. For what is mercy's place, if there is respect for our work? In the third chapter of Romans, Paul plainly teaches that all men are under sin, and that they who believe are justified by grace. Furthermore, in chapter 9:31 he says that Israel in following the law, did not attain to the law of righteousness. That means that they who undertook to do the law by the strength of free will, never really fulfilled the law but only appeared outwardly so to do. Isaiah in chapter 55:2 freely invites to Christ buyers whosoever will: "come," says he, "and buy wine and milk, without money and without price. Why spend ye your money for that which is not bread and your labor for that which does not satisfy? Incline your ear (that is, believe), and your soul shall live, and I shall make an eternal covenant with you, the faithful mercy of David," (that is, the faithful mercy promised and confirmed to David). Jeremy 17:5–8: "'accursed is the one who confides in man, who makes his arm his flesh and draws away his heart from God. For he shall be as shrubs in the desert and will not see when good has come, but shall live in dryness, in the desert, in a land of salt and uninhabitable. Blessed is the one who trusts in the Lord; the Lord will be his reliance, and he will be like a tree which is transplanted above waters, which sends its roots to the water and when the storm has come, he shall not fear," etc. Read the rest for yourself. For this one chapter of the prophet has argued with sufficient clarity that our moral works are nothing but simulation and lies of our flesh.

To this belongs what Scholastic theology has invented about the beginning of penitence and about attritions.[51] Nature does not grieve over a transgression except with self-love and the fear of punishment. Both are plainly sins, and it is impossible but that they bear with them the hatred of that one who inflicts these punishments, namely God. It is indeed a task peculiar to God to arouse in us a knowledge of and hatred for sin. "For the Lord bringeth down into hell and restoreth again, the Lord killeth and maketh alive, the Lord humbleth and raiseth up" says Hanna in her song, I Sam. 11:6. And Jeremy 31:19 reads: "after that thou didst convert me, I did penance," etc. Moreover what advantage is there in pausing here, since Christ has spoken so plainly in John 6:44 that "no man cometh unto me save as the father hath drawn him?" Now indeed simply because the Sophists forget what the Lord has

---

[51] Attritiones: Since Hildebert of Tours (1134) the sacrament of penance was divided into three parts: contritio cordis, confessio oris, satisfactio operis." Alexander of Hales was the first to make a distinction between "contritio and attritio." "Timor servilis principium est attritionis, timor initialis principium est contritionis." cf. Migne: Patrol. lat. 210,665 C. This "timor" is called "initialis" because it is the beginning of wisdom or as Bonaventura says: "Initialis dicitur quia in eo inchoatur sapientia et gratia." Thomas gave the distinction its churchly consciousness when he defined "attritio" as "quandam displicentiam de peccatis commissis sed non perfectam, contritio autem perfectam, i. e., dolorem pro peccatis assumptum cum proposito confitendi et satisfaciendi." Sum. in Suppl. III iae: Qu. I, art. I. Duns Scotus and others define "attritio" as "pœnitentia informis" preceding the "infusio gratiæ," while "contrito" which follows, is considered to be "pœnitentia formata." The first comes under the conception of "dispositio de congruo." Against these then Melanchthon is aiming these words.

said in Zacharias, and are ignorant of the tropes and figures of sacred language, as for instance: "Return unto me and I shall return unto you," it does not follow that the beginning of repentance has been posited in us. Moreover Augustine never once discarded this passage, nor is it at all obscure except to the Sophists who were acquainted with nothing but their little manuals of logic.[52]

The conversion of God toward us is twofold: the one precedes, the other follows our repentance. That which precedes is accomplished when God makes us repent by the afflation of his Spirit, and when he terrifies and confounds us by revealing our sin. But that which follows is accomplished when God consoles us by putting a limit and an end to our sufferings, and declares openly that he is well disposed toward us. Concerning the latter kind of conversion, Zacharias speaks saying: "Return unto me and I shall return unto you," that is, repent and I will end your sufferings, 1:3. For the prophet is exhorting to repentance those who had returned from the Assyrian exile, being warned by the example of their fathers, if they did not wish to experience again the divine wrath and sufferings similar to their elders. From this it cannot be established that the beginning of repentance is in our power. God Himself invites and draws, and when He has drawn us, He condones our punishments and declares that He is placated and reconciled to us. And simply because the words "Return unto me" are enjoined, it does not follow that it is within our power to repent or to be converted. Because God enjoins that he is to be loved above all things, it does not follow that it is within our

---

[52]Parva logicalia: Melanchthon refers to handbooks of logic compiled for beginners. cf. G. L. Plitt, "Jod. Trutfetter" Erl. 1876. S. 17 f.

power to do it, simply because he enjoins it. Rather on account of the very fact that he does command it, it is not in our power to do it. For in doing this God enjoins the impossible, in that he commends His mercy unto us, as we shall see in our discussion of the law.

Why have not the Sophists observed even that sentence recorded in Zacharias 10:6: "and I shall convert them, because I shall have mercy on them, and they shall be as they were seeing that I shall not renounce them." Behold God says he will convert Judah, not because of their good deeds, but of his own mercy. Similar places I commend unto you, my Christian reader, for your consideration. For it shall come to pass that when you shall become more familiar with Scripture, then, without any difficulty, you can solve these arguments of the Sophists.

You understand now, reader, just how much I thought should be said concerning the power of that innate pest. Nor do they require any more to be said, who wish to be fashioned by the reading of the Scripture and meditation, rather than by human commentaries. For no amount of comment can be sufficient for those whose minds are confused by uncertain disputations of the various judgments and opinions of men, and understand nothing but carnal things. There is one who is the most simple and likewise the most certain teacher, the Divine Spirit, who has expressed himself both accurately and plainly in the sacred Scriptures. When your mind as it were has been transformed into these, you can comprehend the nature of this topic just as absolutely, simply, and exactly as the nature of any other theological matter. They who depend on the judgment and opinion of men and not on the Spirit, do not discern these things as such, but discern only dim shadows of them just as those in the Platonic grotto.[53] What philosopher, what Scholastic theologian saw the true nature of virtue or vice? The theologasters measure original sin only by external works. Meantime they did not see the malice and, as it were, the intercutaneous sickness. Although they understood the improbity of some of the affections, nevertheless reason does not consider them all. Reason does not consider even those with which the Spirit wars such as, blasphemy, hatred of God, self-love, diffidence toward God, and the innumerable sins of this kind which are so grafted in man that they cling not only to his sensitive appetite which is only one part, as they teach, but have seized his entire nature and hold it captive.

They call these affections infirmity, but such infirmity as can be overcome by human strength. Scripture says the very opposite, that only through the Spirit of God can the affections of the flesh be conquered, because "those whom the Son has set free, they indeed are free," John 8:36. Therefore do not permit their figments about external works, elicited acts of the will and the like to move you. For God judges the heart and not the external work. For as is recorded in I Sam. 16:7, God does not see as man sees. And if you please from this it will be learned just how much damage philosophy has done to the Christian religion when our theologasters following philosophy have invented good works, that mask of external works which merit nothing but what that parable about the foolish virgins in the gos-

---

[53]Platonicum specus: A reminiscence on Plato: Republic VII, 1 in which Plato shows the relation between knowledge of the world of appearance and the knowledge of truth, that is ideas. They who see only the world of appearance are like men in a deep hole into which a light from above is shining. They do not see the things themselves but only the shadows. Melanchthon later used this picture again to great advantage. cf. C. R. I. 695, 726.

pel teaches. For the virgins signify nothing but Pharisaic righteousness, that is the shadows of external works.

But what else do the philosophers teach except external works? In their disputes about virtues, don't they refer all things to external works and fictitious elicited acts? They are blind and leaders of the blind. We must pray that God may transfer our minds from the judgment of human reason and philosophy, to Spiritual judgment. For the blindness of human reason is such that, without the light of the Spirit, we cannot know the absolute nature of sin or righteousness. The whole notion of human reason is darkness. The Spirit of Christ is light, he alone teaches all truth. Nor can the flesh or human reason fix its eyes on the shining face of Moses, because a veil covers the law and it judges only concerning external works, or fictitious designs or intentions (as they call them), or to use Paul's words "of the letter." But the Spirit searches indeed the deep things and penetrates, I Cor. 11:10. Now of the things which I have written about original sin, I shall, in a few words, indicate the whole by submitting several theses, or, as it were an epitome of what has been said:

1. Sin is a disposition of the mind against the law of God.
2. Because we are born children of wrath, it follows that we are born without the Spirit of God.
3. Seeing indeed that the Spirit of God is not in man, therefore man knows, loves, and seeks nothing but carnal things.
4. Hence in man there is a contempt for God, an ignorance of him, and whatever vice Ps. 13 describes. "The fool hath said in his heart, there is no God."

5. Thus it is that man, by his natural powers or faculties, can do nothing but sin.
6. Now not only a part of man (which they style "the sensitive appetite") is subject to the passions of sin.
7. Since Scripture attests the fact that the heart is impure it follows that all human powers or faculties are likewise impure.
8. For the heart signifies not only what they style the sensitive appetite, but in fact is the very seat of all affections, love, hate, blasphemy, unbelief, etc.
9. And as the heart signifies the seat of all human affections, so also the flesh signifies all of the natural powers of man.
10. Whatever is done through the natural powers is carnal. The constancy of a Socrates, the moderation of a Zeno are all nothing but carnal affections.
11. Paul in I Cor. 2:44 once called ψυχικόν or animal the work of reason, for example the philosophic virtues.
12. And in that very same place, τὸ ψυχικόν is openly condemned of sin.
13. In other places he always calls carnal whatever within us is done without the work of Spirit, no matter how good it may outwardly seem to be. This is apparent from Romans 8:3 where Paul says: "the justification of the law could not be fulfilled through the flesh." Who does not see that here the word "flesh" means the most powerful human faculties which by human judgment appear to be able to conform

to the law? He teaches the same in II Cor. 3 also.

14. What I have wished to advise against is that the Scholastics might not impose it upon anyone, when they distinguish between "theoretical and sensitive appetite," attributing to the senses depraved affections, and freeing the theoretical appetite from vice.
15. This notion of the Scholastics is sufficiently refuted by those scriptural passages quoted. Nor can they joy in Origen as they seem to do, where he has treated of the soul, flesh and spirit. Notwithstanding, what is it to me what Origen thinks, since I am disputing about the meaning of Scripture and not that of Origen?
16. The reason why the Scholastics denied the fact that all the works of man are sinful was that they had fixed their eyes on external works and therefore on the veiled face of Moses, and hence did not judge the affections.
17. They invented freedom of the will for the same reason. For they saw that somewhere in external works, there was a kind of freedom. In such manner does the flesh judge about external works. On the other hand, the Spirit teaches that all things happen necessarily according to predestination.
18. Experience teaches that there is no freedom in the affections.
19. After all things in Scripture began to be referred to external works, then all Scripture at once was obscured, and it was not known what was sin, what grace, what law, what gospel, what Moses and what Christ. This darkness greater even than the Egyptian darkness, we

owe to that impious and execrable philosophy of the Scholastic theologasters.

20. Precisely what that impurity connected with the heart really is, that depravity, that wickedness which we call original sin and which all the saints deplore, but which reason does not know, will become plainly evident when the law will be revealed, when God has opened the eyes of the conscience as I shall discuss below in the topic on the law.

I was duty bound to discuss in this topic the fruits of sin, that is the kinds of vices. In a corresponding manner the Apostles in the Epistle to the Galatians has enumerated the fruits of the flesh, but these each man may discern for himself. It suffices for the Christian to know, that all natural works, all the affections of the human faculties and their attempts, are sins. Now what man can enumerate all the affections, especially if we estimate the kinds of vices by the affections, which ought to be the case? Besides, of those who have estimated the various forms of virtues and vices by the appearance of works, how many have recorded vices for virtues and virtues for vices? Hence I shall leave the judgment of these matters to the individual spirit of each man.

On Law

The topic on Laws will much more clearly reveal the power and nature of sin, since the law is said to be the knowledge of sin. Wherefore if anything will seem to be lacking in the preceding topic, it will be supplied, if I mistake not, in that which follows. Nevertheless

I do not do this in order to heap up all the things that can be said of each individual head, but I am giving only the nomenclature of the most common topics, so that one may see on what the whole of Christian doctrine hangs, and whither Scripture above all must be referred. And, too, I do not wish you to learn these topics from me as a teacher, but as from one who advises from Scripture and not from his own commentary. For believe me, it matters much whether you seek the substance of such things from the fountains or from the caverns.

Here not only sweeter waters are drawn, as the poet has said, but also purer. For how much more certain is that which the Scripture prescribes than what is gathered from the commentaries?

Moreover law is a judgment whereby the good is enjoined and the evil is prohibited. Legal right is the power of acting according to the law.[54] Many things both for and against laws have been spoken by the ancients, and I shall indicate a little later from what fountain these things have flowed.

Of laws, some are natural, others Divine, still others human. Concerning natural laws, I have not yet seen anything worthily written whether by theologians or lawyers. For since they are designated "natural," their formulas ought be collected by a method of human reasoning through a natural syllogism. That is precisely what I have not yet seen done by anyone, and I by no means know whether it can at all be done, since our human reason is so enslaved and blinded. Paul moreover, in Roms. 2:15, teaches by a marvelously elegant and clear argument, that within us there is a

---

[54]This definition of law was formulated by a medieval jurist, cf. C. R. 13,552. The source is otherwise unknown. The text reads: "Jus est auctoritas agendi secundum legem." K. 110.

natural law. He says that the Gentiles have conscience defending or accusing a thing done; and it is therefore a law unto them. For what is conscience but the judgment of our action which is demanded by some law or common formula? And so a natural law is a common judgment to which all men alike assent, and therefore one which God has inscribed upon the soul of each man, adapted to form and shape character. For as in the theoretical disciplines such as mathematics, there are certain common principles or κοιναὶ ἔννοιαι ἢ προλήψεις as for instance: "The whole is greater than its parts," so in the moral disciplines there are first common principles then conclusions—these words must be used for the sake of teaching—as the first rules of all human functions. You have rightly called these "natural laws." Cicero in his book De Legibus following Plato, derives the formulas of laws from the nature of man. Now although I do not condemn this notion, yet I think that it was more urbanely than exactly done.

Moreover, very many impious sayings occur in that disputation of Cicero, as customarily happens when we follow the methods and compendiums of our reason, rather than the precepts of Scripture. For a judgment of human comprehension is, on a whole, fallacious, due to innate blindness. And accordingly even though there are certain forms of character imprinted with us, nevertheless they scarcely can be apprehended. But I do say this that those natural laws imprinted on human minds, I mean the knowledge of those things which they call "concreated characters," were not acquired by our character but were placed there by God to serve as a rule for the judgment of character. Now that this view may agree with Aristotelian philosophy, is not the point I labor. For what difference does it make to me what that wrangler has thought? However, I omit those things which we have in common with the brute beasts such as the preservation and production of life, and the procreation of one's kind; and what lawyers refer to the category of natural law, I simply denominate certain "natural impulses" common to all living things.

Moreover of the laws which belong properly to man, the ones I have submitted seem to me to be the chief:

I. God ought to be revered.

II. Because we are born into a definite society of life, no man ought to be injured.

III. Human society demands that we use all things in common.

The first law concerning the reverence of God we receive from Romans I, where there is no doubt but that the Apostle considers it among the natural laws when he says that God has declared his majesty to all men by the foundation and administration of the world. But whether or not the fact that God is can be deduced by human syllogism, is a matter more for the curious than for the pious to dispute. This latter fact is especially true since it is not safe for human reason to argue about all things, as I said in the outset of this compendium.[55]

The second law which provides that no man be harmed, without doubt is deduced from the common necessity that all of us are born bound and united to

---

[55]Melanchthon apparently flinches from the problem just stated because he deduces the first principle of his natural law not on the nature of man, but grounds it on the Scripture. In (C.) 1522 after an enumeration of the three laws just mentioned, he writes: "Primam legem—principio monui: Posteriores duas leges facile colligat argumentis humana ratio. Primam legem quomodo colligere possit, non video, sic occæcata, post Adæ lapsum. Videmus enim ingeniosissimos quosque in eo fuisse ut nihil esse deum sentirent. Non percipit enim animalis homo ea quæ sunt spiritus dei. Certe de potentia et voluntate dei judicare per sese ratio non potest."

all. Scripture indicates this when in Gen. 2:18 it says: It is not meet that man should live alone, but that he be given assistance for his life. And so the law orders that no man be harmed; that is, that we should all earnestly love one another in order that all might experience our benevolence with zeal and kindness.

Now if you should say: "why then do the magistrates kill criminals?", my answer is at hand. Seeing that the state of human affairs since the fall of Adam is such that it has tainted all of us with sin, so that very often the evil injure the good, therefore it results that all mankind must exert itself to see that the law concerning injury is especially preserved. Hence those who have disturbed the public peace and injured the innocent must be restrained and put from our midst and coerced in order that the many, by the removal of offenders, may be preserved. But still the law remains: Injure no man, but if anyone should have been injured, he who inflicted the injury ought to be removed so that the many may not be injured. It is of more importance to preserve the many than just one or two; therefore he is done away who threatens the many by one or two crimes. Hence in the state there are magistrates, the punishment of criminals and wars, all of which lawyers have referred to "Jus gentium."[56]

The third law concerning the common use of things, plainly takes its rise from the very nature of human

---

[56]The following explanation of the Tertia Lex proves that, the Augustianian Medieval notion that the state grounded on law is a consequence of sinful development in the life of mankind is re-echoed here. It is to be observed that Thomas and his disciples taught that the state would arise even without any Fall from original righteousness. Cf. J. J. Baumann, "Die Staatslehre des Thomas von Aquino." S. 167ff. Here and there one finds in Luther ideas which remind of this view only Luther looks upon the State as some moral good. Cf. Luther: Von Weltlicher Obrigkeit" 1523: "Wenn alle welt rechte Christen das ist recht Gläubigen wären, so wäre kein Fürst, König, Herr, Schwert noch Recht noth oder nutz. Denn wozu sollts ihn?

society. For if among a very few things that common saying should be valid which being interpreted means: "'that friends ought to share all things in common,'"[57] why should it not likewise hold good among many men? Especially so, seeing that they should be so closely united with each other that brothers would cling to brothers, children to parents, and parents to children. Now the law against injury decreed this. But because man's cupidity does not suffer us to use all things in common, this law must be corrected by a higher one: let no man be injured. And too, possessions are to be shared so far as public peace and the welfare of the many may permit. For inferior laws are amended entirely by higher ones, and mutual participation of the many must be urged to a certain limit. Then a third law must be joined: that property is to be divided since the common safety of the man demands it. Moreover because the state of human nature is such that there is need of at least some mutual sharing of property, since property ought by nature be common, it has been ordained that the use of property is to be shared, to be sure through contracts, buying, selling, leasing, farming out, and in other ways. And here you may discern what is the origin of contracts or agreements.[58]

Dieweil sie den heiligen Geist im Herzen haben, der, sie lehret, und macht, dass sie Niemand unrecht thun, Jedermann lieben, von Jedermann gerne und fröhlich leiden, auch den Tod." E. A. 22, 66 ff. and also on 68.

τὰ τῶν φίλων κοινά. Cf. Aristotle: Nicomachean Ethics Book 8, C. II.

[58] The view here expressed, which sees in commercial traffic and its various forms a moment of sin, agrees in the main with the view of the Scholastics, popularized by Gabriel Biel. Cf. Werner: Duns Scotus S. 504. Thomas following Aristotle argued against community ownership. Cf. Baumann, "Die Staatslehre des Thomas Von Aquino" S. 148. The strongly communistic trend of the Reformation in its early stage, which, however, is to be distinguished from the practical communistic groups of Anabaptists, is due partly to what has been said, and partly to the larger preference for Plato on the side of the

Plato saw this when in the fifth book of his *De Legibus* he says that, that state is best administered in which accession is made as nearly as possible to the common statement: "the "possessions of friends are common to all." And further, when not only possessions of friends are held in common, but even when the very members of each one: eyes, hands, feet, mouth, serve public utility. Nor ought any other example of a well constituted republic be sought than that state in which the common statement τὰ φίλων κοινὰ can be observed. And thus agreements (contracts) have been devised, through which each man's possessions are equally shared by the many, lest there should be no sharing of property at all. Now of the general formulas of natural laws you can divide them somewhat as follows:

I. Love God.

II. Because we are born unto a kind of common society, injure no man but assist whomever you may with kindness.

III. If it cannot be that no man is injured, let this be done in order that the smallest amount of people be injured by the removal of those who disturb the public peace. For this duty let magistrates be apjointed, and punishments for the guilty be instituted.

IV. Divide property for the safety of public peace. As to the rest, let some alleviate the wants of others through contracts.

Now whoever wishes, let him add to these from the poets, orators, and historians the particular judgments that are customarily referred to "jus gentium," such as what is everywhere written about marriages, adulteries, restitution, ingratitude, hospitality, permutation

---

humanistic school, whose view respecting community ownership was shared by such fathers as Lactantius, Ambrosius and Chrysostomus.

of property and other like things. For it seemed sufficient to me to note merely the most common forms. But do not indiscreetly consider certain ideas of the gentile writers. For very many of their common judgments imitate the depraved affections of our nature and not our laws. For example that from Hesiod (Opp. et. dies 353–354:)
τὸν φιλέοντα φιλεῖν καὶ τὸ προσιόντι προσεῖναι. Καὶ δόμεν ὅς κεν δῷ καὶ μη δόμεν ὅς κὲν μὴ δῷ.
For in these verses friendship is measured decidedly by utility. Such is also that common saying: δὸς τι καὶ λάβε τι.

To this belongs also what they style "the repulsion of force by force," as is evidenced from the following quotation from the Ion of Euripides (1045–47):
τὴν δ' εὐσέβειαν, εὐτυχοῦσιν μὲν, καλὸν τιμᾶν. Ὅταν δὲ πολεμίους δράσαι κακῶς θέλῃ τις, οὐδεὶς ἐμποδὼν κεῖται νόμος.

And, too, in "jus civile" as they call it, there are very many things indicating human affections more than natural laws. For what is more foreign to natural law than the captivity of slaves?[59] And that which is of interest is uncivilly protected by contracts. But of this later. A good man will adjust civil constitutions to fairness and equity, that is, to divine and natural laws, against which it cannot be right for anything to be instituted. So much for natural laws which, if you can, divide more exactly and subtly.

On Divine Laws

Divine laws are those laws ordained by God in the

---

[59] Spalatin: "das gefenknuss der laybaygen leut." It is noteworthy that Melanchthon grounds the right of personal liberty in the very nature of man. It becomes more noteworthy when we remember that the Pope just a short while before had declared that the faithful should make his enemies the Venetians slaves. Cf. Gieseler: Lehrbuch d. Kichengeschichte II, 4, 182.

Canonical Scriptures. There are three orders of divine laws: some are moral, some judicial, others ceremonial.

Moral laws are those prescribed in the decalogue, to which the studious person refers all laws contained in Scripture touching morals. For how often the same law is repeated in Scripture! Moreover it must be observed here that I do not set forth the decalogue concerning external works alone and digress into counsels and precepts, after the method of the Scholastics. Wherefore in a few words, I shall mention the formulas of the laws.

The first three precepts: thou shalt have no other Gods, thou shalt not take the name of thy God in vain, remember the Sabbath day to sanctify it—these three Christ undoubtedly set forth in one law (Mark 12:30s): "Thou shalt love the Lord thy God with all thy heart, and with all thy soul, and with all thy mind." Moreover it seems that this is the distinction between these three laws, that although they pertain to the same thing, the true worship of God as is the case in the first: "Thou shalt have no other Gods," it is rightly referred to the affections, that we should not love or fear anything except God, and should not rely on our own works, virtue, prudence, righteousness, or plainly on any creature but on the goodness of God alone. Moreover these affections are not in our power, so that no one knows except the spiritually minded, what is the trust of God, the fear and love of God. To this law belong also many utterances of prophecy concerning the fear of God and reliance on God and the like things. The words of this law wonderfully commend unto us the reliance on and the fear of God. For the words: "I the Lord thy God am very jelaous, visiting the iniquity of the fathers upon the children," etc., terrify us with their threats and declare that the power of his wrath is to be feared.

Again when he adds that "I have mercy upon thousands of them that love me," does he not here demand by commending his goodness, that we love him and rely on his goodness? Moreover greater things are demanded than I can follow with words. The Scholastics have taught that to love God is the same as to wish to be God, and because God hears we must not envy his kingdom, and similar things in more obscure words than those which they could have taught even in their schools. For it cannot be known what it means to love God unless the Spirit teaches. By that I mean unless in reality, one experiences the inkindling of the Spirit Himself. You have the work of the first precept: to rely on God, to love and fear God. This is the worship spoken of by Christ in John 4:23: "True worshippers who will worship the father in spirit and in truth." And acceptable external worship of its own accord will follow such an affection as this is.

The second precept stipulates that the name of God be not taken in vain; and it plainly teaches that we should bear witness to that faith itself and likewise to the fear and love of God, by the very use we make of his name. And just as the former precept which demands faith and love has been affirmed, so also this precept. It too demands us to praise the name and glory of God, to invoke his name, to take refuge in it as though running to a well fortified port, "to swear by the name of God." Deut. 5:13 says: "A Psalm of David, to His name." And we know that Solomon (Prov. 18:10) says: "A most strong tower is the name of the Lord." Therefore let us praise and proclaim the beneficence of God toward us, let us give thanks and in the words of the Apostle, "Let all that we do, be done to the glory of the Lord." So you can see that the second has its origin in the first precept.

The third precept orders us to sanctify the Sabbath, to cease from our work, that is to suffer and to bear the work of God in us, which is our mortification. The first demands faith; the second the praise of God's name; the third the tolerance of the works of God in us. They who teach work-righteousness and the power of free will especially violate this precept. For it demands the mortification of free will. And when the people of the New Testament have a perpetual Sabbath, it means that people whose flesh is zealously mortified and whose spirit is quickened. For they are ignorant both of the Sabbath and of Christianity who assert freedom of the will, and are enemies of the cross of Christ justifying themselves by their own works and attempts. They are following the example of the one who gathered wood on the Sabbath (Numbers 15:32ff.)

Thus you see that the three precepts: "we must believe God, praise God and permit God to work in us," are all comprehended in this one saying: "Thou shalt love the Lord thy God with all thy heart," etc. He loves thus who believes, doubting nothing; who fears, praises and suffers with a most ardent spirit. I have not purposed to set forth the whole law for how could that be done in a compendium? But I have desired to warn you of these things so that you may know in what error they are, who think that nothing can be demanded of us that is greater than our human strength. Whoever desires a more extended treatment of the precepts can find it if he will in a little German work of Luther, "on Good works."[60]

---

[60]Luther's "Sermon von den guten werken" is meant. This was completed toward the end of May 1520 and dedicated to the prince John of Saxony. Cf. E. A. 16, 118 ff. Weimar Ausgabe VI, 196; cf. also Theodor Kolde: "Martin Luther" I, 249 f.

At this point the Sophists make two errors. The first is made when they think that the supreme love of God is not required or demanded in this life; and thus also do they judge with respect to the rest of the affections. But this opinion is clearly refuted by this one text: "Thou shalt love the Lord thy God with all thy heart, and with all thy soul, and with all thy mind." For if God demands the whole heart for Himself, then he does not permit a part thereof to be given to a creature elsewhere. Would that Elias were near to show how unfortunately lame they be who think that a part of the heart is to be devoted to some creature and a part of it to God.

This law cannot be fulfilled as long as we are in the flesh; not because it is not demanded, but because all of us are debtors as long as we fail to pay what we owe, and this is precisely what I said before, that all men are always sinners and do always sin. And when I treat on Grace later on, it must be sought again to what degree we are justified, and to what degree we are still sinners.

The second hallucination of the Sophists is when they think we can fulfill these and the rest of the precepts by our own powers. For they think the precepts are enjoined only with reference to external works; for example, that we should not worship in ceremonies and external offices many gods or idols, etc. But I am forced to explain the law as it touches the affections, by these very words: "Thou shalt love the Lord thy God with thy whole heart." Now the flesh especially loves itself, confides in its own prudence and righteousness. For Paul says so in Roms. 8:5: "The flesh seeketh the things which are its own and cannot be subject to the law of God." Therefore, it cannot love God nor rely on his goodness, etc. It is a great and incomprehensible matter to love God, and through all to embrace the divine will with a truly pleasant and cheerful heart, even though it condemns and mortifies. And so I ask you, O Sophist, can you by nature wish hell and eternal punishment? If you deny that you can, then also deny that God can be freely loved by the flesh.

The rest of the precepts, which comprise the second table have been explained by Christ's words in Matt. 5: "Love thy neighbor as thyself." In Roms. 12, Paul enumerates the almost innumerable laws of love. Indeed now, the Sophists have explained even these laws with reference to external works alone, averring that the law is satisfied if you do no murder, if you do not openly associate with harlots, etc. On the other hand, Christ explains the law concerning the affections, and that too in an affirmative manner. By the law: "Thou shalt do no murder," Christ enjoins us to be toward all men in our hearts both right, candid and liberal; likewise that we be open to all sorts of kindness, not returning evil for evil, not litigating our possessions, in a word, not resisting evil but loving our enemies and that, too, freely and candidly. Thus they think that the law "thou shalt not commit adultery" is satisfied, if we do not design an evil deed by the overt act. But Christ teaches that chastity and purity of heart are demanded, so that we do not dare to desire even things evil. As to the rest, the diligent reader will observe for himself in the gospel.

On Counsels

At this time, I point out another error shameful and disgraceful, which the Sophists made when they created counsels out of the divine law. They taught that certain things are not necessarily demanded by God but are only exhorted. For instance, if any one should choose he might obey, and they would free him from danger who would not obey.[61] Moreover they reckon for the most part among the counsels, those things which are recorded in Matt. 5: Loving ones enemies, resisting not evil, abstaining from litigations and court proceedings, treating well those who deserve evil, giving, mutually sharing with the needy, and even giving up principal (in loans).[62] Now all these things I say are demanded and I number them among the precepts. For Christ openly condemns those who love only friends, and puts them on equality with the gentiles and publicans. Likewise Christ makes guilty of judgment that one who is angry with his neighbor or despises his neighbor and says "racha." But if he only exhorted us not to be angry why did he menace us with a judgment? If it is a matter of freedom to be angry with one who offends or not to be angry, why did he threaten penalties? He who threatens punishments does not exhort, but demands. Besides since it is a precept that our neighbors are to be loved, does not love embrace all those things which they number among counsels? And Paul in Roms. 13:9 refers all these things to the law, "Thou shalt love thy neighbor as thyself."

I John 3:19 reads: "Little children let us not love in words and tongue, but in deed and in truth"; that

---

[61]This was taught by Thomas Aquinas: II, 1 quæst. 108. art. 4: opportet quod præcepta novæ legis intelligantur esse data de his, quæ sunt necessaria ad consequendum finem æternæ beatudinis in quem lex nova immediate introducit; consilia vero opportet esse de illis, per quæ melius et expeditius potest homo consequi finem prædictum." cf. also Thomasius, Dogmengeschichte. 2 Aufl. S. 182. Luther had also sharply contended this distinction. cf. opp. lat. 12, 203. Köstlin: Luthers Theologie I, 285. Likewise Didymus Faventinus (Melanchthon's pen name) C. R. I, 307.

[62]Desperato etiam sorte" "Spalatin's German translation is very rich on this score: "auch ohne Hoffnung der Hauptsummen wieder zu erlangen."

is, let us love from our heart and candidly, and witness our love by our zeal and kindness. Now if they number among the laws the passage: "Thou shalt not covet," etc. why don't they consider as laws those things which it embraces? But is it not the work of concupiscence to be angry with an enemy, to avenge one's property, to be unwilling to divide one's money with the poor? They must therefore confess that these things have been enjoined (since indeed they seem to be so) that we should not covet anything. In a word, why don't they interpret the whole law as a counsel seeing indeed that they annul part of it? But you will say: "It is an act against my family if I must share with another." I answer: This is only a pretext for your own cupidity made by carnal prudence. For one's spirit will easily show how far one must share, and it will gladly deprive itself provided it is given to obviate a brother's want. Are you ignorant of the fact that you ought to do to your neighbor as you wish to be done by? "But we will be subject to the injuries of all, if we are not permitted to avenge ourselves." Rightly so. For this is the way of the Cross, that you are subject to injury. "The evil will seize our possessions if we are not permitted to have recourse to judgment." It is the magistrates' duty to take care that no citizen injures another; it is your duty to counsel good in a case of this kind.

But why do I attempt to weaken the arguments of carnal knowledge, when it can never come to pass that he will approve the divine law, except that one who is spiritually minded? Again, you cannot understand if it is by no means agreeable to do so why Christ has enjoined precepts. Carnal arguments of this sort impose themselves upon the Sophists, since it did not seem civil enough to make the riches of all so common, that no man could lay claim to his property.

Moreover it was considered inhuman and ignoble to enjoy leisure, if they could safely enjoy the wealth of others. So at this point, counsels were devised from the precepts and that most pestilent opinion was accepted, that states could not be administered according to the gospel, just as though Christ had handed down some such things as might pertain only to a handful of monks, and not to the entire human race. But what ought to be more common than the gospel which Christ has ordered to be preached to all? Now Augustine in his epistle to Marcellinus (the fifth in the order of his epistles), has completely dissolved such carnel misrepresentations against the law which prohibits vengeance. Moreover it does not forbid magistrates to place penalties for crimes. Nay more, these, as Paul says in Roms. 13:4, carry the sword as a terror to evildoers. But it does prohibit us as individuals from mutually performing this with a desire for vengeance. It is the magistrate's duty to see that the state suffers no wrong. It is your duty to suffer and repress a private injury. But I shall perhaps discuss this more fully in another place.

The only place in the gospels where a counsel appears is that concerning celibacy; and of it, Christ in Matt. 19:12 says: "He who can hear, let him hear." In I Cor. 7:25 Paul says: "Concerning virgins I have no commandment of the Lord: yet I give my judgment, as one that hath obtained mercy of the Lord to be faithful. I suppose therefore that this is good for the present distress, that it is good for a man so to be. "Art thou bound unto a wife? Seek not to be loosened. Art thou loosed from a wife? Seek not a wife," etc. You will not argue at this point whether counsels are superior to precepts, will you? These are the fallacies of the Scholastics who understood neither precept nor counsel. For the precept concerning adultery will not be fulfilled no matter how much of a celibate one may be, since it cannot be otherwise than that concupiscence will incite one, however chaste he may be. But concupiscence has been prohibited by a precept, which indeed one can more nearly fulfill being married than if he were single.

On Monkish Vows

What moreover about monkish vows?[68] In the first place in respect to the very nature of a vow, Scripture neither counsels nor orders that one vow in any respect. Moreover God does not approve of anything except what he either orders or counsels. So then I do not see that anything is added to one's piety through a vow. The Mosaic law did not demand that vows be made in any respect; yet it did permit such. The gospel entirely ignores the servitude of vows, since there is altogether a certain liberty of the spirit. And as to why the custom of vowing has been accepted, as far as I can see it has been done solely through the ignorance of faith and evangelical freedom. The rite of vowing is not so much a contradiction of faith as it is of the liberty of the spirit. The Scholastics even teach that a work done in accordance with a vow excels a work that is done without a vow. Impious men they, to evaluate piety by works rather than by the spirit and faith! But why do they prefer a work on account of a vow, since

---

[68]Melanchthon on good grounds joins this article here. For Thomas had taught Summa II, qu. 108 art. IV that in order to become blessed a person need not entirely give up the things of this world; but if he does this he will reach his goal "vita æterna" more easily. The things of this world according to I John 2:16 are: "in divitiis externorum bonorum, in delectis carnis, in honoribus." To renounce these as far as possible is the content of the evangelical counsels. Perfection is manifested in such denial.

a vow is neither demanded nor does it console? Consider then again, I pray, what is to be vowed. Celibacy, poverty, and obedience are sworn. That celibacy is counseled, I do not deny. But in view of the weakness of our flesh (as even Christ himself said that all could not hear his word about celibacy) of what moment is it to let so many thousands of men share in a thing that is so very doubtful and perilous?

Of the ancient hermits as far as I can gather from history, there were only a very few who contended successfully with the flesh, although they zealously emaciated their bodies by hunger and thirst, and were most fortified by the knowledge of the divine Scriptures against the wiles of the devil. But how shall we conquer in such luxury, in the greatest of ease, so unarmed, so ignorant of the Scriptures and the gospel, with which unless you are most conversant, you will contend unsuccessfully with Satan? And moreover, success teaches how prudently we vow.

Furthermore, poverty is demanded of all Christians by divine law and does not only pertain to monks. However evangelical poverty is not that common mendicity, but means that we have all things in common, that we share, that we give to all who are in need, and that we do a thing with this in mind: the mitigation of another's want. Evangelical poverty is not "to possess nothing," but to so possess that you think you yourself are the keeper of another man's property, and not your own. This is what Paul teaches in Ephes. 4:28: "Rather let him labor working with his hands which is good, that he may have wherewith he may contribute to him that hath need." To this also can be referred what is recorded in Matt. 19:21: "Go sell all thou hast and give to the poor." For Christ thus wished him to be a pauper in order that he might give. Now we call poverty nothing but the reception of something from others. Do you see how far from the gospel the institution of begging really is? Even as poverty is demanded so also is the task of acquiring property, not for our own sake but for the sake of our brothers. So far from being approved is that thing called mendicity!

Finally, they vow obedience. But each one of us owes by divine law obedience to parents, teachers and magistrates. Wherefore, in the monastic institution there is no specific perfection. But just now I do not choose to dispute about monks. They have seen how Christianlike they thought who went so far as to prefer the state of monkery to the class of mankind, judging Christianity not by the spirit, but by external appearance. Formerly monasteries were nothing but schools, and the scholars lived as celibates according to their own will and as long as it pleased them. They used all things in common with their fellow classmates. They yielded and rendered obedience to their preceptors. They sang Psalms, prayed and held discussions. In short, they considered the whole nature of the life to be the first beginning and rudiments of those morally imperfect. And I would that such were the condition of the monasteries today. For if such were the case, we would have holier schools and less superstition and impiety. For in what part of Christian affair does Antichrist more powerfully hold sway than in monastic servitude?[64]

---

[64] See Luther's remarks on these assertions which Melanchthon personally submitted to him: "Methodus tua non stulte dicit, votorum servitutem alienam esse ab Evangelio," etc.: De Wette II, 45. Cf. also Enders III, 223, 232. ct. also Luther's Theses: op. var. arg. IV, 344 ff. W. A. VIII, 313, and his writing "De votis monasticis" opp. V. art. VI, 235, W. A. VIII, 573. On the whole problem cf. Th. Kolde: Martin Luther II, S. 16 ff.

On Judicial and Ceremonial Laws

There remain judicial and ceremonial laws. Concerning these it is not important to say very much in a compendium. Judicial laws concerning judgments and, in addition, the penalties of forensic cases have been handed down by the Jewish people in the Old Testament. Christian writings (gospel) are ignorant of laws of this nature primarily for two reasons. First because Christian people are prohibited from vindicating themselves and poverty and common goods are enjoined. Next because court proceedings are forbidden, in the language of Paul in I Cor. 6:7: "Moreover now, it is indeed wrong that ye have lawsuits among yourselves."

Ceremonial laws respecting sacrificial rites, holydays, vestments, victims and the like things, have also been handed down. There is no doubt but that the mysteries of the gospel have been adumbrated in these, as the Epistle to the Hebrews teaches. Likewise many places in Corinthians and somewhere the prophetic writings bear witness to the same thing, commonly applying allegorically the types of the law to evangelical mysteries. Of such a nature are many of the Psalms. Moreover in passages of this type it is necessary to allegorize, but one must do so with prudence. For as touches allegories even great authors often talk with more than puerile nonsense. Nor do they admit of the allegorical interpretation except that the rites and duties were handed down in this respect, that they were to be signs of other things; that the sacrifices of the Levitical high priest have been handed down in this respect: to typify the sacrifice of Christ.

Unless an individual is thoroughly conversant with the whole of Scripture he will unsuccessfully treat of allegories. But moreover the Spirit will easily judge, nay more, common sense will tell you how far and to what degree, the use of allegories is permissible. However they lead to an understanding of the power of the law and the gospel, provided they are fitly used. The comparison of Aaron with Christ in the Epistle to the Hebrews is wonderful, in that it sets the Christ clearly before our eyes and correctly shows what benefits the world has received through Christ. The comparison points out what the high priesthood of Christ bestows on humanity; and that we are justified by nothing save through the priesthood of Jesus.

Something yet is to be said about the strength of the law and then abrogation. These topics ought to be considered especially at this time. But since this discussion cannot be understood except by comparison of law and gospel, therefore, I shall discuss simultaneously the strength of the law and abrogation later when I treat of the gospel. I shall now add to this topic what ought to be thought about human laws.

On Human Laws

In short, human laws are those created by man. And as they regard the affairs of man, some human laws are civil, others pontifical. Civil laws are those sanctioned by the magistrates, princes, kings, and cities in the government. Paul tells us what ought to be the authority for law of this nature in Romans 13:1–3: "Let every soul be subject to the higher powers. For there is no power save from God. The powers which be are ordained by God. Moreover they who resist, receive unto themselves condemnation. For princes are not a terror to good works but to evil." For the duty of magistrates and civil laws is nothing other than the punishment and prevention of injuries. For this purpose, laws concerning the division of property, the forms of contracting, and the penalties of evil-doers are enacted. For the magistrate is a minister of God, and an avenger unto wrath for him who has committed crime. Moreover it is not permissable for a magistrate to decide against the Divine Law; nor ought he be obeyed against the Divine Law. This is in accordance with Acts 5:29: "It is better to obey God rather than men." And a prudent reader will easily judge from this passage just how far we are subject to human law. I shall have more to say about magistrates when I discuss the condition of men.

What now about pontifical laws? As far as Pontiffs decide litigation and judgments, they are plainly worldly princes. Moreover Divine law has made subject to civil magistrates, Kings and Princes, both that which pertains to litigations and judgments and the Priests themselves as well. But now the Princes have connived and founded for themselves laws, impious and especially tyrannical, concerning the immunities of churches, their own revenues, etc. And here the kindness of charity demanded that those who are the richest should alleviate the public want by their common treasury and wealth, while they prescribe for evil foreboding whoever should demand of a priest revenue, tribute or the like, which were commonly collected for public necessity. But of these things elsewhere. It is enough to have pointed out that the sacerdotal laws concerning civil matters were enacted contrary to charity and through pure tyranny.

Neither Pontiffs nor councils nor the universal church have any right to change or decide any matter of faith. For articles of faith are to be determined in accordance with the order of Scripture. Nor must that be considered an article of faith which has been handed down outside of Scripture.[65] In the first place, Paul (Gal. 1:9) orders that there be no alteration. "If anyone shall have preached unto you other than that which ye have received, let him be Anathema." Likewise who can be a prophetic spirit who differs from the Scripture? Nay rather that spirit is mendacious which proclaims against the truth. And to Timothy Paul writes (I Tim. 6:3): "If anyone teaches otherwise and does not acquiesce to the same words of Christ he is haughty." Moreover there have been many impious things decreed contrary to the Scripture. These I shall discuss later.

In the next place whatever either the Church or a Pontiff has decided beyond the Scripture, according to Paul is not to be considered as an article of faith (II Tim. 3:14): "Abide thou in those things which thou hast learned, knowing from whom thou hast learned them." Paul thinks it important that we know whence we have learned. Now how shall we know the source of those things humanly discerned, if it cannot be determined according to Scripture? For indeed, that is certain to have emanated from the Holy Spirit which the Scripture confirms. It is doubtful whether that which is handed down outside the Scripture comes from the Holy Spirit or from a mendacious spirit. Paul enjoins the Thessalonians (1:5, 21) to prove all things and to hold fast that which was good. Elsewhere he orders us to try the spirits to see whether they are of God. I ask you now, how shall we try the spirits, unless they are examined according to some fixed law or

---

[65]"Nec habendum est pro articulo fidei quod citra scripturam proditum est!" As early as 1519 in his Bachelor's thesis the author said practically the same thing: "Catholicum præter articulos quorum testis est scriptura non necesse alios credere.—Conciliorum auctoritas est infra scripturæ auctoritatem." cf. Krafft: "Briefe und Dokumente aus der Zeit der Reformation," S. 6.

rule, and that too, the Scripture which alone is certain to have been produced by the Spirit of God? To attribute unto councils the authority to create articles of faith is a rash thing. Especially so since for example, it may be that nobody in the whole assembly of the council may have the spirit of God.

In Samaria the priests of Baal prophesied and the Kings of Israel performed all things according to their oracles. Why wonder if at the present time, impious men destitute of God's Spirit prophesy? The priests in Judah who withstood Jeremy and the Spirit of God assumed the same thing when they said (Jer. 18:18) "Come ye and let us think thoughts against Jeremy; for the law will not pass away from a priest nor counsel from a wise man, nor discourse from a prophet." What else is it than what the pope's church says today? Within us is the authority of decision: a council is ruled immediately by the Holy Spirit and cannot err; sacred Scripture is obscure and ambiguous; we have the right and faculty of their interpretation, and the like. But it has been openly proclaimed in Scripture that ecclesiastical princes will err (Ezek. 7:26) : "The law will pass from the priest and counsel from the elders." And in Matt. 24:24 it reads: "False Christs and false prophets shall arise and shall give many signs," etc. Then, too, although the council may have the Spirit of God, yet Scripture indicates that it can err. (Ezek. 14:9) : When a prophet shall have erred and shall have spoken a word, I am the Lord who deceived that prophet." And in I Kings 22:22: "I am the Lord who deceived that prophet." And in Kings 22:22: "I shall go forth and I shall be a lying spirit in the mouth of all the prophets." What importance is attached to saying more? Paul (Gal. I:16) says he did not acquiesce to flesh and blood; do we believe in flesh and blood? I ask you, why do you believe the Nicene Synod rather than the Arminensian? Is it because the authority of the Roman Pontiff approved it?[86] For this reason you prefer the authority of a Pontiff to both a council and Scripture, which is not only impious but foolish as well. Why do you approve of the Synod of Antioch which condemned Paul of Samosata who denied the divinity of Christ, when the whole thing was done without the authority of the Roman Pontiff? In the Council of Alexandria when a decree concerning the three divine hypostases was made against Sabellius, no mention was made of a Roman Pontiff. It is said that there were no Roman Pontiffs in the Council of Nicea. The Greek writers of the Constantinopolitan Synod make no mention of a Roman Pontiff, so that it is very likely that none were there, or else if there, were not outstanding. Stephanus VI rescinded the Acts of Pontiff Formosus by the authority of a council. His judgment was condemned by John X at the Synod of Ravenna.[87] Now when Synods disagree with each other, one of necessity must have been in error. The Council of Lugdunum ought to be considered impious because it approved the books of the decretals.[68] Especially so because the decretals contain so many cruel and impious things.

Moreover, by these papal councils I see nothing done except what is in the interest of Roman tyranny; the

---

[66]Eck answers this question in his Enchiridion Locorum communium (Edition of 1525) with these words: "Arminense conciliabulum fuit non concilium neque legitime congregatum."

[67]Cf. E. Dummler, Auxilius und Vulgarius, Leipsic 1866; cf. also Hefele, Conciliengesch. I. Aufl. IV. Bd. S. 565-77.

[68]The Council of Lyon held in 1245 is meant. Innocent IV selected a number of canons from it and sent the same to the University of Bologna for use in School and Judicial practice. Later Boniface VIII incorporated a collection in his "Liber sextus decretalium" cf. Hefele, Conciliengesch. II. Aufl. V, 1120 f.

subjugation of emperors, the maintenance of the patrimony of Peter, the increasing of the wealth of priests, or the oppression of the Greek church. That heretical order "ad abolendam de hæretics"[69] is well known. It execrates all who think or teach anything concerning the sacraments other than what is taught or observed by the church of Rome. Now the Greeks are not heretics; for the most part they differ with Rome concerning rites and traditions.

Those things which have been decreed in many councils about indulgences are impious. The Synod called by Constantius among other things condemned the evangelical teaching on the distinction of works, namely: that every work is either good or bad and not indifferent, as Matt. 12:33 teaches. But why note anything further since the abominable codices of papal laws are extant from which you may choose what you will. I have made note of these things only to warn you that the vulgar opinion which flaunts itself that councils cannot err has been rashly accepted. Moreover since it is clearer than the noonday sun that councils have often erred and can err, I ask you, reader, why ought that be considered an article of faith which has been decreed by a council without the voice of Scripture? Since it is clear that councils can err, why are not their decrees examined in the light of Scripture? Be it far from a Christian mind to think that he might create an article of faith that is not certain to fall or that cannot fall. Peter denies that the interpretation of Scripture is private: that is, of human exposition.

---

[69]"Ad abolendam de hærecticis": a Decretal of Lucius III. against the Waldenses promulgated at the Council of Verona in 1184. Cf. "Corp. Jur. Can." edited by L. Richeter, II, 751: "Universos, qui de sacramento corporis et sanguinis Domini nostri Jesus Christi, etc. aliter sentire aut docere non metuant, 'quam sacrosancta Romana ecclesia prædicat et observat, pari vinculo perpetui anathematis innodamus."

Shall we permit men to create articles of faith? Why not as Peter says in his Epistle (II, 1:19) follow Scripture as it goes before us. λύχνον φαίνοντα ἐν αὐχμηρῷ τόπῳ Especially so, when the prophet declares they shall not have the morning light who depend not upon the opinion of the law and testimony. I refer to Isa. 8:20. Paul's words (I Cor. 1:3, 11) pertain to the same thing, when treating of Christian doctrine he says: "For no other foundation can be laid save what is laid," etc., meaning thereby that no doctrine is necessary for salvation, no articles of faith other than that contained in the Scripture. The day of the Lord, he says, will prove those things which are built upon it. But if they are to be tested on the Lord's day, why are they accepted not only as a doctrine of true value or stamp, but also as necessary to salvation?

A decree has been made concerning transubstantiation in the Lord's Supper; a decree also has been made regarding the primacy of the pope, and that too, contrary to the ancient synodical orders. Since these decrees were made certainly without the permission of Scripture, why are they accepted as true dogmas? The Apostles in Acts and Paul everywhere prove their doctrine by the authority of Scripture. Christ awakens faith in himself through the Scriptures, when He orders us to search the Scriptures which testify of Him, and also when He says that the Father supports him. He also says that the testimony of two must be received, and many other similar things. In Deut. 12:32 the Lord demands that nothing be added nor detracted from his word. This plainly teaches that it is right for no man to teach as an article of faith, what he does not assuredly know to be the Divine word of God. The Prophets, Christ, and the Apostles knew for a certainty that what they taught was the word of God. Therefore they wished themselves, nay more, their very voices, to be believed.

I am fully persuaded by these things that nothing ought to be considered an article of faith which the Scriptures do not openly touch. Thus the arguments of the Paris theologians are broken down when in their foolish and impious condemnation of Luther they call the dogmas[70] of the councils and schools "Principles of faith" concerning the divinity of the Son. I believe the Nicene council because I believe the Scripture[71] which so clearly proves to us the divinity of the Son that not even the Jews, however blind, could refuse to attribute anything short of divinity to Messiah. The passage in Jeremy 23:6 is well known: "and this is the name they shall call him, our righteous God." And thus I think the rest of the Synods must be judged by the Scripture.

Now shall the church decide about morals, and likewise ceremonies? I do not see why the Pontiff or Synods should decide about morals, unless perchance the papal laws on wars, courts and celibacy pertain to morals. And if measured by the evangelical rule. I ask you how could they have been less piously created even by the Scythians?

---

[70] The Paris Theologians had proclaimed: nonne impium se prodet et infidelem, quisquis orthodoxæ fidei, sanctis, ecclesiæ doctoribus ac sacris conciliis credere dedignatur? Is nempe cui credet, qui catholicæ ecclesiæ fidem habere detrectat? C. R. I, 369.

[71] This remark is to be traced back to an objection of the Louvain theologian Latomus against Luther Latomus, arguing against Luther's thesis that one must hold himself down solely to the Scripture, makes use of the word ὁμοούσιος with which the ancient church had decided the great controversy and which is not in the Scripture. Luther then enjoined in the same sense in which Melanchthon here uses it, in these words: "Quodsi odit anima meam vocem homoousion, et nolim ea uti, non ero hæreticus. Quis enim me cogit uti, modo rem teneam, quæ in concilio per scripturas definita est? Opp. V, 506. —W. A. VIII, 117.

I shall speak of ceremonies which the Papists think is their own realm. In the first place, in order to explain at one and the same time both morals and ceremonies, I say that it is not permitted bishops to order anything that is not contained in the Scripture.[72] For Christ sent his Apostles forth to teach what he himself had said: "Teaching them to observe all things whatsoever I have commanded you" (Matt. 28:30). And therefore he takes away the power of creating new laws and new rites. Christ orders his Apostles to teach nothing but the gospel. How is it then that bishops will prove their right to create laws? Is it from that sentence in Luke 10:16? "Who heareth you, heareth me." But in Matt. 10:41 he wishes a prophet to be received in the name of a prophet. Therefore he does not wish a false prophet to be received. And a false prophet is one who teaches human inventions and the traditions of men.

For the Scriptures call these "dreamers." Moreover I ask you Papists, ye Solons and lawgivers, to produce one syllable from Scripture giving you the authority to make laws! For Scripture does away with the privilege of founding laws when it enjoins: "Let no word be added to nor taken from the law of God." Paul also destroys that privilege in II Cor. 3:6 when he calls bishops of the New Testament "ministers of the spirit." For a minister of the spirit is one who through the law condemns the hearts of all, but who again in

---

[72]Aimed against Thomas Aquinas who attempted to construct out of the gospel which he considered a "lex nova," universally binding church laws. Summa II, 1, quæest. 108 art. 2, concl. This was regarded a necessity. And this necessity the Bishops could suffice, because they were possessors of the Spirit; cf. Erck, Enchir., A. 8. Therefore Melanchthon retorts, "ademit potestatem novas leges, novos ritus condendi." He is here inveighing against the legalistic viewpoint. The "leges" he has in mind for the most part are those "necessariæ ad salutem."

turn, consoles them through the gospel powerful in the Spirit of God. What do human traditions, judging only of external works, make towards such a function as this, I ask? Scripture condemns traditions more often than it can be doubtful just what it thinks about them.

Jeremy 23:28 calls human traditions "chaff:" "what is the chaff to the wheat?" Likewise he calls them "lies and dreams," v. 32. Isaiah 28:8 "vile puke, filthiness." Ezek. 23 calls them: "fornications, the flesh of asses, mare's humor." Other prophets describe traditions in other terms. Paul calls them "coaxing language." But passing by many others, Paul in I Tim. 4:1 indicates the origin of human traditions. "In the last days some will fall away from the faith, giving ear to seducing spirits and the doctrines of demons, speaking a lie in hypocrisy and having their conscience cauterized, forbidding to marry, abstaining from meats which God has created," etc. You see, a false spirit is the author of the traditions about celibacy, the distinctions of meats, etc. And what else are the Papal canons but traditions about celibacy, the distinction of meats, and similar jokes? Matt. 15:9: "In vain do they serve me with the mandates of man."

What then? How do human traditions bind consciences? And do they sin who violate the constitutions or orders of man? I answer that Papal laws are to be borne as we would bear any injury or tyranny: "Who asks you to accompany him one mile, go thou with him two," Matt. 5:41. Moreover they are to be borne only so far as they do not endanger the conscience. Thus traditions are to be violated when they obscure faith or when they are an occasion for sin: Acts 5:29, "it is better to obey God than men." And in addition, he does no sin who violates them without giving offense to his spiritual judgment. Moreover you have clear statements of Scripture which teach that consciences are not to be bound by human traditions. I Cor. 3:22: "all are yours, whether Paul or Apollos"; that is, neither Paul nor Cephas has the authority to bind your conscience. This is also clearly taught in I Cor. 7:23 "ye are bought with a price, be unwilling to be servants of men." But they are made servants of men, whose consciences are deprived of their liberty by traditions. For just as Christian liberty is liberty of conscience, just so the servitude of Christians is servitude of conscience.

The passage in Col. 2:20 is well known. "Seeing indeed that ye are dead together with Christ, why do ye still live in the world vexed by traditions?" And he adds verbatim, as it were, their traditions: "Taste not, touch not, handle not, according to the precepts and doctrines of men, which are indeed things having a semblance of wisdom in superstition and humility, and not the sparing of the body, not in any honor, which ought to be for the necessity of the flesh." In Jeremy 23:16 the Lord forbids false prophets to be heard; this passage should be referred without doubt to this particular case when consciences are endangered. So he says: "Do not hear the words of false prophets who prophesy unto you and beguile you; they speak the vision of their heart and not with the voice of God." I have some rather recent authors who agree with me on this topic and especially does that mighty Gerson think as I do. That is, that consciences are not to be bound by human traditions; and he does no sin who violates them unless he falls into the misfortune of giving offense. I wish Bernard had written more freely about such matters in his work on *Dispensation*. Moreover the Spirit will most certainly judge, II Cor. 3:17: "Where the Spirit of the Lord is, there is liberty." And also I Cor. 2:15 "The Spirit judges all things but he himself is judged by no man."

To be sure I could not relate what sort of things the councils and Popes have created, unless I wished to repeat the whole of canonic law and recount the whole of ecclesiastical history. But I shall state a few examples of the traditions of this nature. From these can be learned what the Scripture so often admonishes namely, that nothing indeed is so averse to piety as the doctrines of men.

In the Council of Nice certain forms of penance were instituted. I do not proclaim by what spirit the fathers decreed them, but I do say that a good portion of the gospel, nay more the very germane power of the gospel, has been obscured by this tradition. For this was the birthplace of "satisfactions." At first these "satisfactions" were endurable when the church still possessed the pure knowledge of the gospel. But a little later what a torment of consciences was created by these "satisfactions." Grace was obscured and what the gospel attributed to faith, began to be attributed to these satisfactions. What is more impious and pernicious than this? Certainly occasion was given to these evils by the Nicene Synod. How much better it would have been to follow the example of Paul in regard to the forms of penance, who received without any satisfaction that Corinthian fornicator when he came to himself, simply warning him (according to I Cor. 2:6) that reproof is sufficient. Moreover the theologasters of our time following the ancient tradition of the Synod of Nice, have made satisfactions a part of penance. There is no error more baneful than this.

What trouble has that Papal confession caused the

consciences of pious folk? How many thousands of souls has it alone utterly lost? While Paul has wished to warn the Corinthians lest that fornicator should be afflicted with too many sorrows! But what do the Roman Pontiffs who invented confessions do but most wretchedly and cruelly trouble terrified but truly pious consciences?

Now with Christianity divided into so many kinds of living, what advantage is it to Christian love and simplicity? Some are laymen, others monks, still other clerics and in these there are innumerable sects which could perhaps be tolerated except that there is rivalry in zeal and ambition. Then to these kinds of living that intolerable burden of celibacy has been added. The Nicene Synod also made a decree concerning celibacy. However what has been accomplished by this tradition is of little importance, since lust could not have been more indulgently spread abroad by any other counsel. In I Cor. 7:25, where Paul treats of virginity he dares not enjoin anything for fear of giving occasion for a snare (setting a trap); and he wishes that to be chosen by which they can serve God constantly and without distraction: εὐπρόσεδρον τῷ Κυρίῳ καὶ ἀπερισπάστως, as the Apostle says in verse 35. But how many less assiduous ones or εὐπρόσεδροι there are who are more vehemently destroyed by God than those whom the flames of passion consume? Paul foreseeing this, does not enjoin celibacy. And what is more, writing to Timothy (1, 4:1) he called the tradition about celibacy a doctrin of demons. But Satan has conquered and the law has been received and promulgated among so many thousands of people, but with great destruction to the Christian cause.

Now already the eucharist has been banished, so to speak, to one particular class of people, the priests;

and what Christ willed to be a common possession of all pious souls is now usurped by priests alone. Thus both the fruits of the mass and the power of the eucharist have been utterly obscured. The eucharist at the present time is nothing but a trafficking of the priests, since Satan discovered that priests ought to be the ones to sacrifice for the people, and that masses could be sold publicly and the like. The use of the mass would not have persisted had not the conditions of living been divided into priests and laity. Oh! the wretched and abominable impiety that rules in the papal masses of today!

But what does it profit to relate more? You can see from these examples that there has been no tradition, however so pious in appearance, but what has been a great evil to the Christian cause. For what seems more becoming than that there should be in the church satisfactions for public crimes? But on the other hand they have obscured grace. What seems more becoming than for bishops to live as celibates? But on the contrary celibacy has been made a way to lust thereby. What seems more reverent (for thus men judge but not the Spirit) than for the use of the eucharist not to be granted to all? But on the other hand the very fruit of the mass is destroyed. So it happens that traditions may indeed have the nature of wisdom, but this very appearance, that false complexion of impious and wicked Jezebel[73] spells disaster.

On the Gospel[74]

I have thus far treated the form of sin and the nature

---

[73] Melanchthon no doubt has in mind the passage in Rev. 11:20.
[74] This whole section should be compared with Luther's statements found in his "Confutatio Lutheriana Rationis Latomianæ," etc. cf. Erlangen Ausgabe. opp. V, Ar, V, 437 ff.

of laws; perhaps I have done so more briefly than the case demands. But I am not writing a commentary. I am presenting in outline merely a common form of topics which you can follow in learning the Scriptures. But now I shall discuss the gospel and grace, and I shall disagree somewhat in these topics with even the higher lights. For the disputation concerning the abrogation and the power of the law has been deferred to this particular topic. Moreover as the nature of sin is not understood except from the formulas of laws, so also the power of grace cannot be known except by a description of the gospel. And as I have so far considered man's condemnation or cursing, I will now discuss his instauration or blessing.

Of the whole of Scripture there are two parts: the law and the gospel. The law indicates the sickness, the gospel the remedy. To use Paul's words,[75] the law is a minister of death, while the gospel is a minister of life and peace. "The strength of sin is the law," I Cor. 15:56, the gospel is the power or strength of salvation to everyone that believes. Nor has the Scripture so narrated law and gospel in such a manner that one would regard as gospel what Matthew, Mark, Luke and John have written, and as law what Moses has recorded. But the plan of the gospel is scattered; there are promises in both the Old and New Testaments. And again, laws are scattered throughout all the books of the Old and New Testaments. Nor are the periods of law and gospel to be discriminated as is commonly thought, although sometimes law, sometimes gospel one after the other have been revealed. Every period that occurs to my mind is a period of law and gospel just as

---

[75] Just as in the section below "on the power of the law" so here Melanchthon is thinking about II Cor. 3:7: "Quodsi ministratio mortis litteris deformata in lapidibus, fuit in gloria," etc.

men in every period are justified in the same way: sin being revealed by the law, and grace through a promise or the gospel.

The periods of revelation vary, for sometimes the law is revealed and sometimes the gospel, and frequently otherwise just as Scripture sees fit. Now you see that in addition to the natural law that is imprinted upon human minds (as I believe), God also made known to Adam certain laws. Examples of such laws are: knowledge of good and evil; and to Cain he revealed that he should not be angry with his brother and that he would die who killed Cain. In this fashion the Spirit of God restored the knowledge of the natural law by a constant proclamation; and this natural law was already obscured in human minds blinded by sin, so that I may almost call the law of nature not some sort of congenital or innate judgment engraved by nature on human minds, but merely laws accepted by the fathers. These laws were passed along forthwith to posterity. For instance Adam taught his offspring about creation, the worship of God, and admonished Cain not to kill his brother, etc. But let me return to the gospel.

The Meaning of the Gospel

Just as the law is that by which the right is enjoined, and by which sin is made manifest, so also the gospel is the promise of the grace or mercy of God, and therefore the forgiveness of sin and the testimony of God's benevolence toward us. Our minds assured of God's benevolence by this testimony believe that He has forgiven all guilt; and being thus elevated, love and praise God and are exceedingly joyful and rejoice in God, as I shall later discuss under the topic "the power of the gospel." Moreover Christ is the pledge of all these promises; wherefore all scriptural promises must be referred to him, who at first obscurely, but later more clearly has been revealed in them.

After Adam fell and was destined to eternal death he would have undoubtedly perished had not the Lord consoled him by the promise of grace. In Gen. 3:15 the tyranny of sin is described: "I shall put enmity between thee and the woman, between thy seed and her seed." But victory is immediately promised. "The very seed of the woman shall bruise thy head." For in my judgment the pronoun refers to the seed rather than to the woman as it is put in our texts.[76] This is the first promise, "the first gospel" by which Adam was encouraged and received a sure hope of his salvation and was therefore justified. Then the next promise was made to Abraham, that in his seed all nations should be blessed. And this promise cannot be understood except as it refers to Christ. This is Abraham's bosom into which they who were received were saved; that is to say, they were saved who believed the promise that was made to Abraham. And this is the promise of which the New Testament boasts. A diligent reader could collect all the promises of Christ in this place, and these promises are nothing other than the gospel. Deut. 18:18: "I shall raise up a prophet unto them from the midst of their brethren like unto thee, and I shall put my words in his mouth, and he shall speak to them all things which I shall command him. Moreover whoever will not hear his words which he shall speak in my name, I shall be the avenger." In II Sam. 7:12 Christ is promised to David: "I shall raise up

---

[76]"Ut in nostris codicibus legitur": Melanchthon follows the original Hebrew text rather than Jerome's Bible which reads: "ipsa conteret." Luther later on began an exegesis of this verse with similar words. cf. opp. lat. I, 242.

thy seed after thee which shall proceed from thy loins and I shall strengthen his kingdom. He shall build a house to my name and stable will be the throne of his kingdom for ever and ever." And on account of this promise Christ is called by the prophets "David's son." Nay more Ezekiel even calls him David. The prophets as a whole repeat the law and give promise of Christ. It would be beneficial for the pious mind to write down and have ready all the divine promises that are wonderfully efficacious to strengthen and elevate the conscience.

In such a manner God revealed the gospel subsequent to Adam's fall, and later on made it clear until finally Christ was revealed. That is Paul's meaning in Roms. 1:1–2: "Into the gospel of his Son, which aforetime he promised through the prophets, in the holy Scriptures concerning his Son." And the gospels do nothing but witness that these promises have been revealed or fulfilled. That is why Matthew begins thus: "The book of the genealogy of Jesus Christ the son of David, the son of Abraham." I call the gospel the promise of grace, blessing, and the benevolence of God through Christ. In Scripture aside from this promise of eternal blessing, there are also promises of temporal things such as that which was made to Noah, and many such things in the law concerning land, wealth, etc. These are not only figures of spiritual promises, but as such are testimonies of the mercy and grace of God, in order to console and incite our consciences to glorify God. But I shall give a more extended discussion of these promises when I consider the topic on faith, what it is, and how it justifies.

You can see how sweetly and gently the wisdom of the Divine Spirit instructs the pious in the Scripture that it pursues nothing but our salvation. The whole of Scripture is sometimes law, sometimes gospel. The books of Moses sometimes treat of law, sometimes of gospel. Thus the gospel is concealed even in the law itself. For what can you find more evangelical than that promise which the Spirit of God has appended for an αἰτιολογία of the first commandment in Deut. 5:10: "Showing mercy unto thousands of them that love me and keep my commandments." And too consider how the legislator Moses suddenly becomes an evangelist, that is, a herald of grace and of mercy in Ex. 34:6: "O Lord God Ruler, merciful and clement, patient and of much mercy and true, thou who preservest mercy unto thousands, who taketh away both iniquity and crimes and sins and before whom no man of himself is innocent." Just name from the entire Old Testament literature a more evangelical discourse. And thus after this manner the Mosaic books teach sometimes law, at other times gospel. I shall say nothing now about any "figures" except those which the letter openly reveals. For these must especially be considered. The sacred histories are sometimes examples of law and sometimes of gospel. For without doubt the horrible misfortune of Saul relates to law and to gospel. Although David had taken another man's wife nevertheless he sought grace, and the prophetic declaration was purely evangelical, II Sam. 12:2: "The Lord hath taken away thy sin, thou shalt not die." Similar examples must be considered in the same manner.

The prophets teach the law when they censure hypocrisy, impiety, carnal security and the like. For they especially condemn hidden vices or hypocrisy. They declare the gospel also as often as they incite, animate and fill shattered consciences with the lively promise of Christ in such a manner that that Apostolic expression resounds: "who shall separate us from the love of God?" Roms. 8:35. The gospels of Matthew, Mark,

Luke and John, treat after a fashion, now of law and now of promises, and in these are examples both of the grace and of the wrath of God.

The examples of Zaccheus, the Centurion, and the Syrophenecian woman all bear witness of mercy. The blindness and fury of the Pharisees are examples of the wrath of God. However the apostolic histories differ from the ancient in this, they witness that Christ is already revealed whom the ancient merely had promised. Then too the promises of grace, righteousness and eternal life are more clearly explained by them than is the case with the Mosaic or Prophetic books. The apostle Paul especially in the Roman epistle (which incidentally I regard as an index καὶ κάνονα of the whole of Scripture) has given a didactic contrast between the gospel and the law, between sin and grace. The rest of the epistles since they are almost παραινετικαὶ whole of Scripture) has given a didactic contrast between the gospel and the law, between sin and grace. pertain to the law although there is not one in which he does not somewhere or other touch on things pertaining to the gospel. A diligent reader will of himself perceive what that is.

I have advised these things chiefly for this reason: to destroy the current error which the impious sophistical professors of theology have produced about the distinction between law and gospel, and the Old and the New Testaments. It is this: that Moses was succeeded by Christ who gave a new law called the gospel, which is contained in Matt. 5 and 6. And further that between the law of Moses and that of Christ there is this difference: the Mosaic law demands only external works while that of Christ demands the affections; indeed the Mosaic law teaches a sort of hypocritical and Pharisaic righteousness. For what is the simulation of external works but Pharisaism?

Moreover the prophets testify that the Mosaic law

demands the affections also, when they so often enjoin upon man to recognize and to fear God, to do judgment and righteousness. These things the Sophists will no doubt tell me were not taught before the incarnation of Christ and the men of their own age. However what sentence is better known than that of Jeremy? The Sophists, though unwillingly, ought to refer it to the law of Moses. For in chapter 7:22 he says: "I did not speak with your fathers nor order precepts upon them concerning holacausts and victims, in the day that I led them out of Egypt: but this word I did enjoin saying: Hear ye my voice and I will be to you a God and ye shall be to me a people." Tell me, Thomas, what has entered your mind that you should teach that the Moisaic law demands nothing but Pharisaism that is, external works, when Moses himself so often demands the affections in no obscure words.[77] And to pass over many places, he surely forbids the coveting of another's property, etc. Ex. 20:17. He had beforehand already interdicted "work" when he forbade stealing and adultery. Therefore you will grant that the following words were stipulated with reference to the affection: "Thou shalt covet not thy neighbor's wife, nor his manservant, etc.," and in Deut. 10:12: "And now, O Israel, what does the Lord thy God demand of thee but to fear the Lord thy God, and walk in his ways and love him, and serve the Lord thy God, with thy whole heart and with thy whole mind, and keep the mandates of the Lord and his ceremonies, which I this day enjoin upon thee, that it may be well with thee." And again in Deut. 5:16: "Circumcise the foreskin of

---

[77]In several places Thomas distinguishes between the Old and New Law. The Old relates to "exteriores actus," the New to "interiores actus": Sed haec ponitur differentia inter novam legem et veterem, quod vetus lex cohibet manum, sed lex nova cohibet animum. Summa II. 1, qu. 108 Art. I.

your heart and harden not your neck, etc." You can find in Moses 600 passages of this nature, so that it is not doubtful but that the law of Moses demands both affections and works.

Christ in like manner explains the law, for grace cannot be proclaimed without the law. And he rebukes the interpretation of the Pharisees and Scribes from the beginning when he says that we shall not enter the kingdom of heaven unless our righteousness shall exceed the righteousness of the Pharisees and the Scribes. The Pharisees interpreted the law thus: you satisfy the law "thou shalt not kill," if you do not kill with the hand; you satisfy the law "thou shalt commit no adultery" if you do not seduce another man's wife. Christ however teaches that the law demands the affections of the heart and not only an external simulation of works. For the law forbade concupiscence. The law even forbade vindication and in the same manner demanded that one love his enemies. Leviticus 19:17: "Thou shalt not hate thy brother in thy heart, but publicly accuse him lest you carry sin against him. Do not vindicate nor be mindful of an injury of the sons of your people, and love thy neighbor as thyself." I do not know why Hieronymus should have preferred to change the word "Proximum" to "Amicum";[78] for thus it reads in our text. Especially so since the Hebrew word connotes "kindred." This was changed by the Septuagint translators to πλησίον and Paul citing this passage of the law follows this translation in Romans 13:9. However the sentiment of this Mosaic passage is as follows: the Jews should love among themselves both friends and enemies, and should treat well those who

---

[78]Melanchthon is translating from the original Hebrew text rather than from the Vulgate which reads: "non quæras ultionem nec memor eris injuriæ civium tuorum. Diliges Amicum tuum sicut te ipsum."

deserve evil. To this is to be added Isaiah 58, which plainly forbids vindication and demands even the love of one's enemies. Also Proverbs 20:22: "Say not! I shall return evil for evil; wait on the Lord and he will set you free."

Now as far as I know, you will never find in the law the words: "Thou shalt hate thy enemies." Thus it is sufficiently clear that Christ made no reference to the sentiment of the law but to Pharisaic tradition in order to condemn it. The Jews had received a certain precept concerning the Canaanites that they should slaughter them, Exodus 23. Some are of the opinion that Christ made allusion to this when he says: "concerning the persecution of enemies it has been said," Matthew 5:14. But if this is true, what else would Christ have wished, since the gospel has been revealed and the "middle wall" has been torn down as Paul says, and the distinction between Gentiles and Jews has been done away and erased, than that just as it had been commanded of the Jews beforehand to love both friends and enemies, we likewise should love both Gentiles and Jews, both friends and enemies? Moreover what of the fact that Israel had a command only concerning the Canaanites? What of the fact that they are ever commanded to love foreigners.[79] To this pertains also what was decreed concerning interest namely, that money is to be lent on "interest" to foreigners, not to kindred. Now since none are foreigners but all are kindred, interest is entirely interdicted.[80]

---

[79] Because Melanchthon would permit of no fundamental difference between the laws of the Old Covenant and the duties of the Christian life, above all he did not sufficiently recognize the popular formulation and the last questions must remain for him unanswered.

[80] This principle pertains to the practices of the Mosaic law carried on among the national life in general. His view was shared by many Every kind of tribute taking was admitted in its sphere as interest. There were times in which the church decisively opposed the taking

Although it cannot be denied but that Christ made innovations in the law, as for instance the matter about divorce and also when it had been enjoined upon the Jews to defend the legals with the sword, nevertheless Christ does not order the gospel to be defended by arms, as is proven by his words to Peter: "Put up the sword in its place. He that taketh up the sword will perish by the sword." Matt. 26:52. Nevertheless it is not the primary and proper function of Christ to found laws, but to forgive. Moses is a lawgiver, Moses is a judge, but Christ is the Savior even as he himself witnesses in John 3:17: "God has not sent his Son into the world to judge the world, but that the world through him might be saved." The law condemns seeing indeed that we cannot satisfy it; but Christ grants the forgiveness of sins to them that believe. Often indeed Christ proclaims the law because without the law sin cannot be known, and unless we perceive it we cannot understand the power and fulness of grace.

Therefore law and gospel ought to be declared at the same time and both sin and grace ought to be shown. Two cherubim have been placed in the Ark, law and gospel; wherefore it happens that you cannot rightly and successfully teach the gospel without the law or the law without the gospel. And as Christ has joined the

---

of interest, but it had already found many ways by which in the interest of its own property, it got around the prohibition, and gradually with the increase in commercial relations one did not hesitate to raise interest, and Joh. Eck dared to intercede in a "Disputation" at Bologna in behalf of the legality of the act. cf. Wiedemann: Joh. Eck. Regensb. 1865 S. 60 ff. Luther entered upon the much mooted question in his two "Sermons on Interest" in 1519. E. A. 16, 77 ff. W. A. VI, 1 ff. He also rejected the exaction of interest, especially when the capital was not on property. Luther was not so certain whether the law forbade it or not. cf. Th. Kolde, "Martin Luther" I, 217 ff. On the other hand Melanchthon stands more on the legalistic viewpoint. Further literature on the problem: Otto: Joh. Cochlæus, Breslau 1874 S. 60 ff. Funck: Gesch. des Kirchl. Zinsverbotes, Tüb. 1877. M. Neumann: Gesch. des Wuchers in Deutschland. Halle 1865.

law with the gospel, so also the prophets joined the gospel with the law. You have many examples of this fact even in the speeches of the Apostles in the book of Acts and moreover, also in all the Epistles of Paul in which, at first, he invariably discusses the nature of the gospel and subsequently quotes various passages.

On the Power of the Law

That the gospel is not law but the promise of grace, I have already said. Now it remains to teach, however it may be, what is the power of the law and what that of the gospel. For in some degree it may be learned from this, what is the distinction between law and gospel. Indeed, in the first place, the Scripture differs with human reason on the power of the law. Scripture calls the law the power of wrath and of sin, the sceptre of an executioner, lightning, thunder. Human reason calls it a correction for crimes, a principle of living. For this language Cicero uses when he speaks of laws. Nothing is more universally celebrated than the praises of laws. So much so that to the flesh Paul might seem crazy to call the law "the strength of sin." I Cor. 15:56. Thus the Jews (John 9:28) who professed to be disciples of Moses were unwilling to recognize Christ. Wherefore, in order to discuss the power of the law with exactness, I shall compare the two classes of mankind.

To the first class belong those who carnally understand the law, but do not perceive that it demands the impossible. These are blind and see neither sin, nor law, nor righteousness. Moreover, they are the hypocritical Sophists of all ages. Paul calls the righteousness of this class "the righteousness by the works of the law." He especially means those who hear the law and control their hands, their feet, and their mouth, but not their heart. For they would prefer to be without the law, no matter how holy they may seem to themselves. This class takes joy in pleasures, wealth, and honor. Of what sort these are, none has said better than the Spirit of God. In the first place, they are without faith, that is, their heart understands nothing about God. As Scripture says: "It does not seek God," meaning thereby that their heart does not magnify but despises God. Then, too, according to Psalm 13, "they turn aside," that is, since they neither fear nor believe God, they turn off to their own counsels. They despise God and make their way to wealth or honors through these counsels. In addition, they even try to justify themselves by their own works. The Scripture has often reproved this class of men, calling them "workers of iniquity." In Psalm 5:10, David thus describes hypocrites: "In whose mouth there is no right or candor, whose inward parts are vanity, whose throat is an open abyss." To this class of men, there is no difficulty in the law. For they live according to a false and carnal knowledge of the law. Therefore, the law cannot accomplish in them what it ought, but they devise unto themselves idols, images of man[81] and the shadows of carnal virtues. Moreover, they are impelled to simulate good works by a carnal affection, either from the fear of punishment, or the pursuit of gain; and are foolishly secure, since they do not see the sickness of their own mind.

The pride, haughtiness, pertinacity and φιλαυτία of this class of men are incredible. They are so far

---
[81] A play upon Ezekiel 16:17 "Et tulisti vasa decoris tui de auro meo atque argenteo meo, quæ dedi tibi et fecisti imagines masculinas et fornicata es in eis."

from satisfying the law that there are none who are farther. The Pharisee in Luke 18:11 who says—"I am not like other men."—belongs to this class. And Isa. 28:15 describes the drunkards of Ephraim in the following language: "We have made league with death, and with hell have we made a pact." And in Jeremy we read "They know not to blush." Matt. 7:23: "Ye workers of iniquity." Paul witnesses that he was such before his conversion, in Roms. 7:8: "I have once lived without the law," that is, there was a time when I seemed to exceed illustriously the law, a time when I surpassed all my equals in the hypocrisy of works. For the law did not then condemn, nor accuse, nor arraign me. And such indeed are all men, who attempt to exhibit the law through natural powers according to the capacity of reason, when they do not understand either the law or their own powers. These are they who behold only the back of Moses, who see only his veiled face, as Paul says in II Cor. 3:17, when he asserts that the Jews cannot understand evangelical righteousness because they behold Moses with veiled hearts. He means that the Jews cannot see what the law demands, as we can who are nothing but sin and an accursed thing.

Thus far, indeed, concerning the nature of those who attempt to do the law through natural powers according to the faculty of human reason. Anybody could estimate with his own heart, just who these are. Paul's words do not properly pertain to them: "The law is the strength of wrath, the strength of sin, the ministration of death," etc. Although the law is condemnation even to them because they make of it an idol unto themselves. And in the next place, they do everything with a sort of ineffable pride and vexation of the heart.

To the second class of mankind, belong all those

to whom pertain these words of Paul: "The law is the strength of wrath," etc. God reveals the law to these, and shows them the condition of their hearts. Indeed, God terrifies and confounds them by the sense of their sin. These are precisely the ones in whom God works through the law. The law does nothing in hypocrites; but they of themselves reproduce a sort of shadow of the law, by means of a kind of hypocritical righteousness. In these the law does its true and proper work. It shows them sin. This is truly done because it is done by God. And Scripture calls this work: "Judgement, the wrath of God, the fury of God, the aspect and face of wrath," etc. Psalm 96:2 ff. says "Judgment is the correction of his throne, fire will go before him and burn up his enemies round about. His lightnings shown upon the earth, the earth saw and was moved. The mountains melted like wax from before the face of the Lord, the whole earth from before the face of the Lord." Psalm 75:9: "From heaven thou hast made judgment to be heard, the earth trembled and shook." And Zech. 11:13: "Let all flesh keep silence before the Lord." Isa. 11:13: "He will shake the earth by the strength of his mouth, and with the wrath of his lips will he kill the impious." Habk. 3:6: "He looked upon and dissolved the nations, and the mountains were forever removed." But what profit is there in heaping up many passages, since there is plainly another part of Scripture, the law, and its function is to kill and to condemn, to show the root of our sin and to confound us? It not only mortifies avarice or lust, but it mortifies the very head of all evil, self-love, and the judgment of reason, and whatever nature possesses that may seem to be good in itself. From this it will appear, how stinking are the moral virtues, how bloody are the rags of the righteousness[82] of the saints! To be sure, even Moses should exclaim in Ex. 34:7: "Before thy face not even the innocent is innocent." And Nah. 1:3: "Cleansing he will not make innocent." And David in Ps. 142:2: "Enter not into judgment with thy servant"; and Ps. 6:2: "Lord, try me not in thy fury." In Isaiah 38:13, Hezekiah says: "As a lion he breaketh all my bones." And this is what John has said in a few words, as is his custom in all things, 1:17: "The law was given by Moses, but grace and truth came through Jesus Christ." Truth is set over against hypocrisy, and grace over against the fury of God. Wherefore, since grace, that is, the mercy and the favor of God, has come through Jesus Christ, it is necessary for the law to be the producer of hypocrisy since it coerces the unwilling and those raging against God, and of wrath since it condemns us as guilty.

In his most diligent discourse about the power of the law, Paul in Roms. 7:7 says: "I had not known sin, save by the law: I had not known lust, except the law had said: Thou shalt covet not." Likewise in chapter 3:20: "The knowledge of sin cometh by the law." Just as though he says, hypocrites are falsely persuaded that righteousness is acquired by the law, when all the law does is to show sin to the heart. Then too, "sin taking occasion through the law, worked in me all manner of concupiscence," that is, when I began to feel the burden of the law—indeed nothing came from the law —it happened that, concupiscence being the more irritated, began to rage against the judgment and will of God. For "without the law sin was dead"; that is, had not the law shown me sin in my heart, had not the

---

[82]"Palutus menstruo panus": cf. this statement with the passage in Jeromes' Vulgate Isaiah 64:5: "Et facti sumus ut immundus omnes nos et quasi pannus menstruatæ universæ justitiæ nostræ."

sense of sin terrified me, sin would have died, it would not have raged. "For I was alive without the law once." There was a time when I seemed to myself to be just, when I did not see the law, and therefore sin. In that state, sin was at rest, nor did it openly rage against God. "But when the law came, sin revived." Moreover, "I died," that is, when God had shown me sin by the law, sin was resusitated. I became confused, alarmed, horrified; in a word, I died, and then indeed, it was clear what the power of the law really was. To be sure, the law was given that we might live; but when we cannot do the law, it is an organ of death. In a word, what is the reason why the law should slay? The law is spiritual, that is, it demands spiritual things such as: truth, a faith that glorifies God, love of God. But I am carnal, incredulous, ignorant of God, foolish, a lover of self, etc.

The Apostle Paul has never so copiously treated of the power and nature of the law, as in that place which I have cited. There seems to be nothing lacking in it. There is no obscurity, no impediment, all is plain and open; so that there can be no doubt as to his meaning. But if the studious reader of Scripture desires, he may add to this other partisan passages which are scattered throughout his other epistles.

In I Cor. 15:56 he says: "The sting of death is sin, the power of sin is the law." For sin would not confound and terrify, had it not been shown us by the law. Therefore sin would not be powerful had it not been excited and manifested through the law. So also death would not be powerful, did it not terrify us by the powers and work of sin. In II Cor. 3:6, the law is discerned by the spirit in the following manner: "Our sufficiency is from God, who has made us fit ministers of the New Testament, not of the letter but of the spirit.

For the letter killeth, but the spirit maketh alive." It will be more clearly known why he calls it letter and Spirit, from the following v. 7: "But if the ministration of death engraved with letters upon stone was in glory, so that the sons of Israel could not behold the face of Moses on account of the glory of his face, which is done away, how much more will the ministration of the Spirit be in glory?" Now the ministration of death is the law, which when it has revealed and manifested sin, confounds, and terrifies, and slays the conscience. The ministration of the Spirit is the gospel, as I shall discuss later. It consoles, makes erect, animates, and vivifies minds which were aforetime terrified.

In the third chapter of Galatians, when the Apostle would teach in a long disputation that righteousness is not obtained by means of the law alone, he adds what cannot be but ineptly opposed, v. 19: "why then the law?" that is, if the law were not profitable unto the attainment of righteousness what, I ask, was its use? And he answers: "On account of transgression, the law was handed down;" meaning thereby, that transgression might be increased. For the knowledge of sin will increase sin, which when it the more implacably rages, is first coerced and then by nature unworthily suffers to be confounded, and is enraged at divine judgment.

Many types of Scripture even teach that this is the power of the law. Exodus 19. When God had given the law, many people were wonderfully terrified by the thunder, smoke, lightning, clouds, the clanging of the trumpet, and such horrible spectres. All of which merely designates the terrors of a shattered conscience. For is not the voice of the people the voice of a corrupted conscience, when they say in Exodus 20:19: "Let not the Lord speak unto us, lest we surely die?" And Moses indeed, not only as a minister of the law, but as an evangelist, wonderfully alleviated the people's consternation by his words: "Fear not, God has come to prove you, and that his fear might be in you that ye might not die." O the plainly evangelical word of Moses! And unless the conscience hears it, how will it endure that horrible face of the judge? But I shall speak of evangelical consolation later on.

Now this light from Moses' face shined so brightly that the peoples' eyes were dulled. And that is why from then on, he never showed himself to the people except with covered face. For human eyes and human minds endure not the splendor of divine light.

Finally: the brightness, the flames on the mountain and the splendor in Moses' face plainly indicate, to use Paul's word, the glory of God by which he confounds the human heart. The judgment of God is that knowledge of sin. Here Sophistic attritions and feigned contritions fail, here also fail the seared consciences of hypocrites. Here God scrutinizes the very depths of the heart. For so far is human reason from seeing its own sins, that it is quite necessary even for the saints and those full of the Spirit, to pray for their ignorance. Now David exclaims in Psalm 18:13: "who understands his faults?" And in Psalm 24:7: "Remember not my ignorance," and many other passages of this kind. Jeremy 17:9 says that "the human heart is depraved and inscrutable." And in verse 10 he says: "I the Lord probe the heart, I try the reins." In chapter 31:8, these are his words: "Thou hast reproved me, O Lord, and I was instructed, even as an ungovernable bullock: convert thou me and I shall be converted; for thou art the Lord my God. For after thou didst convert me, I did penance, and after thou didst show me, I smote my thigh: I am confused and I blush when I remember the ignominy of my youth." And who is there that thinks he fulfills the law, when it is enjoined that we should deny even ourselves? Matt. 16:24.

Finally, the proper function of the law is the revelation of sin,[83] or to speak more clearly; the consciousness of sin; and as Paul says in Col. 2:14: "The handwriting in dogmas, which was written down against us." Thus Paul much more elegantly and clearly defined the conscience, than do the sententious Sophists, who conceive of I know not how many practical syllogisms,[84] in their description of the word conscience. For what else is the conscience of sin but judgment of the law showing sin in our heart? For when Paul says in Col. 2:14: χειρόγραφον τοῖς δόγμασιν ὃ ἦν ὑπεναντίον ἡμῖν he means that consicience is a hand writing and that too in decrees, that is what is charged against us by decrees, by the law.

You have it that the function of the law is the revelation of sin. Moreover, when I say sin, I include every kind of sin, both external and internal: hypocrisy, incredulity, self-love, contempt and ignorance of God, which in themselves are truly the roots of all human works. Indeed, in justifying sinners, God's first work is to reveal our sin: to confound our conscience, to shatter it, to terrify, in a word to condemn, as is indicated by the example just quoted from Jeremy. And Paul says

---

[83]In this, Melanchthon goes back to the notion of Luther. The latter, in a sermon preached in 1516, but in which he did not make such clear distinction between law and gospel, as does Melanchthon in the text, had said: Sicut opus dei est duplex, scilicet proprium et alienum, ita et evangelii officium est duplex. Proprium officium evangelii est enunciare proprium opus dei, id est gratiam, qua pacem et justitiam et veritatem . . . alienun autem evangelii opus est parare domino plebem perfectam, hoc est peccata manifestare et reos arguere eos, qui justi errant sibi, etc. W. A. I, 113. He uses evangelium in its widest sense: evangelium est nihil aliud nisi annunciatio operum dei, so that the law falls under it. cf. Köstlin, Luthers Theologie, II, 498.

[84]Practices syllogismos: Spalatin wrongly translates this as follows: "uebliche Syllogismen." What the author means is: Syllogisms consummated by means of disputations. Similarities are found in the

in Gal. 2:19: "I am dead to the law through the law." David, in II Sam. 12:13 when confused by the prophet's rebuke, exclaims: "I have sinned against the Lord." And in I Kings 21:27 it is recorded that, "Ahab tore off his garment," etc. And as the Scripture says, "he walked with his head hung down."

In II Chronicles 33:12, it is written of Manasses that he was afflicted: for I must use the words of Scripture. And in Acts 2:37 it says: "When they heard these things they were pricked in their hearts." It is sufficient to have indicated at this point, that this work of the law by which the Spirit of God is wont to terrify and confound consciences, is the beginning of repentance. For nature of itself cannot know the hideousness of sin, so far is it from being able to hate it. "For the natural man does not know the things that are of God." I Cor. 2:14. And Rom. 8:5: "The flesh seeketh the things that are of the flesh." The Sophists treat these matters about the beginning of repentance in the fourth book of Sentences, while I so to speak treat them at the very beginning of my work.[85] For

---

Summa theol. II, qu. 99 of Albertus Magnus, who defined conscientia as "habitus motivus et cognitivus sicut intellectus practicus." And then the relation between conscientia and lex naturalis is compared together with a conclusion. Further examples are to be found in Antonius Florentinus in his Summa theol. I tit. 3 c 10. cf. Gass: Die Lehre vom Gewissen, Berlin 1869. Also Seeberg: Dogmengesch. II, 98. Melanchthon in his Loci of 1553 accepts Florentinus' definition and explains it as follows: conscientia est syllogismus practicus in intellectu, in quo major propositio est lex Dei, seu quodcunque Dei nobis aliquid præcipiens. Minor vero et conclusio sunt applicatio approbans recte factum vel condemnans delictum etc. C. R. 21, 1083. For further light on the scholastic syllogisms see: Appel: "Die Lehre der Scholastiker von der Synteresis" 1891, S 30 ff.

[85]With Peter Lombard the doctrine of the sacraments is discussed in the fourth and last book of his Sentences. The position which the Scholastics gave to the seven Sacraments as means of grace, is not so false. On the other hand, the criticism of Melanchthon is clear, since the chief problem of theology is considered to be something entirely different and has nothing but practical relations for him.

the justification of man, and therefore, true baptism[86] is begun by mortification, judgment, and confusion; and these are brought about by the Spirit of God through the law, and just as the Christian life must take origin here from the knowledge of sin, so also Christian doctrine must begin with the function of the law.

It is not worth my while to dispute about whether this fear is servile, or whether as they say, it is filial. I shall leave that sort of question to individuals of leisure. However, very many dispute about this matter in such a way, that it is very apparent that they themselves understand neither servile nor filial fear. It is certain that none can be affected with a hatred for sin, except through the Holy Spirit. It is likewise certain that those who are thus terrified, flee from the face and sight of God unless the Spirit of God brings them back, recalls them, and strengthens them in such a manner that they exclaim with Paul: "Lord what wilt thou have me to do?" Acts. 9:6. The passage in Exodus 20:19 when the people cry unto Moses: "Let not the Lord speak unto us, lest we surely die," establishes the fact that terrified individuals flee the sight of God. In Psalm 138:7 David says "Whither shall I go from thy spirit and whither shall I flee from thy face?" There are manifold testimonies of this nature in the Scripture; but it seems sufficient for me to have mentioned but a few, from which the distinction between law and gospel can be more surely comprehended. However, you see what a difference there is between feigned and true repentance.

---

[86] The expression "verum baptismum" is fundamental. It seems as if Melanchthon wishes to oppose the prevailing notion of the sacrament as an opus operatum. Luther in his "Babylonian Captivity" asserted the same viewpoint: "Significat itaque baptismus duo, mortem et resurrectionem, hoc est, plenariam consummatamque justificationem." E. A. op. V. Arg. V, 85.

On the Power of the Gospel

Those whom conscience has terrorized to such a degree, would be driven doubtless to despair as usually happens in the case of condemned individuals, unless they were consoled and encouraged by the promise of the grace and the mercy of God, which is rightly called the gospel. If an afflicted conscience believes the promise of grace in Christ, it is revived and vivified by faith, as is wonderfully declared by various examples.

In Genesis 3, the sin, repentance and justification of Adam are described. After Adam and Eve and transgressed—and sought a covering and περιζώματα for their nakedness—for thus are we hypocrites accustomed to relieve our consciences by our own satisfactions—they were called to account by God. And indeed, that voice was unbearable. But here girdles profited nothing, here no pretext excused their sin. The conscience lies dead, convicted and guilty, with sin placed before its very eyes by the voice of God. They flee, and Adam offers a reason for his flight, when in Gen. 3:10 he says: "O Lord, I heard thy voice in the garden and was afraid, for I was naked." Behold! a confession and an ἐξομολόγησιν of the conscience. Meanwhile, Adam wretchedly struggles with himself until he hears the promise of mercy, the words spoken concerning his wife: "Her seed shall bruise the serpent's head." Something made for the confirmation of their consciences, for God clothed them, signifying without doubt the incarnation of Christ. For that flesh in a word covers our nudity and takes away the confusion from troubled consciences, into which especially fall the taunts of reproachers. Ps. 68. Sometime ago, I mentioned how confused David was by the word of Nathan. And he would have utterly perished had he not heard at once the gospel: "The Lord hath taken away thy sin, thou shalt not die." II Chron. 12:13. Some are of the opinion, that we are to seek nothing but allegories in the histories of the Old Testament. But here you can see how much instruction there is in this one example of David, even if you consider the letter alone. Nay more, this alone is to be seen, in that by which the Spirit of God has largely exhibited the works both of wrath and also of mercy. What word could be more evangelically conceived than this: "The Lord hath taken away thy sin?" Is this not the sum of the gospel or of the preaching of the New Testament: sin has been taken away? You may add to these, if you will, a heap of gospel traditions. For instance, Luke 7:37 ff. A woman sinner washes the Lord's feet with her tears, and he consoles her with these words: "Thy sins are remitted unto thee." And what story is more commonly known than that of the prodigal son, in Luke 15, who confesses his sin, and upon his confession, the father lovingly receives, embraces, and kisses him. Luke 5: Peter dumbfounded by a miracle and therefore shocked at heart, exclaims: "Depart from me, O Lord, for I am a sinful man." Christ consoles and restores him with these words: "Fear not," etc.

From these examples, I believe it can be understood just what is the difference between the law and the gospel, and what is the power of the law and what that of the gospel. The law terrorizes, the gospel consoles. The law is the voice of wrath and of death, the gospel that of peace and life, or as the prophet says, the voice of the bridegroom and bride. And he who is thus encouraged by the voice of the gospel and believes God is already justified, as I shall subsequently show. It is not a thing unknown to Christians, how much joy, how much gladness this consolation affords. Those joyful words of the prophets by which they describe Christ and the church, pertain to this. Isa. 32:18: "And my people will dwell in the beauty of peace and the tabernacles of trust and in rich repose." Likewise: "Joy and gladness will be found in it, and the voice of praise." In Jer. 33:6: "I will reveal to them the declaration of peace and truth. And it will be to me for a name and joy and praise and exultation to all the nations of the earth." Sophon. 3:9: "I shall give the people an elect lip that all may call on the name of the Lord." Psal. 20:7: "Thou wilt rejoice him with gladness, etc." And Psal. 96:11: "Light has arisen unto the just, and gladness in the heart of the righteous."

But what is to be gained from the multiplication of incidents, seeing that both from the promulgation of the gospel and the advent of Christ alike, the power of the law and of the gospel is made sufficiently clear. And indeed, Exodus 19, which I reviewed a little while ago, describes with what a terrible spectacle the law was promulgated. For just as the Lord then terrorized Israel, so likewise are the consciences of everyone terrified by the voice of the law and together with Israel exclaim: "Let not the Lord speak unto us, lest we surely die." Ex. 20:18. The law demands the impossible, and a guilty conscience is convicted of its sin. Hence, fear and confusion so disquiet the conscience, that no remedy would even appear unless he who has humiliated it, brings consolation. There are some who seek consolation in their own powers, efforts, works and satisfactions. But they accomplish no more than Adam did with his girdles.

There are those who set themselves against sin by the strength of their will. But experience teaches that they continue wretchedly to fail. "For a horse is deceptive for safety, and will not be safe in the abundance of his strength," Psalm 32:17. And also: "Help me, Lord, for vain is the safety of man." Ps. 107:13. On the other hand, the advent of Christ is described by Zech. 9:9: "Exult thou daughter of Zion, be joyful thou daughter of Jerusalem. Behold thy king cometh unto thee, the just one and the Savior, himself poor." In the first place, when he orders exultation, he tells of another work of this king than that he is law, and therefore elicits joy from the conscience which rejoices when it has heard the word of grace. Then, secondly, there is no tumult but all is calm; so that you understand that he is author of peace and not of wrath. That is why Zechariah calls him poor, because in setting Christ forth as an evangelist, so to speak, he has made him gentle. Likewise Isaiah 43:3: "A broken reed he will not crush, a smoking flax he will not extinguish."

The Apostle in II Cor. 3:13 ff. thus compares the face of Moses with that of Christ. The face of Moses terrorized by its splendor as I have stated above. For who can bear the majesty of divine judgment when even the prophet deprecates it? "Enter not unto judgment with thy servant," Psalm 142:2. When the disciples see the glory of Christ on Mt. Tabor, with what a strange and wonderful joy they are filled! So that Peter, ignorant of himself, exclaims: "Lord it is good for us to be here, let us build three tabernacles," Matt. 17:4. For here is the aspect of grace and of the mercy of God. And just as the sight of the brazen serpent saved, so are they saved who have their eyes of faith fixed on Christ, John 3:15 f. Therefore, the Apostles have most aptly called εὐαγγέλιον "Joyful news". For even the Greeks call εὐαγγέλιον "Joyful news," the public proclamation of things well done. We have an instance of this in Isocrates: δὶς ἤδη τεθείκαμεν εὐαγγέλια.

On Grace

Just as the law is the knowledge of sin, so likewise is the gospel the promise of grace and righteousness. Moreover, because the words grace and righteousness, and certainly the gospel are to be considered, I must in this place subjoin the principles of grace and righteousness. For in this manner, the nature of the gospel can be more fully understood.

Indeed, I ask, who can rightly expostulate on this point with the Scholastics who have so foully abused that sacrosanct word grace when they us it, to express the quality that is in the minds of the saints? And above all especially the Thomists, who posited quality or grace in the very nature of the mind: that faith, hope and love are in the powers of the mind.[87] And even here too, how anile and how foolish are their disputes about the powers of the mind! But let those impious men become exceedingly filthy; let those despisers of the gospel suffer anguish for their buffoonery and jest. You, my reader, pray that the Spirit of God will reveal his gospel to our hearts. For the word of the Spirit is such that it cannot be taught except by the Spirit, as Isaiah 54:13 says: "all are θεοδιδάκτοι»

1. In the books of the New Testament, the word "gratia" is generally used to express the Hebrew word חן Now this word was changed to χάρις by the Septuagint translators, as in Exodus 33:12 "Thou hast found favor in my sight," etc. And it often ap-

---

[87]Thomas treats "gratia" in II, 1 Quest. 110. It is distinguished from the general activity of God in man, without which no one can do even the smallest thing. It is something higher and extraordinary which makes for higher ends. It is infused in man and because of it he becomes a "homo gratus." Melanchthon, under the influence of Luther's Commentary on Galatians, inveighs against this notion, which would make the forgiveness of sins dependent on a state or condition of man. cf. C. R. I, 311.

pears elsewhere. For it plainly signifies what we express in Latin by the word "favor." And I would that the translators had preferred the word "favor" to "gratia." For then the Sophists would not have had occasion for their absurd talk in this place. Moreover, just as grammarians say that Julius favors Curio when they mean that in Julius there is favor by which he embraces Curio, so also in Scripture grace signifies favor, and is the grace or favor in God by which he embraces the Saints. Away with Aristotelian figments about qualities! For grace is nothing (if it is to be most exactly defined) but the benevolence of God toward us, or the will of God that has commiserated us. Therefore, the word "grace" does not signify some quality in us, but rather the will of God itself, or the benevolence of God toward us.

2. In Romans 5:15, Paul distinguishes the gift from grace: "If by the sin of one many have died, much more the grace of God and the gift in that grace which is of one man, Jesus Christ, has abounded unto many." He calls grace the favor of God, the favor by which God comprehends in Christ and for Christ's sake, all the saints. Then because he favors us, God cannot but pour out his gifts upon those whom he has commiserated. It is just as if men assisted those whom they favor and shared their possessions with them. Indeed, the gift of God is the Holy Spirit whom God has poured out on all his saints. John 20:22: "He breathed on them and said: "Receive ye the Holy Spirit," and Roms. 8:15: "Ye have received the Spirit of the adoption of sons, by which we cry: Abba, father." Moreover, according to Gal. 5:22, the works of the Holy Spirit in the hearts of the saints are faith, peace, joy, love, etc. It is a thing to be wondered at, how superciliously the

Sophists treat Peter Lombard[88] (who by far perceives more correctly than they) because in one place, he called the Holy Spirit "grace" rather than "Parisian," that is, that well-known fictitious "quality."

3. But I use simply the nomenclature "gratia" following the terminology of Scripture, which signifies that "gratia" is the favor, mercy and gratuitous benevolence of God toward us. It is the gift of the Holy Spirit himself, whom God pours into the hearts of those whom he has compassionated. The fruits of the Holy Spirit are faith, hope, love and the rest of the virtues. And thus indeed about the word "grace." In a word, grace is nothing but the forgiveness or remission of sins; the gift is the Holy Spirit who regenerates and sanctifies the heart, Psalm 103:30: "Send forth thy Spirit and they shall be begotten. And thou wilt renew the face of the earth." The gospel promises grace as well as a gift. There are various passages of Scripture at hand, but it is sufficient to cite just this one, Jer. 31:33: "After those days saith the Lord I will put my law in their inwards, and will write it upon their hearts." These words certainly have reference to a gift, while those which follow refer to grace: "All shall know me from the least to the greatest, saith the Lord, because I shall propitiate their iniquity and their sin will I no more remember."

On Justification and Faith

1. We are justified, when mortified by the law, we are raised up by the word of grace that is promised in

---

[88]Lombard identified grace with the Holy Spirit, cf. Sent. I dist. 17, 2: "His autem addendum est, quod ipse idem Spiritus sanctus est amor sive charitas, qua nos diligimus deum et proximum; quæ charitas cum ita est in nobis, ut nos faciat diligere deum et proximum, tunc Spiritus sanctus dicitur mitti vel dari nobis." Because of this identification of infused love with the Holy Spirit, the Scholastics severely criticized Lombard.

Christ, or in the gospel that forgives sins; and when we cling to Christ nothing doubting but that the righteousness of Christ is our righteousness, that his satisfaction is our expiation, that his resurrection is ours. In a word, nothing doubting that our sins are forgiven and that God loves and cherishes us. Our works however good they may be do not constitute our righteousness. For righteousness is faith alone in the mercy and grace of God in Jesus Christ. That is what Paul means when he says: "The just live by faith." Roms. 3:22 reads: "Righteousness of God is by the faith of Jesus Christ." That is to say, not only is the hypocrisy of works which men impute for righteousness now made manifest, but also righteousness of the kind that God imputes unto us for righteousness is now revealed, to be sure, the righteousness that is by faith of Jesus Christ. For in Roms. 3:5, Paul says: "To him that believeth faith is imputed unto righteousness." And Gen. 15:6: "Abraham believed God and it was imputed unto him for righteousness." But indeed I wish these two passages to be commendatory to you for this reason, that you may understand that faith is fitly called righteousness. For the Sophists are offended by such language when I say that faith is righteousness. But the more properly we contemplate both the nature and power of faith, the more deeply must its ὑπογραφὴ be sought out.

2. It is a well-known fact that the herd of Sophists call faith the assent to those things set forth in Scripture. Hence then, that is faith even what the impious possess.[89] Even the unjust believe, and there is a neu-

---

[89]For Thomas' definition of faith, Sum. II, 2. Quæst. IV, which essentially follows Hebrews 11:1. In respect to its nature, faith is an "Actus" proceeding from two principles (Actus, qui ex duobus activis principiis procedit.) The human will gives faith its direction. The end is the second principle. All acts of the human will receive their

tral quality in the mind common to the impious and the pious. And when they cannot escape from the fact that Scripture says "the just live by faith," and likewise that "righteousness is by faith," then they devise one kind of faith that is formed, that is, that which is joined with love, and another kind of faith that is formless, that is, that which is even in the impious who have no love. And indeed intelligent men pretend that the apostle falsely attributed unto faith that which was of love, in order to allure unto faith by this bait, as many persons as possible. And now they have hatched up "faith infused" and "faith acquired," "faith general" and "faith specific," and I know not what other monstrous notions. But I shall dismiss this trash, for later on I shall prove that the Sophists are wrong by the very nature of the case in such a manner that they will grant me faith is not what they have said it is.

3. The word spoken by the prophet in Psalm 52:1 is well known! "The fool hath said in his heart, there is no God." Very well-known is Paul's word in I Cor. 2:14: "The natural man perceiveth not the things of the Spirit." And Ezek. 29:9 reads: "The river is mine and I have made it." Such passages as these witness that the flesh knows nothing and perceives nothing but carnal things. The existence of God, his wrath, and his mercy are spiritual concepts. Hence, they cannot be known by the flesh. Moreover, whatever nature knows of God without the Spirit of God renewing and enlightening our hearts, whatever it may be, I say it is but a frigid opinion and not faith. Therefore it is nothing but simulation and hypocrisy, ignorance of

---

form and characteristic through the object to which they are directed: "Actus voluntarii speciem recipiunt a fine, qui est voluntatis objectum." Love. whose object alone God can be, is that which gives faith its perfection. Thus faith can now be reckned as a theological virtue or comfort in the fullest sense of the word.

God and contempt. Although this hypocrisy is not seen by carnal eyes, nevertheless, the Spirit judges all things. Take Saul for an example. From all outward indication it seems that Saul was faithful, but the events in the case show hypocrisy, because he did not believe (from the heart, I say,) that those things which he was doing were divinely administered; that they were gifts and works of the mercy of God, whereas he judged them to depend on his own counsels. For (and I speak of heart affections), Saul neither feared the wrath of God nor trusted God's benignity. He shows himself contemptful of God when he sacrifices without waiting for Samuel, lest he be anticipated by the Philistines. Note also I Sam. 13:9 and again I Sam. 15, when Saul erected a trophy to himself after the fashion of the gentiles. Saul had an idea of the existence of God, and that God is a vindicator of sin and is merciful; or otherwise why would he have sacrificed? But there was no faith. Or to use the word of Scripture, "he did not hearken," his heart was ignorant both of the severity and goodness of God. O horrible and miserable sight! If one happens to see such impiety of heart with spiritual eyes. Examine, I ask you, your life and its fruits, estimate as far as you are able, the filthiness of your heart. Do you turn aside as Scripture says, and turn your mind to your own cupidities? And are you not disturbed about provisions, hunger, life, children, and wife, all because you trust God too little? Because you fail to weigh the fulness of the divine mercy?

Do you not fall into other sins because you despair of the grace and mercy of God toward you? For you would undoubtedly do and suffer all things with a most joyful heart, could you but conceive a sure hope of your salvation. Do you not do a thing, do you not aspire to wealth, or in a word, for anything whatever it may be, all because you do not fear the judgment of God? But you would certainly fear it if you believed with your heart, if you could but discern with your mind the power of the wrath of God. And it is this folly, this ignorance, this blindness of the heart that I mean, when I deny that faith is in human nature. To be sure, faith is something greater and more certain than what the flesh can comprehend.

Moreover, this sophistic faith which they first call "formless" and then "acquired,"[90] and by which the impious give assent to the evangelical histories much as we are accustomed to do in the case of the histories of Livy or Salust, is no faith at all but is merely opinion. It is an uncertain, inconstant, fluctuating cogitation of the human mind concerning the word of God. You have it what ought to be thought about scholastic faith; and you also have it that the Scholastics teach nothing but mendacity, vanity and hypocrisy. But if I seem to have spoken too severely concerning their teaching, may they not be angry with me but with Paul who calls a "feigned faith" hypocrisy, I Tim. 1:5: "The end of the law is love with a pure heart, a good conscience, and faith unfeigned."

Besides, in another place he indicates a faith that is feigned. And he has this to say of hypocrites in Titus 1:15: "To the pure all things are pure, but to the defiled and unfaithful nothing is pure, but their minds and consciences are filthy." They profess to

---

[90]Duns Scotus distinguishes "fides acquisita" from "fides infusa." He says in Sent. III. Quæst. 23: Certum est, quod in nobis est fides revelatorum credibilium acquisita," and explains it: Credo fide acquisita evangelio, quia ecclesia tenet scriptores veraces. Quod ego audiens acquiro mihi habitum credendi dictis, illorum. Credo etiam Roman esse, quam non vidi, ex revelatu fide dignorum. Sic et revelatis in scriptura per fidem acquisitam ex auditu firmiter adhæro credendo ecclesiæ approbanti veritatem autorum illorum."

know God but in reality deny him, since they are abominable, disobedient and false to every good work. If in this passage, the faith of the impious were truly faith—for he is certainly speaking about those who are outwardly pious—he should not have called them unfaithful but as the Paris theologians say, those who are "without love." In writing to Timothy, Paul attributes a fictitious faith to hypocrites. And here he calls them "unfaithful." Why then do I not distinguish between a "faith formed" and a "faith formless?" Plainly because that opinion which the hypocrites hold conceived without the Holy Spirit concerning things to be believed and the divine history, is not faith.

Nature does not assent to the word of God and consequently will not be moved. By way of teaching a sort of historical faith, I used to call it "unformed faith acquired"; but from now on I call it not faith, but a mere opinion. What I have said pertains to this, that you may know that Scripture most simply uses the word faith; and that Parisian quality cannot be called faith, which they say even the impious and the despisers of God possess. The condemned do not believe in order to give glory to God, but because they are compelled by experience, which cannot be called true faith. The same thing can be said of those who give up to despair, as was said of Cain or Saul. For what difference is there between them and the condemned? What sort of thing is faith then? Faith is the constant assent to every word of God; a thing that cannot be done except the Holy Spirit of God renews and illuminates our hearts. Moreover, the word of God is both law and gospel. In addition, threats are subjoined to the law. But fear without faith does not justify. Now moreover, even those who despair, those who are condemned can be justified. For those who fear to this degree do not glorify God nor believe the whole word of God, because they do not believe the promises. Therefore faith alone justifies.

4. And so, faith is nothing other than reliance upon the divine mercy promised in Christ, and therefore any sign whatsoever. This reliance on the benevolence or mercy of God first pacifies the heart, and then incites us to give thanks to God for his mercy, so that we of our own accord and joyfully do the law. Moreover, as far as we do not believe, there is no sense of the mercy of God in our heart. And when there is no sense of the mercy of God, there is either contempt of God or hate. Wherefore, how greatsoever works of the law are done without faith, sin is committed. That is what Paul means (Roms. 14:23 when he says: "Whatsoever is not of faith is sin." This sentence most clearly expresses the power and nature of faith. For whatever is done, is done by nature or out of hatred for God; of such a kind are the works of those who do good works against their will, from the fear of the law and punishments. For when we feign good works without faith, does not our heart meditate thus? "Indeed, I have done what I could, but I know not whether God approves or disapproves of my works. He is a severe judge and I know not whether he has commiserated me." With such a cogitation, how can it be that we are not angry with the judgment of God? And in this hypocrisy, with great anxiety of heart the majority of men live; and how depravely they do judge appears, if you please, from this. For they should not contemplate their own works but the promise of the mercy of God. For what is more wicked than to judge the will of God according to our works which he has declared unto us with his words? Now a large part of mankind lives with contempt of God; it will work

in such and such a manner, it will have its way thus and thus even though it is displeasing to God.

For this reason, it is most beautifully said in the book of Ecclesiasticus 32:17: "In all thy work believe with faith in thy mind. For this is the keeping of the commandments." Whatsoever kind the works may be: eating, drinking, working with the hand, teaching, I add that even they are plainly sins. You should not look at works: look at the promise of the mercy of God with trust in him doubting nothing, but that you have in heaven not a judge, but a father who cares for you just as human parents care for their children. But if there were no signification of the divine will toward us other than the fact that he has willed to be called father in that prayer which we daily pray, this alone should be sufficient argument that nothing is demanded of us before our faith. Now since God so often demands faith, since he so often approves of it alone, since he has commended it unto us by rich promises and in addition by the death of his son, why do we not commit ourselves to such a great mercy as this, and believe it? Scholastic theology has taught human works and satisfactions, for faith, for an anchor of consciences. May God destroy that scandal of his church!

5. You have it in what sense Scripture uses the word faith especially as regards its meaning namely, to trust the gratuitous mercy of God without any respect to our works whether good or bad, because we all receive from the plenitude of Christ. They who thus trust, truly assent to the whole word of God, both the threats and promises of divine history. Scholastic faith is nothing but a dead opinion. For how do they believe the whole word of God, who do not believe the promised remission of sins? For it is of no value what the

Sophists say, that the impious believe that the remission of sins pertains not to themselves, but to others. For I ask, is not the forgiveness of sins promised to the impious also? But I do not intend to be disputatious, but am content to have indicated in a few words what is the meaning of the word faith. Luther's little book on *Christian Liberty* is at hand. He who wishes can seek from it further commendations of faith. However, I am of the opinion that the power of faith will be more clearly learned from scriptural examples.

In Genesis 15:1, God promises Abraham his mercy in these magnificent words: "Fear not, Abraham, I am thy protector and thy exceeding great reward." A little later he promises him posterity. Then follows the word: "Abraham believed God and it was imputed unto him for righteousness." What did Abraham believe? Nothing but that God exists? Nay rather he believed the promise of God and then declared that faith by an illustrious example, as when he would have sacrificed his son nothing doubting but that God would have given him posterity, even though his son were slain. Now since faith is to give assent to the word of God, what Abraham really believed is made clear enough from the promise when God adds that he is Abraham's protector. Therefore, they believe who consider God as a protector, a father, and not only as a judge.

In Exodus 14, the Israelites through diffidence murmur when their flight was cut off by the sea and the mountains, and by the enemy pursuing them in the rear. Moses commanded them to stand still and see the mighty works of God, adding a promise, verse 14: "The Lord will fight for you and you shall be still." What now if the Israelites had disputed about faith after the fashion of our schools? What if they had disputed about the fact that it is enough to believe the history, or that God is, and that he dispenses punishments to the wicked, rewards to the good; or that they themselves are also evil and it could be that God wishes to punish both, the Egyptians first and then the Israelites? But no, they did not do this. They believed the divine word, the divine miracles, and trusted in God's mercy, and believed that they themselves were guilty of death, so that they committed themselves through faith to the channel. And having experienced by this example God's will toward them, and seeing that they were safe while the Egyptians perished in the waves, "They feared the Lord and believed the Lord and his servant Moses." And these examples have been exhibited to us to teach us to believe not with that sophistic faith, but with such reliance on the word of God as you see manifested by Moses in this place.

Moreover, what kind of faith does he demand in Numbers 14, when the people despaired of the occupation of Palestine? "How far will this people withdraw from me? How long will they not believe me in all the signs which I have done before them?" Thus spoke the Lord in Numbers 14:11. In chapter 20:12, he is irate with Moses and Aaron because they would not believe that water would come from the rock. Surely Aaron and Moses believed that God existed, but doubted the Divine word which had promised water from the rock. This incredulity the Lord censures.

Moses speaks of this faith in Deut. 1:31: "Thy God has carried thee as a man carries his little son, in all the way that thou hast walked, until thou hast come to this place. And indeed thou hast not believed the Lord thy God who has gone before you in the way," etc. They certainly possessed "unformed faith," they had "acquired faith," but they did not trust the promises of God's mercy. Nor were their hearts incited by reliance upon the mercy of God. They lived with incredulity, despising the work of God and unworthily bearing God's work, the restoration from Egypt. Therefore, though doubtless good men in other respects, they suffered for their incredulity. This is the hypocrisy of men who are to such a degree falsified by good works. However, their heart is not animated with trust and joy in God although God requires trust alone, although he has given his son as a confirmation of the trust, lest we doubt his good will toward us, in order that we may put our hope in God and not forget God's works and seek his commandments, Ps. 77:7. Likewise I Chron. 5:20: "They called upon God when they fought and he heard them, because they had believed on him." See also the incident when the prophet Ananias censures Asa, King of Judah, for trusting in the aid of the Syrians. But I do not know of an instance where Scripture has more plainly shown the power of faith than in the example of Jehosaphat in II Chron. 21, when he confounded the Ammonites and Moabites by a mere song, and ordered his army to do nothing but halt in confidence. The example of Ezekiel is also of this nature.

Isaiah (chapter 7) required of Achas such a faith as this, when he forbids him to seek aid from the Assyrians, promising him divine assistance and adding: "If you will not believe, you shall not endure."

All the sacred histories are full of incidents of this nature. It will therefore be of benefit to the pious and studious reader, both for learning the nature of faith and for the confirmation of his conscience, to gather up these various examples. However, I shall note several places even from the New Testament literature, in order that it might be understood that the spirit of both Testaments is one and the same.

I begin with Acts 15, where Peter says that the

fathers were not justified by the works of the law but by faith although they were living in the law, and adds that their hearts were purified by faith. Unless you understand these things just as he sets them forth concerning the reliance on the grace and mercy of God, you err very much. For how could it be that scholastic faith purifies hearts! Peter means that all the works of the fathers like David, Isaiah, and Jeremy, were sins, and moreover, he means that they were justified alone by their reliance on the mercy of God promised in Christ. The prophets just as often testify of him. This reliance on the good will of God is to be extended throughout the whole life, throughout all our works, throughout all corporal and spiritual temptations.

6. One and the same is the faith whereby God is believed, whereby his goodness is trusted in any temptation whatsoever. The test (temptation) of the woman sinner in Luke 7 was a spiritual one, and Christ encouraged her with these words: "Thy sins are remitted." Likewise verse 50: "Thy faith has saved thee, go in peace." Very many were physical, as when he healed diseases and rebuked the incredulity of his disciples in some physical matter, as for instance when they were solicitous about bread. For he chides them thus: "What think ye among yourselves, O ye of little faith?" etc. Matt. 18:8. And how often he teaches them the father's care for them in physical matters! Matt. 6:32: "Your Father knows what things ye need." And 10:31: "Ye are better than many sparrows." And such physical things are not to be despised but are as the very first principles of faith to be exercised.

7. I advise these things lest we labor somewhat in distinguishing the divine promises. For some pertain to physical things, as is the case with all those of the Old Testament, while others are spiritual, and

therefore properly pertain to the New Testament. For I feel that only the just believe the physical promises from the heart, and God has declared his mercy by the promise of physical things. Thus the saints could easily argue that their souls are much more a care to God if their bodies had been; and that he does not cease to be a father of souls, who has played the part of a father for their bodies. That is what I have already said: that the promises of physical things through themselves were the promise of grace; obscure indeed, but nevertheless clear enough for those who have the Spirit of God.

In Numbers 14:19 ff., when Moses prayed for the sin of the people, their sin was pardoned. And in Exodus 20:5 ff., the law was given with a promise of grace: "I am the Lord thy God, showing mercy unto thousands of them that love me and keep my commandments." And too, sacrifices for sin were handed down, and we must believe that they were signs of the remission of sins to believers. I do not seek allegories, but I wish a history to promise mercy in the very fact that physical benefits have been promised. Many stories in Genesis beautifully accord with this notion, as when Jacob says in Gen. 28:20: "If the Lord shall have been with me and kept me in the way which I go, and given me to eat and clothing to wear, etc., the Lord will be to me a God." Moses has commended faith in the mercy and goodness of God, by examples of works and of physical promises. Deut. 8:3: "Want afflicted you and he gave you food, manna, which ye knew not nor your fathers, that he might declare unto you that man does not live by bread alone but by every word that cometh out of the mouth of God." Indeed that is the word of life by whatsoever the human heart learns the mercy of God. Examples of this kind of faith are enumerated in Hebrews 11, many of which pertain to physical things. And too, what prevents me from accommodating the whole chapter to this place?

In the first place, he defines faith as follows: "Faith is the substance, that is, the expectation of things hoped for, the assurance of things not apparent." The Sophists by their peculiar explanations have turned this ὑπογραφή of faith towards their dreams, and towards that little carnal opinion they call faith, with the result that the apostolic sense is by no means clearly understood.[91] However, I simply repeat those most simple words: "Faith is the assurance of those things which are not apparent." I prithee, what is assurance? On the other hand, nature holds nothing of divine and spiritual things for a certainty, except it has been shown them by the Holy Spirit. But now, he calls it "expectation of things hoped for." Therefore that is not faith to believe in threats alone. Nay more, Scripture calls that fear.

But that is faith to believe also in the promises, that is, to rely on the mercy and goodness of God in the face of the injuries of this world, in the very face of sin, death and of the very gates of hell. Do you not see then, that the "expectation of things hoped for" is

---

[91] Cf. Gabriel Biel sentt. lib. III dist. 23 qu. 2, C. The Vulgate reads: "Est autem fides sperandorum substantia, rerum argumentum (Augustine reads 'Convictio') non apparentium." Peter Lombard: "quia per fidem subsistunt in nobis etiam modo speranda et subsistunt in futuro per experientiam." According to Biel "fides" can be called "substantia rerum sperandarum" because it is the origin of them. "Sic ergo fides dicitur substantia rerum sperandarum—in quantum est quædam inchoatio futuræ beatudinis, quia fides est prima virtus infusa sine qua res sperandas nemo consequi potest." On the contrary, Luther already in his lectures on the Psalms had emphasized the factual possession of future things by faith. This thought now appears again in Melanchthon. "Certitude" is his translation of ἔλεγχος In his view, however, "historica fides" stands in no relation to Justification at all. And where Scripture seems to speak of "historica fides" it has a content exceeding mere "assensus."

called faith? Consequently they do not believe who do not await the promised salvation.

On the other hand, you will say, I believe that salvation is promised, but that it will come to others. For thus the flesh perceives. But hear thou, were not these things also promised to thee? Has not the gospel been preached to all nations? Therefore thou dost not believe unless thou dost believe that salvation has been promised to thee also. For it is sure impiety and infidelity not to believe every word of God, or to be unable to believe that the remission of sins has been promised to thee.

Moreover, the Epistle to the Hebrews subjoins examples of this definition, 12:3: "By faith we understand that the world was made by the word of God," so that the invisible things to wit, of his divinity and virtue were made visible even by the works of his power. For thus this passage agrees with that one in Romans 1:20. The Sophists surely will bawl because I foolishly find here another kind of faith besides historical faith, seeing that the Epistle of Hebrews here speaks only of history and particularly of the creation of the world. But, hear now, how will this example agree with the definition of faith prescribed, if it pertains only to historical faith? Moreover, he calls faith in the history of creation not only that vulgar opinion of which the Gentiles and the Saracens are convinced, but the very knowledge of the power and virtue of God deduced from the creative work. For this faith was none other than that which Peter or Paul possessed, if you please. For Peter thus understands the power of God in the resurrection of Christ and thus he understands his goodness and mercy when he believes that Christ was a victim and satisfaction for him. He therefore trusts in no work of his own, but simply in the mercy of God which was promised in Christ. Thus he who judges the creation of things by the Spirit, sees both the power of God the author of such things and his goodness, when he perceives that he receives all things so to speak, from the creator's hand, such as: life, food and offspring; and when he entrusts these to the creator to regulate, rule, administer and give in accordance with his goodness as he pleases. Such faith is not a frigid opinion about the creation of things, but is a most lively knowledge both of the power and goodness of God pouring itself out upon all creatures, ruling, and administering all creatures. If I could explain it as the dignity of the case demands, how many pages would I use on this topic alone? However, he who truly believes, will easily estimate by the Spirit what faith in the creation really is.

Perhaps the Sophists will laugh, but let them truly laugh although they cannot refute what I know to be so firm, that not even the gates of hell can dislodge. Paul calls faith in the creation a more august and venerable something than sophistic opinion, when he says in Roms. 1:10: "The invisible things of God especially his eternal Godhead and power are clearly seen by the things which are visible."

Moreover, what else is God's power (virtus) or Godhead but his power (Potentia) and goodness? Acts 14:16 reads: "He has not left himself without testimony, imparting gifts, giving rain from the heavens and fruit-bearing seasons." And how cheerfully David amuses himself by the meditation of creation in Psalm 104:24: "Thou hast made all things in thy wisdom, the earth is filled with thy possession." Likewise verse 27: "All things wait on thee, that thou mayest give them meat in season; what thou givest they gather, and opening thy hand all things will be filled with goodness."

I ask you, can flesh lead to such a mystery of the creation? Or can that chaos of carnal dreams called philosophy do so which, when it says things happen by contingency, plainly denies the work of creation?

Thus the people of the law, as it were, recognized the power and goodness of God in that they were freed from the Egyptian servitude. For Exodus 20:2: "I am the Lord thy God who brought thee out of the land of Egypt, out of the house of bondage, etc." and as before the law was given, the fathers recognized in those things which God did with Abraham, Isaac, Jacob, just why Abraham called him God, so also before them the very creation of things was a certain sign and form whereby God was recognized. Thus Abel and the other saints believed although their faith was also aroused by the promise that Eve's seed should bruise the serpent's head.

Therefore it is subjoined in Heb. 11:4: "By faith Abel offered a more pleasing sacrifice than Cain." Both undoubtedly had a knowledge of history, otherwise why would Cain offer up a sacrifice? Therefore, when he attributed faith to Abel and not to Cain, he does not mean some sort of historical opinion but a faith glorifying God, a faith judging well of God and trusting his divine mercy, etc. By such a faith Abel overcame, and through it received the testimony that he was righteous. The author of the epistle has diligently noticed this fact, in order to show that faith is that which is imputed for righteousness and not a sacrifice, not a work.

"By faith Enoch was translated that he should not see death," verse 5. That is, because Enoch believed God, he was pleasing to God; so much so that God in him would show the fathers an argument and a hope for a better life, when he translated him. For what does it profit us to investigate why Enoch was translated, provided we understand that God showed to the fathers in him, a sort of example and a most certain proof of immortality, to confirm their faith? The following verse (6) reads: "Without faith it is impossible to please God, for he that cometh to God ought to believe that God is, and that he is a rewarder of those who seek him." You see how this cannot be understood of sophistic faith, for it is certain that hypocrites do not trust in God that he has commiserated them, or that he wishes them well and will save them. For if you question their hearts they will answer thus: I know not whether I can be saved. I indeed know that salvation has been promised; I know that God is merciful; but perhaps he will not deal with me according to his mercy. Such majesty as that does not seem reasonable to me, and the like of such answers. However, not even these things which the impious speak of the judgment of God really proceed from their heart. For they despise the judgment of God, and do not fear it until they are confounded by God. We would be completely subdued however could the heart but conceive the magnitude of God's goodness and the fulness of his grace, and could believe thus: God is not forgetful of you; his mercy is so great that if you believe him he will preserve, keep, and save you. Therefore trust him.

Those whose hearts are encouraged by the sense of the goodness of God to such a degree that they believe those things will come to pass what God has promised, indeed truly believe these things: that God is a rewarder, nay more, they believe these things, and in a word truly believe God himself. For the impious do not believe them, but hold a sort of frigid opinion to which no depth of heart adheres.

By faith Noah, when he had received a response, fearing those things which were not yet seen, prepared an ark for the salvation of his household. Behold Noah's faith embraces two things: threats and promise. And that is what I have said before, to wit: that the impious do not believe one word of God, neither the threats nor the promises. Noah attributed true glory to God, and therefore fears God's threats and relies on God's promise of salvation, and therefore his mercy. Now in those days, don't forget, there were many hypocrites who feigned the truth. They feigned belief in the existence of God and thought he was an avenger of the wicked, and a savior of the good. But they were by no means moved by those threats of God. And why, you ask? Because they did not believe with their heart, because they were not moved by the promise of salvation through the ark, because they did not confide in the mercy of God upon them.

Therefore, sophistic faith is nothing but pure deceit, pure mockery or wantonness of souls. Nevertheless, the impious and the godless (ἄθεοι) Sophists teach that their faith feigned after good works is enough, although there is no good work but what is performed either with hate for or contempt of God. For whatever is done without trust in the mercy and goodness of God, is done with hate for and contempt of God. As Paul says in Roms. 14:23: "Whatever is not of faith is sin." And in Heb. 11:7: "By the Ark he condemned the world." Especially so since one was saved by faith, and the rest were lost through unbelief. Then how solicitous the author is in his admonition that the sum of righteousness is faith in the mercy and grace of God, when he adds: "And became heir of righteousness." I do not speak of figures nor seek out allegories, but I confine myself strictly to history. Noah was justified by faith alone in the mercy of God, not by any works of his own. He had received this from God's promise that he would be saved from the waters, and then too, from the promise handed down to the elders, concerning the head of the serpent, that is, concerning the fact that the sting of death would be destroyed.

By faith Abraham, when called to go into another country which he should receive for an heritage, obeyed and went. What is more, he knew not whither he was going. Abraham trusted the mercy and goodness of God, nothing doubting that whosoever the people might be, God would be his protector and savior. He therefore committed himself to God's word and left his native land, none otherwise than the children of Israel committed themselves to the word of Moses when they crossed over the Red Sea.

Moreover, so great was that faith of Abraham that although his whole life was spent roaming around in uncertain places, it was nevertheless unshaken. He seemed to himself to be sufficiently strong and wealthy; he seemed to think he dwelled in a safe place because he lived under the shadow of God's wings. And now, in the very fact that he saw no certain dwelling place in Canaan for himself and son, he perceived that he was a sojourner in this land, and he wished to be a citizen of the eternal city. By faith also Sarah received the power to conceive and retain seed. For the word of God vivifies and creates all things when Sarah believes it, especially the promise of seed, how it could be that she would become fertile, not only with a "sterile," but with a "worn out" womb. "For all things are possible to him that believes." Mark 9:22. But how severely besieged was Abraham's faith? With what a strong ram was it shaken when he was ordered to sacrifice Isaac in whom alone he knew posterity was promised?

Moreover, how firm was young Isaac's faith when he hesitated to yield in no way to the command of his father and to the divine will? Do you think you could execute such a cruel command upon your son, especially when posterity had been promised in him? Don't you think that the son would have been obstreperous toward the father unless both, trusting in divine mercy, had committed themselves to it? Nor did faith fail. The son is saved and restored to the father. You see that here a prelude to sin and death, to justification and resurrection, and hence to the whole New Testament is made.

Did not Abraham and Isaac and all the pious saints before the gospel was revealed learn from this, that something even in death, was to be hoped for from the will of God? Did not the fathers conceive from this example the faith of a conquered death, and saw a prelude to Christ who was to bruise the serpent's head, that is, the sting of death? By faith Isaac blessed Jacob and Esau believing that in the future, they would occupy the promised land. Now this is the more wonderful because he wished the blessing of Jacob, which he had stolen from his elder brother whose blessing it rightfully was, to be confirmed, doubtless from faith in the divine word: "The elder shall serve the younger," Gen. 25:23. By faith Joseph blessed the sons of Isaac, although already an exile, but nothing doubting that they would return to Canaan and would become the progenitors of many peoples. Nor did the parents of Moses doubt but that they would return to Palestine, which was the reason for their concealing the infant, the hope of the race. Then, too, that is why they entrusted him in secret to divine mercy rather than slay him.

Add to these the other examples if you care to do

so. I have merely outlined a form of examples to be treated and have taught that the author of the Epistle does not speak of sophistic hypocrisy but of faith; that is, of trust in the mercy or grace of God.

You do not here see a distinction of divine promises, but simply that the word faith is the promise of the mercy or grace of God, or that it is a question either of eternal or temporal matter.

Moreover the promises of spiritual things in general can be deduced from the promises of material things not only by means of allegory, but by a clear and manifest argument of the Spirit. The sacrifice of his son taught Abraham what was to be hoped for in death. Now it is of no avail to distinguish promises, because all the rest are directed to that first promise made concerning the seed of Eve, that is, Christ. Therefore posterity was expected because that seed was awaited, to wit, Jesus Christ. And so the promise made to Eve was renewed in the one made to Abraham. Gen. 22:18: "In thy seed shall all peoples of the earth be blessed." This can only be referred to Christ. For Paul interprets it so in Gal. 3:16: "In thy seed, which is Christ." And Jacob clearly declares in Gen. 49:10 that posterity and the kingdom of grace promised for Christ were awaited: "The sceptre shall not depart from Judah, nor a leader from his feet, until he shall come who is to be sent, and he shall be the expectation of the Gentiles." What else did he mean but that the promises of the Kingdom and hence of corporal things are to be referred to Christ and consummated in him? That is why Paul, without any discrimination whatever, cites the promise made to Abraham.

In Gal. 3:8, Paul cites Gen. 12:3: "In thee shall all nations be blessed." And in Roms. 4:16 ff. he says that the inheritance of the world was promised to Abraham and that they are Abraham's sons who believe with Abraham, regardless of race. And further, that all believers are kings in Christ the King. As Psalm 8:7 says: "Thou hast put all things under his feet." Again, those who manifestly believe on Christ after the gospel has been revealed, have all physical blessings in him. "For if God spared not his own son, but delivered him up for all of us, how will he not give all things together with him?" Roms. 8:32. It likewise appears from the very nature of the kingdom that, inasmuch as all creatures—death, hunger, the sword, principalities, heights, depths, sin and, in a word, whatever human weakness is wont to fear—have been made subject to Christ, they have been made subject to his brethren likewise. They are in our power, they have been subjected beneath our feet, unless of course we do not believe that Christ reigns.

This relates to what I have said before, how that faith is to be spread throughout every vicissitude of our life and death. And why, you ask? Because we use no creature rightly except we use it by faith. Indeed we abuse all creatures through diffidence. That is, by not believing that we please God in the use of a creature, showing distrust in the use of a creature for the mercy and benevolence of God toward us. He abuses poverty, death and misfortunes who does not believe that they are the works of divine mercy, or who shows diffidence here, fleeing to human aid and doubting that he can conquer them in Christ. Thus Abraham would have abused that sorrowful command to sacrifice his son, had he not freely obeyed and entrusted himself to divine mercy, being confident that God would deal with him after the manner of paternal affection. He none the less misuses money, life and success, who does not recognize in them gifts of divine mercy, and who does not use them faithfully as though they were another's gifts, etc.

Finally, he possesses all things and can do all things, who possesses Christ. For Christ is righteousness, peace, life and salvation. You see that the divine promises agree in this manner. For they are wholly individual signs and tokens of the goodwill of God toward us, which he commends and recommends to us, sometimes by a work, sometimes by a gift. Throughout the history of all scripture the whole is incumbent on this: to teach and to accustom us to confide in his goodness. And if anyone contemplates this goodness in its manifold and varied promises, how can he restrain himself from pouring out his mind and soul into that gulf of such great mercy? Moreover, the goodwill of the father has been merited by Christ[92] whom he gave to be our intercessor, our victim, and our satisfaction. "For God so loved the world that he gave his only begotten son for the world," John 3:16. Because he favors him, he favors us. Because he has made all things subject to him, he has made them subject to us.

Thus all promises are to be referred to him who has merited the mercy of the father for us; who has procured the father's favor for us. John 1:16 says: "Of his fulness all of us have received, grace for grace," favor toward us for favor toward Christ. Occupy your spirit by meditating accurately upon the promises. For Christ can by no means be learned apart from the promises. And unless you know Christ you will not know the father. Bend all the cogitations of your spirit hither, bend your attention hither so as to learn from the promises what is offered you in Christ. Moreover I ask you, where, in a word if you please, is Scholastic

---

[92]Spalatin is good: "Nun hatt der Herr Christus den guten und gnedigen willen gottes verdient."

theology mindful of the promises? If at all, it is done in such a manner that the grace of Christ is obscured, and Christ is made not a pledge of mercy but a legislator and an exactor much more severe than Moses even seemed to be.

Thus far, I have spoken of the promises which are to be referred to that one made to Eve, by which it was signified to Adam and Eve that both sin and death and the penalty of that sin would sometime be abolished to wit, when Eve's progeny should bruise the serpent's head. For what do the serpent's head and his plots signify but the reign of sin and death. If you recall the remaining promises to this one, you will see that throughout all scripture, the gospel is simply the forgiveness of sin through Christ or the preaching (declaration) of grace.

However, as I said a while ago, all the promises, even those of corporal things, are tokens of the benevolence or mercy of God. And he who believes them is justified because he thinks well of God and attributes praise to him for his clemency and goodness. He does not yet believe every word of God, who hears the threats and confesses the history. But he believes every word of God who believes the promises in addition to the threats and the history. It is not enough to be believed that the reason why he took on flesh and was crucified and resurrected from the dead was that he might justify as many as should believe on him. But if you believe that these things were done for your good, for your salvation, then happy is your belief.

Hence, whatever they may call faith in addition to this kind of faith, is nothing but deceit, mendacity and false madness. Is there any reason why justification is attributed to faith alone? I answer that since we are justified by mercy of God alone, and since faith is plainly a knowledge of mercy by whatever promise you embrace it, our justification is attributed to faith alone. They who wonder why justification is attributed to the mercy of God also wonder why justification is attributed to the mercy of God and not rather to human merits. For to trust in divine mercy, is to have no respect for any of our works. He does injury to the mercy of God who denies that the saints are justified by faith. For since our justification is a work of divine mercy alone and not a merit of our own works, as Paul plainly teaches in Roms. 11, it is necessary for justification to be attributed to faith alone, by which alone without doubt, we receive the promised mercy.

What then about the works that precede justification, I mean the works of free will? They are all of them the accursed fruit of an accursed tree. And although they may be examples of the most beautiful virtues such as were Paul's before his conversion, nevertheless, they are nothing but deceit and mendacity, because they proceed from an impure heart. Now impurity of heart is ignorance of God, not fearing God, nor trusting him, nor seeking God, as I have pointed out before. For the flesh knoweth nothing but carnal things. Roms. 8:5: "The flesh seeketh the things which are of the flesh." And I Cor. 2:14: "The natural man does not perceive the things which are of the Spirit of God; who has known the will of the Lord?" Nature understands, knows, and seeks glory, wealth, tranquillity and dignity of life. The philosophers name many such things among the chief goods; one names εὐθυμία, another ἀναλγησία. It is apparent that nature affects nothing divine. For it is neither terrified by the word of God nor incited to believe. And what are such fruits of a tree but sins?

Indeed the works that follow our justification although they proceed from the Spirit of God who has taken possession of the hearts of those justified, are nevertheless of themselves unclean, because they are performed in a heart that is still impure. For justification has just begun and is not fully completed. We have received the first fruits of the Spirit (Romans 8:23) but not yet the "titles."[93] We are still waiting with groaning as Paul says in Roms. 8:23, for the redemption of our body. Hence because there is still some impurity in these works they do not deserve the name righteousness. And wherever you turn, whether to the works that precede or to those that follow justification, there is no place for our merit. That is what Paul means in Gal. 2:20: "Moreover because I now live in the flesh, I live in the faith of the son of God who loved me and gave himself for me." Mind you he does not say: I now live in my good works; but, I live in the faith of the mercy of God. Moreover, the reason why those works that follow justification are not imputed for sin is faith alone. But concerning this, I will speak later.

Therefore when justification is attributed to faith or to the mercy of God, human efforts, human works, and human merits are done away with. They owe their beginning and growth to mercy, so that the righteous-

---

[93] In order to understand this and the following assertions, the reader must bear in mind that Melanchthon understands "justificatio" in the Augustianian sense. In a preliminary draft of the Loci called "Theologica Institutio" he describes it not as a new relation to God but as the actual possession of true "justitia" quæ et solida et constans esset et ex animo bearet nos." Thus "justificatio" and sanctificatio" fall in fundamentally together. Later this notion gradually receded into the background. cf. Herrlinger: Theologie Melanchthons S. 6 ff. Luther in his writing "de libertate Christiana" brings the passage just quoted from Romans 8 into a new relation. cf. E. A. opp. V Arg. IV, 235. W. A. VII, 59:1 . . . "Propter quod apostolus Rom. 8 appellat primitias spiritus, quod in hac vita habemus, accepturi scilicet decimas et plenitudinem spiritus in futuro."

ness of the entire life is nothing other than faith. That is why Isaiah (16:5) calls the kingdom of Christ a kingdom of mercy: "And a kingdom shall be prepared in mercy." Now if we are justified by our own works, then it would not be a kingdom of Christ and of mercy but of us, a kingdom of our own works. And Hosea 2:19 reads: "I shall engage thee forever, and I shall engage thee in righteousness and judgment and in mercy, and in commiserations; and I shall engage thee in faith and you shall know that I am the Lord." And Psalm 88:15: "Mercy and truth go before thy face." Mercy is gracious favor that has no relation whatsoever to our merit. Truth is the work of God, truly and not hypocritically justifying us. But what does it profit to collect more passages when Isaiah in the 53rd chapter in the first place, condemns all of our righteousness in these words: "All we like sheep have gone astray, each has defaulted to his own way, and the Lord has put the iniquity of us all on him"; and then later says that not by our works, not by our plans, but Christ by the knowledge of himself, will justify man. Behold, the knowledge of Christ is justification, and moreover, that knowledge is faith alone. To those who know the power of sin, to those whose consciences are smitten by the knowledge of sin, it is a pleasure to hear this doctrine of faith. But our gospel is veiled from the hypocrites in whom the god of this world has blinded their unfaithful minds, that the light of the gospel of the glory of Christ, who is the image of God, might not shine upon them.

You will say: Then we merit nothing at all? Why does Scripture so often use the word "reward?" My answer: It is a reward and should be, not because of any merit of our own, but because the father has promised and as it were already bound himself under obligation to us, and made himself a debtor to them that have merited nothing of the kind. For what could be more clearly spoken against our merits than what Christ said in Luke 17:9 f.: "For what does he thank that servant? Because he has done what he had ordered? I think not. So also ye, when ye have done all which is commanded you, say: We are unprofitable servants, because we have done what we ought to do." And Paul in Roms. 6:23 says: "The wages of sin is death, but the gift of God is eternal life." He calls eternal life a gift, not a debt, although it is a debt because the father has promised it and has put his faith under obligation to us.

Nor do those passages of Scripture give any offense which may seem to proclaim merits. Of such a nature is that passage in Roms. 2:10: "glory and honor to everyone working good." Also Matt. 25:35: "I was an hungered and ye gave me to eat," etc. For there are many passages of the like in Scripture. I answer in a word; Scripture speaks not only of the external appearance of a work or of its "disguise" and "rouge," but of the work as a whole. That is, it speaks both of the external work and then especially of the will or of the affection that is the author of the work. Scripture calls a good work an "external simulation" not of the work, but the whole work: that is, the good affection and the fruit of that affection, none otherwise than as common sense customarily speaks of it. For who calls that a good work which he knows proceeds from a malignant heart? And so when Paul says "glory and honor to him working good," I don't see any need for these explanations, and the less so since it is self-evident. For Paul does not say "to him feigning a good work," but to him working with heart, affection, and hands in the work. They who do not explain Paul's words in connection with the whole work, and the life and soul of the work, but only of the external form of the work, pervert what he has most simply and correctly stated. The principle is generally accepted in the schools and common sense teaches, that no work is good without the affection. Let them consult common sense who interpret Scripture with respect to part of a work and not the whole. And what of the fact that in the same place, Paul most beautifully refers a life well lived to faith, and teaches that all good works take origin in faith as if faith were a fountain. For he says "To those seeking glory and honor through perseverance in good works." Now what is "seeking" but that recorded in Hebs. 11:6: "He that cometh unto God ought to believe that he is and that he is a rewarder of them that seek him." They seek who believe, who by reliance on the word of God are carried off to glory. Likewise, how could the power and nature of faith be more certainly expressed than by the word "Perseverance," since it is impossible for any man unless he has great faith, to continue and to endure in good works, midst the allurements of the flesh and the world and midst so many affections?

Again, Paul in the same passage (Roms. 2:8) refers a badly ordered life to unbelief when he says: "To the contentious and those who believe not the truth." What does the phrase "not to believe the truth" mean but to show distrust? They are contentious who oppose the truth, who follow carnal opinion. For whoever openly sins does so either out of contempt of God or else out of despair of his mercy. Sennacherib moved his armies against Israel because he considered God to be nothing. Because he despaired of mercy, Cain therefore ventured anything afterwards. For there is no man who would not most zealously conform to the law of God, if he knew God would commiserate him. But because we are contentious, we debate with ourselves, and perceive something more difficult than is really the case concerning the fulness of divine wrath and mercy. And so from contempt of both the wrath and mercy of God, we turn aside to our own cupidities and venture to do anything, being impious, blind, mad, solely out of love of glory or possessions or pleasures. A sorry plight, if it falls your lot to behold the impious madness and the insane impiety of your heart!

You see then, how appositely Paul has referred a well-ordered life to faith and its opposite to incredulity. The circumstances in the case explain the other passages in such a way that they do not need the assistance of foreign explanations. I leave the treatment of these to the industry of spiritual readers. For I do not wish the Sophists to be "ill-employed by leisure."[94] by whom, there is nothing which has been so well and so simply said but what is not perverted, distinguished and dissected into a thousand forms. Surely there is no obscurity in that passage of Matthew which I have quoted, if you rightly judge the matter. Now I do not press the argument that when he calls them "blessed of his father" he signifies they have attained salvation by divine blessing, and not works; for it cannot be denied but that Christ is speaking of the works of faith when he says in Matt. 25:35: "I was hungry and ye gave me to eat," and in verse 40: "What ye have done unto the least of these my brethren, ye have done unto me." For since the just believe they do to Christ what they

---

[94]Male feriati: Spalatin translates this: die uebelmiessige Sophisten." The phrase means those who celebrate joyful festivals in leisure or idleness. The phrase is borrowed no doubt from the Latin poet Horace, cf. Carm. IV, 6, 14: "feriatos Troas."

do to them, in this they rightly contend. Such a faith distinguishes works. Hypocrites do not feed on and drink Christ, but themselves. For they serve their own glory, no matter how much they may display the appearance of beautiful virtues. It is enough to have pointed out these things, in order that the studious may have a plan for the treatment of such passages, for I must not play the part of a commentary too much.

On the Efficacy of Faith

Now this fact must be considered also: that just as works are the fruits of the Spirit, they are also indications, testimonies, and signs of it. Christ says as much in Matt. 7:16: "By their fruits ye shall know them." For hypocrisy cannot forever be dissembled, and faith unable not to assert itself to most eagerly serve God as a pious son serves a pious father. For when by faith we have tasted of the mercy of God, and have known the divine goodness through the word of the gospel which pardons our sins and promises grace, the soul cannot but love God in return and be joyful, and express its gratitude by some reciprocal service as it were for such great mercy. Paul has most graphically said the same (Roms. 8:15): "By faith we cry: Abba, father." Now because such a mind subjects itself to God, false ambition, jealousy, malice, envy, avarice, pleasures, and their fruits, are banished and it knows things that are humble; it hates itself and abominates all its own cupidities; in a word, as Paul (Roms. 6:21) says: "Now are we ashamed of those things which we aforetime enjoyed." Therefore it imparts itself to all its neighbors, and serves them, placing itself at their disposal, considering their wants as its own, doing all things with everyone candidly, sincerely, without self-seeking and with no malice. Such is the efficacy of faith as it appears from the works of those whose hearts are possessed by true faith.

Concerning such a faith as this, Paul (Gal. 5:6) says: "In Christ Jesus circumcision profiteth nothing nor uncircumcision, but faith which is powerful through love." He says faith in Christ is powerful and then this faith is of the type that imparts itself through love in the use of a neighbor. I John 4:7: "Everyone that loveth his brother is born of God and knows God. Who does not love, does not know God, for God is love." And II Peter 1:5–8: "Add to your faith virtue, to virtue knowledge, to knowledge temperance, to temperance patience, to patience piety, to piety brotherly love, to brotherly love, love." Now if we possess these things, they will cause the knowledge of our Lord Jesus Christ to be by no means unfruitful. Now by this gradation, Peter has ingrafted the remaining virtues to faith as though beautiful branches to a root, so that virtue, that is the vehemence and passion of a mortified flesh follows faith. But this vehemence is ruled by knowledge, so that its duty to the body is performed.

There may be some way whereby the subdued body may serve the spirit εὐπροσέδρως, to use Paul's word, that it be not destroyed. Again it serves the necessity of the body so that it does not run to excess, but that it may be temperate. Now in addition to temperance there follows the bearing of evils. For there are many who are temperate but at the same time implacable when offended. Piety follows hard after tolerance, that is, we bear adversities placidly not only before men, but also before God, giving thanks to him that mortifies us, being not at all indignant at the will of God, even as the Israelites who perished in the wilderness in the rage against God's will. Piety mothers love; that is, that we do well by those who persecute us, and that we treat our enemies with kindness. In fine, from the fact that it proceeds from a sincere heart, that we love all in general with equity and sincerity, you have the sum of the Christian life; faith together with its fruits. Now the classes and orders of the virtues I do not distinguish like the philosophers and Scholastics, into moral and intellectual. Nor do I make fine distinctions between gifts and fruits as for instance Aquinas did in his works.[95] For faith alone of its kind is that sense of the mercy of God, which is at once the very fountain and life and ruler of all good works.

On Love and Hope

It is evident from this, how the love of God and the love of neighbor which they call "Caritas," proceed from faith. For the very knowledge of the mercy of God causes us to love God in return. It causes us of our own accord to subject ourselves to all creatures and this is "love of neighbor."[96]

Moreover, hope also is a work of faith. For faith is that by which the word is believed, while hope is that by which one awaits what has already been promised through the word. What makes us anticipate is

---

[95] Cf. Thomas Summa II, 1 quæst. IXVIII, 8. For a lucid discussion of Aquinas' distinction between "Dona" and "Virtutes," Cf. Gass: "Gesch. d. Ethik," Berlin 1881, S. 336 f. Also Frohschammer: "Die Philosophie des Thomas Von Aquino," Leipg. 1889, S. 483 f. The "fructus" were treated in Quæst. 70. They were pointed out in Gal. V as proceeding out of the power of the Holy Spirit working in the Christian.

[96] Qui proximi amor est: cf. Luther's "De Libertate Christiana." In this he speaks of the "primitiis spiritus" and adds: "ad hanc partem pertinet, quod supra positum est, christianum esse omnium servum et omnibus, subjectum. Qua enim parte liber est, nihil operatur, qua autem servus est, omnia operatur." Opp. V. arg. IV, 235-W. A. VII, 59.

faith in the word of God. Ps. 9:11: "All they hope in thee who have known thy name." And too, there is no reason why the one should be separated from the other. Certainly Scripture employs promiscuously the words hope and faith, awaiting and enduring. And just as faith is reliance upon the gratuitous mercy of God without respect to any of our works, so also hope is the expectation of salvation without any respect to our merits. Nay more, it is not hope concerning God except there be nothing of merits. For how does he hope for mercy who demands some reward, as though it were due his merits? Let the afflicted conscience rejoice; let the evangelical sinner[97] be glad because there is not respect of merits. The hypocrite is truly indignant that Christ is an offense to the Jews and foolishness to the Greeks, but to them that believe, salvation and wisdom.

What is written in I Cor. 13:2: "If I have faith so as to remove a mountain and have not love, I am nothing," is made the basis of an objection to them that defend the righteousness of faith. However, I ask you Sophists, why is it, that although you see that the whole of Scripture is to teach that justification is a work of mercy and Paul reiterates it in so many clear words as for instance in Roms. 1:17: "The just lives by faith"; and Roms. 4:5: "To him that believes on him that justifies the ungodly, his faith is imputed unto righteousness"; likewise Roms. 10:10: "with the heart it is believed unto righteousness," and similar pas-

---

[97]"Evangelicus peccator": A beatiful oxymoron which Luther voiced as early as 1516: "Omnis sanctus conscienter est peccator, ignoranter vero justus, peccator secundum rem, justus secundum spem; peccator revera, justus vero secundum reputationem Dei miserentis," E. A. opp. V arg. I, 251. Cf. Harries: "Luthers Lehre bis zum Jahr 1517 mit besonderer Ruecksicht auf die Frage nach dem Verhaeltnis von Rechtfertigung und Heiligung zu einander," Jahrbuechern fuer deutsche Theologie 1861, S. 798.

sages—why is it, I again ask, that you have so placed this one passage in Corinthians of all Scripture over against the remaining Pauline epistles, as to compensate the rest by your explanations and yet be unwilling to qualify this one by interpretation? I shall set it forth simply as it has been said, without any gloss.

In the first place, it is indeed quite clear that Paul is here talking of love toward neighbor, to which your schools do not attribute the beginning of justification. For I do not tarry longer with that fiction that the love of God and of neighbor are the same thing. In the next place it cannot be denied but that Paul has here used the word faith for the gift or faculty of performing miracles, as chapter 12:9 also witnesses with the following words: "To another faith by the Spirit." It is granted moreover that the charismata of performing miracles such as: prophecy, knowledge of tongues, and eloquence, can be conferred even upon the ungodly.

It is my judgment that one should not especially separate justifying faith from the gift of miracles, since here as in almost the entire Epistle he demands love in addition to faith, as elsewhere in all his epistles he demands good works from believers or from those who are justified. Paul thinks correctly when he calls that man nothing, who may have all sorts of faith whatever but is without love. For although faith alone justifies a man, yet love is also demanded, to be sure, the second part of the law Roms. 13:9: "The whole law is renewed in this! Thou shalt love thy neighbor as thyself." Moreover, love does not justify a man; the more so because no man loves as he ought. Faith alone justifies, a faith that relies not on its own merits, but only on the mercy of God.

There remains the passage in James 2:17: "Faith without works is dead." Well said by James. For he censures those who judged that a mere historical opinion about Christ is faith. Besides, just as Paul often calls faith "feigned" and sometimes "true," in like manner James sometimes styles it "living" and sometimes "dead." A living faith is that efficacious and burning reliance on the mercy of God, productive always of good fruits. That is what he means in chapter 2:22, "Faith is made perfect by works. Likewise because his works declare Abraham had a living faith, therefore Scripture is fulfilled when it says, 2:23: "Abraham believed God and it was imputed unto him for righteousness." And so finally, James[98] effects this, that a dead faith (that is, that "frigid Parisian opinion") does not justify. A living faith justifies. That is indeed a living faith which spends itself in works. For he says so in 2:18: "Show me thy faith without thy works and I shall show you my faith by my works." Be it noted, however, that he does not say: "I will show you my works without faith." Moreover, what has been said, squares most aptly with this exposition namely, that if faith does not possess works it is of itself dead. Therefore it is quite clear that James is merely teaching that the faith of those who do not produce the fruits of faith is a dead faith, although from external appearances, they may seem to be believers.

---

[98]Luther had answered Eck's interest in the passages in question by his "resol. super propositionibus Lipsiæ disputatis a. 19," with this: Stilus epistolæ illius longe est infra apostolicam majestatem nec cum Paulino ullo modo comparandus. Deinde de fide viva loquitur Paulus. Nam fides mortua non est fides, sed opinio." E. A. opp. V. ar. II, 278. Melanchthon admits only the second and under the impression of the powerful intercession of Carlstadt for the authenticity and canonicity of James (in the writing aimed against Luther "de canonicis scripturis Aug. 1520) makes an attempt to secure a reconciliation. On his position and that of his contemporaries regarding James cf. G. Kawerau: "Das Schicksal des Jacobusbriefes im 16. Jahr." 1889, VII, S. 359, in Ztschr. f. Kirchl. Wiss.

It will not be useless to point out that concerning which I perceive there are contentions everywhere, namely: "How may man know whether he is in the favor of God, and how can it be ascertained whether there is faith in his heart?" The question is a twofold one. For in the former, the question is concerning the will of God toward us, and not of our affections; whereas in the latter, the question concerns our affections alone. Now the Scholastics indeed taught—and it was a most foul error—that neither could be known. And it is clearly evident from this that the whole bunch of them possessed nothing of the Spirit. Now in reference to the flesh I ask, how can it know what the divine will toward it is, since it is entirely ignorant of God? And moreover, how will the flesh which does not fully understand its own affections judge of spiritual affections? Jer. 17:9: "The heart of man is depraved and inscrutable." Therefore, the Scholastics simply imagined that there were several qualities in the soul of man of which we ourselves are ignorant. Besides, they taught that God wishes that we do not seek to know so that the conscience may forever fluctuate in uncertainty with itself. Now what is this but teaching despair? Indeed that is my opinion.

In the first place, as touching the divine will, faith is nothing but a sure and constant reliance on the divine benevolence toward us. The will of God is known, but by faith from the promise of the gospel. For you do not attribute true glory to God if you do not believe that God wills himself to be manifested by the gospel. They know themselves to be in the favor of God who estimate the will of God in accordance with his own word, and not from human merits. Thus Paul in Roms. 4, when he teaches by several arguments that righteousness is by faith, finally adds this most powerful reason!

If Justification were by our works rather than by faith, the conscience would never be at rest, longing now for this and now for that in life and labor; and the result would be nothing but despair. Consequently (in Roms. 4:13–6) he says: "Therefore not by works, that the promise may be firm according to grace." And how often do the prophets glory in security! Hosea 2:10: "I shall cause them to sleep with confidence." Jer. 23:6: "In those days shall Judah be safe and Israel shall dwell in confidence."

Now what do the words "fiducialiter" and "confidenter" and the like signify but security? This security is most beautifully expressed in the words of Micah 4:4: "A man shall sit under his own vine and under his own fig tree"; and the words of Isaiah are very clear, 32:17 f., "And the work of righteousness will be peace and the labor of righteousness silence and security forever and ever; and my people will sit in the beauty of peace and in the tabernacles of confidence and in rich repose." To this degree do the prophets describe that Christ's kingdom will be a kingdom of security.

Moreover what security would there be if our consciences are forever in doubt as to the will of God? It is necessary therefore that we be certain of the grace and benevolence of God towards us. That is what the Lord says in Jer. 9:24: "Let him that glorieth glory in this, that he understandeth and knoweth me." God wishes that his will be known and that we glory in his will.[99] What is more impious than to deny that the divine will either ought not or cannot be known?

---

[99] Cf. Lutheri opp. in Psalmas E. A. opp. ex. Lat. 15. 262: "Fides autem esse nullo modo potest nisi sit vivax quædam et indubitata opinio qua homo certus est super omnem certitudinem sese placere deo, se habere propitium et ignoscentem deum in omnibus, quæ fecerit aut gesserit, propitium in bonis ignoscentem in malis."

Especially so when he has already expressed it by his own word?

May I now ask the Sophists whether they believe what is in the Apostles Creed on the remission of sins? Also, whether they believe the word of the Priest when they are absolved? If they do believe they necessarily know that they are in the favor of God. But if they do not believe, why do they confess? Wicked Rome and Eck the author of the Roman Bull[100] have condemned a certain article of Luther on faith which teaches that faith is necessary for absolution. They reply then by asking why people hear absolution unless they believe. This is a more obscure and pernicious impiety than anyone can think. I do not doubt but that it has been the death of many a soul which was driven to despair by this carnal, sophistic, Parisian dogma. May the Lord destroy the lips of all who speak a lie!

A Christian mind will easily learn from the teacher experience that Christianity is nothing but that sort of life which is indeed certain of the mercy of God. Roms. 12:7: "That ye may know what is that good and perfect will of God, well-pleasing," etc. Therefore the Sophists will say, "is there nothing then that we fear?" Rightly so, if fear is without faith it shall have been impious. Moreover fear which is joined to faith is not ignorant of mercy. But it exclaims with Job (9:28): "I was afraid of all my works." The saints fear because of their works, but trust however in the mercy of God. Hypocrites trust in their works, and are ignorant of God's mercy, nay more even of the

---

[100]Melanchthon refers to number 10 of the 41 principles branded as false in the Bull "Exsurge domine": peccata non sunt ulli remissa, nisi remittente sacerdote credat sibi remitti: imo peccatum maneret, nisi remissum crederet: non enim sufficit remissio peccati et gratiæ donatio, sed oportet etiam credere esse remissum. cf. C. Mirbt: Geschichte des Papsttums, S. 115. cf. Also Luther's "Assertio omnium articulorum." E. A. opp. V. arg. V, 192. W. A. VII, 119 and P. 370 ff.

fear of God. Just as the prophet has said in Ps. 35:2: "The fear of God is not before their eyes."

Luke 18:10 records what appears in a hypocrite. And the use of Scripture will teach the collation of fear and faith. It is enough to note that fear ought to be referred to our works, and faith to the mercy of God. Faith is the author of holy fear. That faith which is devoid of trust in the godness of God is by necessity impious.

The passage is Ecc. 9:1: "No man knows whether he is worthy of love or hate, but all things are reserved for the future," does not prove that a man is ignorant whether God has pardoned his guilt or not.[101] Besides, I could make it out from this, that a man is ignorant of the fact whether God is angry with sin or not. Nor can I wonder enough at the sublety of Satan on this score, when I see that by the abuse of this passage of Scripture, not only faith has been banished from the hearts of men, but also fear. What is that κυβείαν καὶ πανουργίαν πρὸς τὴν μεθοδείαν πλάνης as Paul calls it (Eph. 4:14) but Parisian theology which so cunningly subverts the Scripture?

---

[101]This was the occasion of much worry to Luther as a monk. cf. E. A. 31, 286. Also Köstlin, Luthers Theologie, II, 470. In Augsburg, Cardinal Cajetan had opposed Luther's assertion: "oportere eum qui ad sacramentum accedit, credere se consecuturum gratiam sacramenti," with this: "potius incertum esse omnem accedentem, gratiam consequeretur necne." Lutheri Acta Augustana opp. V. arg. II, 369. W. A. II, 7. Also the Council of Trent rejects the evangelical notion of security or certainty of faith, when it teaches in Sess. VI cap. IX: "Sed neque illud asserendum est, oportere eos, qui vere justificati sunt, absque ulla omnino dubitatione apud semetipsos seatuere se esse justificatos, neminemque a peccatis absolvi ac justificari nisi eum, qui certo credat se absolutum et justificatum esse; atque hac sola fide absolutionem, et justificationem perfici, quasi qui hoc non credit, de dei promissis, deque mortis et resurrectionis Christi efficacia dubitet: nam sicut nemo pius de dei misericordia, de Christi merito, deque sacramentorum virtute, et efficacia dubitare debet: sic quilibet, dum se ipsum, suamque propriam infirmitatem et indispositionem respicit . . . cum nullus scire valeat certitudine fidei."

In the book of Ecclesiastes, Solomon's general argument appears to be as follows: that human arguments must not judge the judgments of God and hence, he refutes the calumnies which wicked philosophy makes against the judgments of God. I would that this book instead of pestilent philosophy might be exhibited to youths, teaching them how weak hearts might be made strong by the faith and fear of God. As is now the case, philosophic impiety and the wicked works of poets and orators excite natural impiety, which has in turn to be suppressed and removed wholly by the word of God. Therefore Solomon (Ecc. 9:1) says thus: "They are wise"; but that is no reason why they can rely upon either their righteousness or wisdom. "For their works are in the hand of God" . . . How wonderfully in one and the same verse Solomon has taught both fear and faith, when he forbids us to rely upon our righteousness or wisdom! Again since the works of the righteous and the wise are in God's hands, he enjoins us to trust in him who has the very spirit of the wise and just in his power. There follows then this passage: "There are those whom God dislikes; but they cannot be known by man from external appearance, but all things are reserved for the future." That is, human reason judges that those are pleasing to God upon whom God has bestowed gifts, wealth, wisdom, righteousness, and glory; again, it considers those to be hated by God who lack these things.

But insofar, rational judgment is false. For he loves the very most, those who are poor and unfortunate, the vile and the dejected; and he hates the very most, those who immoderately accumulate wealth. You have an example of both in the children of Israel and Pharaoh. Therefore this establishes the fact that we cannot discern between the pious and the impious on the grounds of external events as for instance human reason judges. For if each man would interpret Solomon according to the judgment of his own conscience, then I do not see how a sinner could be ignorant of the hatred of God since nothing is more certain than the fact that God is offended by sin. Then to grant especially that Solomon should be accepted concerning the judgment of the conscience of the saints, you would only make out from this that the saints are not yet secure except in so far as they believe, according to Romans 8:24: "By hope are we saved." But just as they know mercy by faith, so do they trust themselves by faithful fear to the divine will to be judged and condemned, in order to give God the glory. For thus we pray: "Let thy will be done."

You have the example of David in II Sam. 15:25 f.: "If I have found favor in the eyes of the Lord, let him restore me and show it to me, and his tabernacle; if however he has said "you are not pleasing to me," I am ready. Let him do what is good in his own eyes." For fear cannot be separated from faith. Faith beholds only the mercy of God; while fear beholds God's judgment and our works. Paul speaks thus in Roms. 11:20: "Thou standeth by faith; do not be puffed up in thy mind, but fear." Likewise since this whole book of Solomon is for the purpose of teaching that the flesh ought not judge of divine counsels and that having denied ourselves we should both fear and believe God, I am by no means foolish in the opinion that this much can be maintained: we are ignorant of those whom God has chosen and of those whom he has rejected; hence saints may not be haughty nor sinners despair. Besides, as far as I understand them these are Solomon's words: "Every man is ignorant of love and hate in their appearance, the more so because all things come to pass equally to the just and the unjust."

From this it is clear that Solomon is speaking not of the judgment of the conscience of each man, but of the manner of discerning between the pious and impious externally and by other means. What stands written in the Latin text: "all things are reserved for the future," seems to me to be an interpolation for the sake of clarifying the text. For to my knowledge, it is contained in neither the Hebrew nor Greek translations. But these things require a more extended disputation elsewhere. Let the thought be most certain that we who are justified ought to be always most sure of the remission of sins and the benevolence of God upward. Therefore sacraments or signs of the mercy of God have been added to promises, as I shall later discuss, to most certainly testify that we have attained the benevolence of God. Just as a money lender is sure that he will receive his money from the man whose signed αὐτόγραφον of the transaction he possesses, so likewise certain signs, baptism and participation in the table of the Lord have been added to the promises or αὐτογράφοις of Christ, that Christians might be certain that their sins are forgiven. Indeed the saints most certainly know by faith that they are in favor, and that their sins are forgiven. For God who has promised that he will forgive the sin of believers does not fail, although the believers themselves may be uncertain whether they will persevere.

So far, I have said that we ought to be certain of the benevolence of God toward us. What now about the works of God in us? Can we know whether we have conceived the Spirit of God in our heart? I answer: The fruits of the Spirit bear us witness as to what has transacted in our hearts. Gal. 5:24: "They who are of Christ have crucified the flesh." Moreover each person knows whether he hates and abominates sin truly from his heart, and that is the "crucifixion of the flesh." Each person knows whether he fears God, whether he believes God. Hypocrisy indeed emulates the Spirit of God, but temptation discerns it, during which only the faithful endure. Whatsoever you do, see to it that you first believe. For God wills that true glory be attributed to him. Moreover, I shall bring together under several heads, this whole discussion on the law, gospel, and faith.

Summation: Law, Gospel, Faith

1. Law is that teaching which prescribes what ought and what ought not to be done.

2. The gospel is the promise of the grace of God.

3. The law demands the impossible: love of God and neighbor. Roms. 8.

4. They who attempt to express the law through human powers and free will, only feign external works and fail to express the affections which the law demands.

5. Therefore they do not satisfy the law but are hypocrites: "White-washed sepulchres without," as Christ calls them in Matt. 23:27, and Gal. 3:10: "Those who are by the works of the law, are under the curse.

6. Hence it is not the function of the law to justify.

7. But the proper function of the law is to reveal sin and therefore to confound the conscience, Roms. 3:20 "The knowledge of sin is by the law."

8. To the conscience which now knows sin and is confused by the law, Christ is revealed by the gospel.

9. Thus when John preaches repentance, at the same time he shows Christ: "Behold the Lamb of God that taketh away the sins of the world." John 1:29.

10. Faith, by which we believe the gospel showing us Christ, and by which Christ is received as the one who has placated the father, which through grace is given, constitutes our righteousness, John 1:12: "As many as received him, to them gave he the power to become the children of God."

11. If indeed such faith alone justifies us, there is plainly no respect for our merits or our works, but only of Christ's merits.

12. Such a faith pacifies and exhilarates the heart, Roms. 5:1: "Being justified by faith we have peace."

13. And it results that for such kindness, for the fact that sin is forgiven for Christ's sake, God is loved in return and thus the love of God is the fruit of faith.

14. This same faith causes us to be ashamed of the fact that we have offended such a kind and liberal father.

15. And in addition, it causes us to abominate our flesh together with its concupiscences.

16. Human reason neither fears nor believes God but is utterly ignorant of him and despises him, according to Ps. 13:1: "The fool hath said in his heart there is no God." And Luke 16:31: "If they do not hear Moses and the prophets they will not believe even if one would get up from the dead." By this Christ means that the human heart does not believe the word of God. This madness of the human heart Solomon (as instanced by Ecclesiastes 8:11) has reproached: "Because no judgment is quickly brought against the evil, and the sons of man without any fear perpetrate evil things."

17. Because the human heart is utterly ignorant of God, it therefore turns aside to its own counsels and cupidities and sets itself up in the place of God.

18. When God confounds the human heart through

the law by a knowledge of sin, it does not yet know God and certainly not his goodness, and therefore it hates God as though he were an executioner.

19. When God arouses and consoles the human heart by showing Christ through the gospel, precisely then does it know God; for it knows both his power and goodness. This is what Jeremy means when he says in 9:24: "Let him glory in this, that he knoweth me."

20. He who has believed the gospel and knows the goodness of God, his heart is now made erect so that he trusts God and fears him, and consequently abominates the counsels of the human heart.

21. Peter has most aptly said in Acts 15:9: "Hearts are purified by faith."

22. Mercy is revealed by promises.

23. Sometimes these promises are corporal, sometimes spiritual.

24. In the law corporal things are promised such as: the land of Canaan, the kingdom, etc.

25. The gospel is the promise of grace or the forgiveness of sins through Christ.

26. All corporal promises depend on the promise of Christ.

27. For the first promise was of grace or the promise of Christ. Gen. 3:15: "Her seed shall bruise thy head," that is, the seed of Eve should bruise the kingdom of the serpent lying in wait for our heel, that is, sin and death.

28. This promise was renewed in the one made to Abraham, Gen. 12:3 and 18:18: "In thy seed shall all nations be blessed.

29. Wherefore since Christ should be born of Abraham's posterity, the promises which were added to the law concerning the possession of the land, etc., are obscure promises of the coming of Christ. For

these corporal things were promised to the people lest they should die before the promised seed would come, and also that God might in the meantime indicate his mercy and try the people's faith by these corporal things.

30. Upon the birth of Christ, the promises which had been made were consummated and the remission of sins was openly accomplished, for which purpose Christ was to be born.

31. The promises of the Old Testament are signs of the coming of Christ, and therefore of the promise of grace that was to be published in the future.

32. Just as he does not really know God who merely knows that God exists but does not know his power and mercy, in like manner he does not truly believe who merely believes in the existence of God but not his power and mercy.

33. Therefore he truly believes who in addition to threats believes the gospel also; who turns his face to the mercy of God or to Christ who is the pledge of divine mercy.

So far on faith; I shall add a few words on love (caritas) later after I shall have finished the subject on the distinction of law and gospel.

"On the Distinction between the Old and New Testaments and likewise on the Abrogation of the Law."

It can be easily detected what is the difference between the Old and New Testaments from what I have written on the law and the gospel, and the function of each. On this problem as well as on the distinction between law and gospel, the schools wretchedly labor when they call the Old Testament a certain law that demands only external works, and the New Testament a law that demands both works and affections. For this reason it happpens that the majesty and fulness of grace are obscured. And grace ought to be placed in an illustrious position in full sight of all, as it were, and should be shown and alone declared. I shall relate the matter in a few words. Seek from former considerations what the law is and what the gospel. Here I shall discuss the use of the terms.

Those who call the Old Testament simply that which is law, seem to me to be following a custom of speech and not reason. And further, they seem to be using the word Testament commonly for a constitution or institution. I call the Old Testament a promise of physical things joined with a requisition of law. For God both demands righteousness through the law and promises a reward for it: the land of Canaan, wealth, etc., as appears from Deut. 29:10–13: "Stand all of you this day before the Lord your God, your chiefs and tribes and elders and doctors, all the people of Israel, your wives and children and sojourners who are with you in your camps, and the camp followers, etc."

On the other hand, the New Testament is nothing but the promise of all good things without the law. The New Testament promises good things without condition since nothing in turn is demanded of us. And from this you see the fulness of grace and the abundance of the divine mercy. In a word, it is the glorious gospel that bestows salvation gratuitously, without any regard to our righteousness or any of our works.

May not the human heart exclaim aloud concerning such profuse grace? Who believes this report? But this distinction between the Old and New Testaments is indicated by Jer. 31. But in order for it to be more fully known, the subject of the abrogation of the law must be discussed.

Since the law is divided into three parts, I shall relate to what extent each one has been abrogated, especially since they do not seem to have been nullified in the same manner. And then the unanimous opinion of writers is that the judicial and the ceremonial laws have become obsolete, while the moral laws have been renewed. I shall first speak about the moral laws.

That part of the law called the decalogue or moral precepts has been antiquated by the New Testament, is proven from the quotation which the author of Hebrews uses when he says that the law has been divinely abrogated, because the people have made it invalid. Heb. 8:9 and Jer. 31:31. Moreover Israel sinned not only against the ceremonies, but against the decalogue which Christ in the gospel calls the chief part of the whole law. Likewise when the prophet calls the gospel a "New pact," he perceived that the old is antiquated as Hebrews 8:13 says: "by calling it New he has made the first Old." And in I Tim. 1:9 we read: "The law was not founded for the righteous man." In both Romans and Galatians there are to be found many such witnesses of liberty. For who is ignorant of that well-known passage in Gal. 5:13?: "Ye are free, but notwithstanding do not give liberty an occasion for the flesh." Nay more, most vile shall have been our Christian liberty and more than servitude, if it abolishes merely the ceremonies, the portion of the law most easily borne. For who does not sacrifice a sheep with less difficulty than he controls wrath, love or like passions? And so it must be confessed that the decalogue even has been antiquated.

Therefore the question arises shall we be permitted to do as we please? To kill at will, or to lie at will, etc.?

This same question occurs in Roms. 6:15 when Paul says: "Seeing that we are not under the law, shall we therefore sin?" Moreover Christian liberty consists in this, that every right of the law to condemn and accuse us has been taken away. The law curses those who have not once for all absolved the whole law. But does not the whole law demand the highest love toward God, the most vehement fear of him? Since our whole nature is entirely foreign to these matters, although we may exhibit an exceeding wonderful Pharisaism, nevertheless we are guilty of the curse. Christ has taken upon himself this curse of the law, this right of the law, so that although you have sinned, although right now you have sin—for I must use the language of Scripture—nevertheless you are saved. The power of death, the power of sin, the very gates of hell have been broken by our Samson. That is what Paul writes to the Galatians 3:13: "Christ has redeemed us from the curse of the law, having been made a curse for us." Likewise 4:4: "When the fulness of time came, God sent his son, born of a woman, born under the law, that he might redeem those who were under the law." And Roms. 6:14: "Sin shall not have the dominion over you: for ye are not under the law, but under grace."

This is the security which the prophets always so heartily celebrate namely, that they are above any power of the law who are in Christ; that is, although you sin, although you have sinned, you cannot be condemned. For it says in I Cor. 15:54, 55: "Death is swallowed up in victory. O death, where is thy victory?" etc. These things ought to be impressed upon Christians firstly in all other cases, but especially when they come to die; for to the dying this is the one remaining, truly sacred anchor, as the old proverb puts it. And this is the liberty which Paul almost everywhere preaches, whereas on the other hand he scarcely touches upon ceremonies in one or two other passages. Nor is the New Testament anything else but a promulgation of this liberty. This is what the prophet has most appositely signified in Psalm 2:6: "I have set my king upon the Holy Hill of Sion." Here the father says he will ordain a King for Mount Sion. Afterward, he reveals what sort of a kingdom it will be, obviously when God will rule by his word and not by human strength or the power of the world. Therefore he adds, 2:6: "I shall declare a mandate, the Lord hath said unto me: thou art my son." What will this new declaration be? Was the word of God, to be sure the law, previously declared on Mount Sion or not? Now indeed this is abrogated by a new declaration when the word about the Son Christ is instituted.

But if nothing else is declared except that the son is Christ, it follows that the righteousness of the law and works are not to be exacted nor anything else demanded, but that we kiss the son. This is what he more clearly says later: "Blessed are all they who trust in him." Your own righteousness will not save you, nor your own wisdom; but this son will save you, this son who is your king, your fortress, etc. There are many such passages in Scripture which commend this liberty unto us. For on the whole, what is the gospel but a publishing of this liberty?

Finally: Christianity is liberty, because those who have not the spirit of Christ can by no means do the law, and are guilty of the curses of the law. They who have been renewed by the spirit of Christ, going of their own accord even without the law dictating, are let to do those things which the law has ordered. The will of God is the law. And the Holy Spirit is but the living will of God and a motion. Wherefore when we have been regenerated by the Spirit of God which is the living will of God, we will already of our own accord, the very things which the law has demanded.

In regard to this notion Paul has said in I Tim. 1:19: "The law was not made for the just man." And in Roms. 8:2: "The law, which is the spirit of life," that is, the law as a motion of the Spirit giving life, "has made me free from the law of sin and of death." Besides St. Augustine copiously treats of Christian liberty in a book titled *The Spirit and the Letter*. In Jer. 31: 31–34 you have as follows: "Behold the days come saith the Lord that I shall make a new covenant with the house of Israel and the house of Judah, not after the covenant which I made with your fathers in the day in which I took their hand to lead them out of the land of Egypt, a pact which they made void and I was angry with them, saith the Lord. But this shall be the nature of the covenant which I shall make with the house of Israel: after those days, saith the Lord, I shall give my law in their inner parts and write it on their hearts, and I shall be to them a God, they to me a people. And a man shall teach his neighbor and a man his brother saying: Know the Lord. For all shall know me, from the least to the greatest, saith the Lord. Because I shall propitiate their iniquity, and their sin shall I no more remember." In this passage the prophet mentions a twofold covenant, the one old and the other new. The old one or justification by the law, has been made void. For who could fulfill the law? Moreover, because the exaction has been done away with, the law must now be written upon hearts in order to be expressed. Therefore liberty does not mean that we do not do the law, but that we will and desire spontaneously from our hearts that which the law demands. This is exactly what no can could do formerly. Ezek.

11:19: "I shall take away the stony heart from their flesh, and give them a heart of flesh, that they may walk in my precepts and keep my judgments and do them, and may be to me for a people."

You have it to what extent we are free from the decalogue. In the first place, that although sinners yet it cannot condemn those who are in Christ; then secondly, that those who are in Christ are driven by the Spirit to do the law, and by the Spirit do it. They love and fear God, administer to the necessities of their neighbors, and desire those very things which the law has demanded, and would do them even had no law been given. For their will, to be sure the Spirit, is nothing other than a living law.

To this degree even the fathers before the incarnation of Christ were free, as many as had the spirit of Christ.[102] Peter sees this same thing in Acts 15:10, when he denies that they could do the law: "Neither we," says he "nor the fathers could endure. But by faith were they justified." That is, although the fathers could not satisfy the law, they knew that they too were free through Christ and were justified by faith in Christ, not by the merits of their own works or righteousness. For Peter is not merely Speaking of ceremonies here, but of the law as a whole. For the law of ceremonies can by no means be kept without also keeping the decalogue. For ceremonies are not done before God except they are done by a faithful, spontaneous heart. And what is more, Peter was *not* arguing that the external works of ceremonies could not be done. For

---

[102]Quotquot spiritum Christi habuere: Melanchthon has fallen into the mistake of failing to see that the history of the Old Covenant has gone over into the form of a history of the people of the Old Testament. Luther likewise shared this erroneous idea for some time. cf. Köstlin, Luthers Theologie I, 162.

what is easier than the discharge of a few little ceremonies? If you enumerate how many more papal rites there are in the church today than you see in Moses, you can collect the Mosaic ceremonies in a very few verses, but larger volumes of decrees and decretals are not enough to contain the papal rites. How different are the Roman Pontiffs from Peter in whom they glory as their predecessor. Peter abrogated these few little ceremonies handed down by divine law, while they in every age invent new and foolish ones. Therefore it can be seen that Peter has argued in Acts not only of ceremonies, but of the law as a whole.

In Romans 6, 7, and 8, Paul gives a long disputation about this freedom, teaching that only the new man is free. Hence, we are free insofar as we have been renewed. Insofar as we are flesh and age, we are under the law; although what is left of the old, is condoned in believers for the same of their faith. In a word, as far as we believe, we are free; and as far as we show diffidence, we are under the law. Luther in his Antilatome[103] has copiously treated the subject of sin in saints or the residue of the Old Man in regenerated persons, so that I find it unnecessary to say any more about the subject. Especially so since Paul so clearly states that he is still a captive of sin. Augustine and Cyprian have done likewise in several places. For here we have just begun our justification and have not entirely completed it. Thus Paul forthwith orders us to be changed by the renewing of our minds. And in Philippians 3:12, he says that he has not already attained, is not yet perfect, but that he follows on "to

---

[103] In Antilatomo: The work of Luther which made its appearance in August 1521: "Rationis Latomianæ pro incendiariis Lovaniensis scholæ sophistis redditæ confutatio." See the Erlangen Edition of Luther's works V. arg. V, 397 and especially page 463 ff.

apprehend." Therefore when the abrogation of the law is discussed, it must be considered in how far the gospel antiquated the decalogue rather than that ceremonies and judicial laws have been abolished. For from the abrogation of the decalogue, the fulness of grace can be most nearly discerned, if you please, since he has argued that believers are saved from the exaction of the law and with no respect of works. Therefore the law has been abrogated, not however to the degree that it does not exist, but only that it does not condemn and cannot be made to do so.

Concerning judicial and ceremonial laws, I would that they had more exactly discussed the matter who have referred liberty to these alone. And with respect to these it must be accurately observed what Paul says, I Cor. 7:19: "Circumcision is nothing," and in Galatians 5:6: "In Christ Jesus neither circumcision nor uncircumcision profiteth, but only the new creature." Likewise note I Cor. 10:26 where he writes: "The earth is the Lord's and the fulness thereof." These things prove that this is Christian liberty, that you can use external matters of this nature or not use them. Thus Paul circumcises one and refuses to circumcise another. Sometimes he accommodated himself to those who observed Jewish rites, sometimes he withstood them. Let us have this same liberty. They do no sin who are circumcised, nor do they sin who omit it. Besides it is rather unfortunate that Hieronymus has fabricated concerning ancient ceremonies. And yet today they generally follow him. But they sin who think circumcision is necessary, and are circumcised for this, that they might be justified or that they might do a good work. Again, they also sin who omit circumcision in this respect, that they may be justified. When Hieronymus forbids circumcision, he errs just as much as the Jews erred when they demanded it. If anyone ordered the eating of pork flesh, he shall have erred as much as the one who forbids it. And this was Paul's method. He refused to circumcise Timothy when he saw that the Jews demanded circumcision and therefore the doctrine of faith was obscured, since they attributed justification to circumcision and not to faith.

The same thing must be observed in moral works, that just as you eat and drink not with a view to being justified, so also you give alms not with a view to being justified. But as you eat and drink to satisfy the bodily needs, so also give alms and love your brother, in order to serve common necessity and that by this you may coerce lust and subject the body to the spirit. As eating, drinking, sleeping, standing, and sitting do not justify, so also not only circumcision, but such moral works as chastity, serving the necessities of your brethren and the like do not justify. For faith alone justifies according to Roms. 1:7: "The just man shall live by faith." Moreover this freedom in moral matters as necessary as it is to know, is so obscure that it cannot be understood save by the spiritual.

Therefore what I have said stands: the judicial or ceremonial laws are not abrogated to the extent that he sins who might use any of them. But Christianity is liberty of the sort that it is left with us to use them or not use them, even as it is within our power to eat or drink. But I would desire Christians to use that form of judicial laws handed down by Moses, and in addition, many of the ceremonies. And since human necessity indeed demands judicial and ceremonial laws (as is my belief), it would be better to use the Mosaic laws in preference to Gentile laws and Papal ceremonies.[104]

THE LOCI COMMUNES

To come nearer to the point, one and the same is the reason why the whole law, not only ceremonies and judicial formulas, but the decalogue as well, was abrogated: because it could not be fulfilled. Peter in Acts gave this reason for the abrogation of the law; and also Jeremy when he teaches that a new covenant is to be entered into because we have made the old one null. And in this passage he makes no exception of any part of the law, seeing that he is speaking apparently of the law as a whole. However the law is antiquated only in those who have believed the second covenant, and that is the gospel. And so, those who have the spirit of Christ are forthwith free from every law.

Moreover, this is why the saints do the decalogue: because the decalogue in addition to righteousness of heart, does not demand certain distinctions of place, seasons, events and persons; and because the Spirit is the very justification of the heart. The decalogue cannot but be fulfilled even though the law has been abrogated. For as the sun cannot but shine when it rises, so also the decalogue cannot but be kept when the Spirit has been diffused into the heart of the saints. Again, the spiritual man is free to this degree; that unless the Spirit himself according to his nature in conjunction with him would effect the fulfillment of the decalogue, we ourselves indeed would not do so. Now when the Spirit produces this kind of will which is

---

[104]This thought which Jakob Strauss in a false comprehension of the principle of Scripture had attempted to advance by setting up the Mosaic law by an abrogation of the existing laws of the country, was shared by many during this period. Luther had often declared that the Scripture is a worldly law-book and set the Mosaic law over against the existing laws (nostra jura civilia sub quibus vivimus) cf. De Wette, II, 489. Enders IV, 305. Moreover Melanchthon a year and a half later had returned from the view expressed above, and attempted to weave it in upon Strauss in this sense.

itself the fulfillment of the decalogue, the law is done not because it is demanded, but because the spiritual man cannot do otherwise.

Judicial and ceremonial laws aside from righteousness of the heart, are external observations circumscribed by things, persons, places, and seasons. Because the Spirit with himself does not necessarily discharge these observations, there is therefore no reason why we are to do them. The Spirit of God cannot be in the heart without expressing the decalogue. Therefore the decalogue is necessarily to be done. The Spirit can be in the human heart even without these external observations. Therefore these judicial and ceremonial laws are not necessarily to be done. It is apparent from this that the decalogue for the most part contains negative laws, in order to signify that there is not certain work circumscribed by persons, places, and times demanded, but rather that righteousness of heart is demanded. The remaining laws distribute and dispense external matters. I am content with having pointed out that the decalogue has been antiquated not to the extent that it no longer is, but that it does not condemn us if we are in any way delinquent; and also, that it might be fulfilled. And to such a degree is this the liberty of the conscience which perceives by faith, that sin has been forgiven.

Therefore people think that the ceremonial laws have been abrogated for the most part, because they were shadows of the gospel, of which there is no more need since the body, that is, the gospel itself is now manifest. Now I by no means know whether Paul ever followed this reason or not.

In Col. 2:16 he says: "Let no man judge you in meat or drink or in feast days or new moons or sabbaths, which are shadows of things to come, but the body is

Christ." Perhaps in this passage he may seem to be talking of the nature of a type. Certainly in Galatians he rejects ceremonies on the grounds that they do not justify. The same is argued throughout the entire epistle of the Hebrews, namely, that not only the ceremonies but the whole law has been abrogated for this reason: it could not justify, or as I have said above, it could not be fulfilled. In chapter 7:18 it is written: "Rejection of the former mandate because of its weakness and uselessness." And when he discussed the priesthood, he concluded that the Levitical priesthood was annulled on the grounds that it has not effected the remission of sins, but that our Highpriest Christ effects it. You see that this one reason for the abrogation of the law is pressed and urged in the Scripture: the law was abrogated because it did not justify or, because it could not be kept. The schools do away with ceremonies alone because they were types of the gospel. The decalogue remains because it does not seem τυπικὸς (Typical).

But what has this to do with the commendation of grace? The Scripture talks of the abrogation of the law so that everywhere in it, it commends the fulness of grace unto us. It does away with the ceremonies in such a manner that it appears that the whole law has been done away. It so rejects the ceremonies that it is evident that the ceremonies have been abolished. Not that they may not be performed, but because they can be performed or omitted without endangering the conscience: because they do not condemn when omitted, nor justify if you have performed them. It is enough to have pointed out these things. Seek the general nature of them in Galatians and Hebrews. When Augustine somewhere seeks for the cause of the abrogation of the law, he talks of nothing but figures.

Scripture therefore abrogates the law because it does not justify. Why then was the law? To reveal sin or convict of sin, and to show openly that we need the mercy of God.

Now about the forms of judicial laws. I am of the opinion that they have been abrogated because they are external observations just like cermonies, which a free spirit may or may not use at will. It is not permissible for a Christian to contend in court, but that is not the reason why the law was abrogated. For although they sin who make litigations[105] it is necessary nevertheless that laws and courts exist by which the profligate may be restrained. Nor do they sin who judge or declare the law. The Mosaic law was not given to be litigation material to citizens, but to be a formula of judgment for magistrates. Therefore there ought to be no dispute whether one who litigates can use the Mosaic law. For he is not a Christian who litigates. Ought a Christian judge use the Mosaic law alone? Here I answer, it is a judge's prerogative to use it or not. For it is a disposition of external matters in no way pertaining to Christianity just as eating and drinking. Paul demands that a judge be only a wise man and one in whom the Spirit of Christ dwells. I Cor. 6:2: "Know ye not that the saints will judge of the world?" Likewise verse 5: "For is there not any wise man among you who can judge?", etc.

It is clear from these passages that he requires not some certain law, but the judgment of a spiritual man. Sometimes he even approves of the sword of the nations (concerning which I shall have something to say

---

[105]Melanchthon overlooks the fact that to a Christian who goes to court without hatred, it is more of penalty or suffering than a deed or act committed in sin. Therefore because of it he can say: "Ut peccent, qui litigant."

later) and calls it an ordinance of God. Moreover laws constitute the most powerful part of the sword. And thus the sword of the nations and the laws of the nations were used by Naaman the Syrian and Nebuchadnezzar and by others, if they were pious princes of the nations. And I do not doubt but that Daniel and other Israelites did so among the Assyrians. Certainly the Roman guard stationed in Judæ used the sword of the nations. And in Luke 3:14 John gave his approbation in these words: "Extort money from no man, do not any calumny and be content with your wages." Such an one was Cornelius in Acts 13:7–12.

I have enumerated these things that it may be understood that civil and external dispensation of things in no way pertains to the righteousness of the Spirit, precisely as plowing a field, or building a house, or mending shoes do not refer in any way to the righteousness of the Spirit; and also that it is within the right of Christians to use or not use the Mosaic forms of judging, although I would wish that these laws were received in preference to the Gentile and often foolish laws. For we have been ingrafted to that "Olive Tree."[106] And it would be becoming to prefer the word of God to human constitutions. Nor is there today scarcely any other use for Roman law than that forensic pettifoggers in their litigations may have something on which to feed themselves.

To what degree the law has been made old, I am of the opinion can in some measure be learned, from what I have already said. The Spirit by using the Scriptures

---

[106] It need scarcely be remarked, that this presumptive scriptural ground (Roms. 11:24) contains a false transmission of the historical aspect of salvation over to the sphere of natural life. Therefore came the natural antipathy for the Roman law which Melanchthon shared with many of his contemporaries, and which appears in many flyleaves of this time.

will indeed teach with greater certainty. Nor can this liberty be understood save by the spiritual.

Moreover you may say, if they are free who have the Spirit of Christ, were then David and Moses likewise free also? Mos certainly so. For that is what Peter means in Acts 15:12 f: "Neither we nor our fathers could bear, but we believe that we are saved through the grace of our Lord Jesus Christ, even as also they." That means: the fathers knew that all their works were sins; they knew too that they did not merit salvation by any works of their own but yet were without the mercy of God. And so they believed and were saved by trusting in mercy; and when they had received the Spirit of God, they sensed that they were free from the curse of the law, and hence from every burden or exaction of the law. But the reason why they did not omit ceremonies was that this freedom had not yet been revealed, the gospel of freedom had not yet been promulgated. Wherefore they bore the law in no way unwillingly, although perceiving that they were justified by faith. You can see that they never properly used their freedom, as is evidenced from I Sam. 21:6: David ate the shew bread which was a thing unlawful for all save a priest. But David made an illustrious prophecy concerning liberty when he said: "The way is indeed polluted but it is sanctified by the vessels." That is, they are pure because they were faithful, and all things are made holy by the faith of the saints such as food, works, etc. Paul says the same thing in Tit. 1:15: "To the pure all things are pure, to the polluted nothing is pure."

Summation: We are free by faith from the whole law, but this same faith, that Spirit of Christ which we have received, mortifies the remainder of sin in our flesh. Not because the law demands it, but because that is the very nature of the Spirit that it cannot but mortify the flesh. This is what Paul says in Roms. 8:1: "There is now no condemnation in them that are in Christ Jesus." He means thereby those who believe: and since they are already redeemed from the curse of the law, since they are already saved, these very persons walk not after the flesh; that is, since the Spirit rules in them, therefore the remainder of the flesh is crucified. Indeed laws will be prescribed for believers by which the Spirit will mortify the flesh. For liberty is not yet consummated but only begun, until the Spirit increases and the flesh is killed. There is a use for the decalogue in the mortification of the flesh, but no use for ceremonial or judicial laws. It thus results that believers have use of the decalogue, but not of the rest of the laws.

On the Old and the New Man

I have said that liberty is not yet entirely completed because sanctification is not yet perfected in us. For we have begun to be sanctified by the Spirit of God and are sanctified until the flesh is forthwith killed. Thus it is that the nature of the saints is twofold: spirit and flesh, the new man and the old man, the inner man and the outer man. "Flesh" not only designates "body" as I have argued above, but plainly the whole man; or as Paul in I Cor. 2:14 calls it, ψυχικὸς, that is, he who is subject to the natural affections and emotions. The "old man" and the "outer man" signify the same as "flesh." Flesh is all the human affections according to nature. Not only to be hungry or thirsty but also to love wealth, glory and the like. Again "spirit" means first the "Holy Spirit himself," and secondly his "motion" in us. The "new man" or the "inner man" are "spirit" because they have been regenerated by the Holy Spirit. John 3:6: "That which is born of the Spirit is spirit." Therefore we are holy as far as we are "spirit" or as far as we are renewed. In the flesh, in the old man, in the outer man, there is still sin. Thus says the Apostle in Gal. 5:17: "The flesh striveth against the spirit and the spirit against the flesh." The Parisian Sophists say that concupiscence in the flesh of saints is not sin, but "infirmity." Luther has fully refuted them in his work titled *Antilatomus*. And too, what is clearer than the fact that whatever is averse to the law of God is sin? Then why don't they call concupiscence sin? Do not the saints seek their own? Do not the saints have love of life, glory, security, tranquillity, and possessions? The reason the Parisians have not called these things sin is that they have not considered the nature of the affections, but have thought that one sins by external actions. They do not see the root of works. Thus it happens that they foolishly judge concerning the fruits. What work is so good but that in it nature does not seek something of its own?

Granting that you have put away the love of glory, notwithstanding you have not yet put away the fear of punishments. Therefore the flesh pollutes works be they ever so good. Now if one sins in no other respect, have we not most cruelly and violently transgressed by the very sluggishness or inactivity of the spirit? One ought burn with love for God and trust in him; one ought be terrified by the fear of God, for these things are demanded in the first precept. But who fulfills them? Let us confess then that it is a fact that sin is in our flesh. And this is the glorious mercy of God, that sin is forgiven unto those who believe. Nor does the abrogation of the law mean anything else but that the right of the law has been taken away by

Christ to this degree, to wit, the condemnation of sinners. There are some who divide man into three parts, spirit, soul, and body. I do not condemn this view, provided they grant me that strictly speaking, spirit is not a part of man's nature but is divine agitation, and body and soul, that is nature without the spirit, cannot but sin, and moral virtues do not absolve it from sin.[107] Paul in Philippians 3:8 says that he considers as losses and dung, that righteousness which he had rendered by natural attempts with the assistance of the law. Why then do the defaming Sophists boast of natural works even to the point of doing violence to the gospel? For nothing so obscures the fulness of grace as that impious doctrine of moral works.

Paul rejoices that he is found in Christ, not having his own righteousness from the law, but that righteousness that is through the faith of Christ and that comes from God. But the Sophists consider even a merit of the law as righteousness.

On Mortal and Daily Sin

In the above discussion of sin I purposely omitted to treat of the forms of sin, mortal and venial, as is the usual division. Every work of a man who is not in Christ is a mortal sin, because it is the evil fruit of an evil tree, the flesh. "The mind of the flesh is death," says Paul in Roms. 8:6. In verse 7 he says: "The carnal mind is enmity against God." And further,

---

[107]Sunt qui tres hominis partes: In this and the subsequent discussion the author does not correctly distinguish trichotomy. If the three parts belong in a similar manner to the nature of man, he cannot say of the last two only, "mind and body," that they are sinful. And too on the other hand, the question arises was the Spirit as "agitatio divina" already in those who have not been "born again?" According to our position one would have to deny it, and Melanchthon says man as a creature lives "per agitationem divinam."

verse 8: "They who are in the flesh cannot please God." In these passages "flesh" must be construed necessarily as meaning the whole nature of man, and, too, the most illustrious powers of nature as I have said before.

Indeed no other part of man is any more flesh than that supreme faculty of reason, because in it is ignorance of God, and contempt for him; likewise incredulity and similar pests, the fruits and works of which are all human functions. On the other hand, all the works of the saints are venial sins, to be sure, because believers are forgiven through the mercy of God. God never takes the Spirit from the saints so that they fall into the manifest crimes rightly denominated moral sins. And I do not gainsay this denomination provided they know that I call them mortal to this degree: whatever is done by those who have not the Spirit of God.[108] What the Sophists now call "mortal sins"[109] were one time generally called "crimes," and what they now call "venial sins" were given the names of "acts openly evil" and "daily sins."

I believe that one ought especially notice what I have said about the law and the gospel, and the Old and New Testaments. I am aware of the fact that these very things have been treated with less dignity than the case demanded, but I do not wish to be called Rabbi. The use of Scripture will abundantly supply what I have left out. I have thought it sufficient to indicate

---

[108]These sentences also allude to the already expressed view of the "Mechanical comprehension" of the work of the divine Spirit in the regenerated. But human self-determination and responsibility in the development of the Christian life are not sufficiently calculated by the author.

[109]Quæ isti venialia: on the history of the concept mortal sin cf. Zöckler, especially the section that deals with the seven principal sins. Luther attacked the problem in his sermon on repentance. Erlangen A. 16, 46. Vide: O. Zöckler: Lehrstueck von den sieben Hauptsuenden. Muenchen, 1893.

what you should seek after in Scripture above all else. Moreover you will seek after law and gospel. The law reveals sin and terrifies the conscience. Sin is forgiven by the gospel, and the Spirit is revealed, who inflames the heart to do the law. If you should rightly consider the word testament, the Old Testament shall have been a τύπος of the New Testament and not a testament as one in which the testator has departed. In the New Testament the testator has departed. In the Old Testament sheep were slaughtered as a type of the testator, which did signify the death of the testator. But these require more discussion than the nature of this commentary admits. At this place it is also customary to dispute about the letter and the Spirit, but I prefer you to consult either Augustine or Luther in preference to me, although I have made bold to touch upon them above when I discussed the nature of the law.

On Signs

I have said that the gospel is the promise of grace. Moreover next to promises is the place of signs. For in the Scripture signs are added to the promises for a mark. These signs remind us of the promises and are sure testimonies of the divine will toward us. They also bear witness that of a certainty we will receive what God has promised unto us. Gross errors are made in the use of signs. For when the schools dispute about the difference between the sacraments of the Old and the New Testaments[110] they deny that the sacraments of the Old Testament had any power to justify. They attribute to the New Testament sacraments (though

---

[110] The history of the distinction between the Old and New Testament sacraments which was first set forth by St. Ambrose, has been carefully and minutely traced by Ludw. Hahn: Die Lehre von den Sakramenten, Breslau 1864, S. 43 ff.

by a manifest error)[111] the power to justify. For faith alone justifies.

Moreover, what is the nature of signs can be most easily understood from Paul's epistle to the Romans. In the fourth chapter the following discussion of circumcision is contained. According to Paul, Abraham was not justified by circumcision, but before it and without its merit. He did however later receive circumcision as σφραγίδα δικαιοσύνης; that is, as a sign, by which God would witness that Abraham was just, and by which Abraham himself would be conscious of the fact that he was just in the sight of God, lest fluctuating in a doubtful conscience he might give himself over to despair. If you understand this function, what can come about more joyfully than signs? It is not enough for signs to remind one of the promises; it is a matter of great importance though that they are a sure testimony of the divine will toward us.

Thus Moses (Gen. 14:11) calls circumcision a sign: "That it may be unto you for a sign of the covenant between me and you." Because circumcision is a sign it reminds Abraham of the divine promise, and not only him alone but all who were circumcised. Because

---

[111] Justificatio according to scholastic formulation consisted of "remissio peccati" and "infusio gratiæ." Man is placed in another state or relationship by the last element, and is made righteous. The mediation of this grace is made in a particular manner through the sacraments: "They are the canals or channels through which grace passes and is branched off into different dirertions." The passion of Christ is the principal source of human salvation, but in the language of Thomas the sacraments are still very necessary: Quia operantur in virtute passionis Christi et passio Christi quodammodo applicatur hominibus per sacramenta." While the power of the sacraments has this ground, it is not possible to ascribe such efficacy to the Old Testament sacraments. cf. Summa III, qu. 61 art. I. Although Melanchthon does not share the same view of "Justification," he must nevertheless deny the efficacy of the Old Testament sacraments. Above all he must deny their magical power. Luther at Augsburg contended against Cardinal Cajetan, in his work "Resolutions to the 95 Theses."

circumcision is a sign of the covenant, that is, because it signifies that the covenant will be ratified, it confirms the conscience of Abraham. Hence it results that he doubts nothing but that it will come to pass just what has been promised. Doubting nothing, I say, but that God will fulfill just what he has promised. But what did God promise to Abraham? Was it not that he would be a God to Abraham, that is, did he not promise to embrace Abraham, to save and justify him? So Abraham doubted not but that these things were sure, having been confirmed by circumcision as it were a mark.

Run through the whole of Scripture if you will and seek out the nature of signs from the sacred histories, but not from the impious Sophists. The Lord extends Hezekiah's life because of Isaiah's prayer. Now that the king may know for a certainty that this promise will be kept, God confirms it by the addition of a sign: the shadow of the horologe should be turned back ten degrees (II Kings 20). Lest Gideon should doubt that Israel would be liberated under his leadership, he was confirmed by two signs (Judges 6). Isaiah (7:13 f.) upbraids Ahaz for disdaining the sign of the divine will toward him. For he believed not the promise. But why heap up any more incidents of this sort when Scripture abounds in such examples? I believe the use of signs can be learned from the examples already given.

Signs do not justify, as Paul says in I Cor. 7:19: "Circumcision is nothing," and so baptism and participation in the Lord's table are nothing but witnesses καὶ σφραγίδες of the divine will toward you. And your conscience, if at all in doubt, is rendered certain by them of the grace and benevolence of God toward it. As Hezekiah could not doubt the fact that he would recover when he had both heard the promise and had seen it confirmed by a sign; as Gideon could not doubt the fact that he would be a victor, when he was confirmed by so many signs; just so, ought you not doubt the fact that you have attained mercy, when you have heard the gospel preached and received its σφραγίδας baptism, and the body and blood of the Lord. But if you will, Hezekiah could have been restored to his health even without a sign had he been willing only to believe the bare promise. Likewise Gideon would have been victorious without a sign, if he had believed. So you can be justified without a sign provided you believe.

Indeed signs do not justify, but the faith of Hezekiah and that of Gideon likewise had to be supported, strengthened, and confirmed by such signs. In such manner is our weakness strengthened by signs lest amid so many insults of sin, it may despair of God's mercy. Just as you would consider it a sign of divine favor were God to talk face to face with you, or show you some peculiar pledge of mercy such as a miracle, so in like manner it behooves you to perceive concerning these signs that you believe that God has commiserated you when you receive baptism or participate in the Lord's table just as certainly as you would seem to believe, if God talked face to face with you or showed you some other miracle that pertains particularly to yourself. For signs were instituted for the purpose of exciting faith. Now however, both faith and the use of signs have been extinguished, by those who extract gain from them. The knowledge of signs is most salubrious, and I by no means know anything else that so consoles the conscience and more efficaciously confirms it than the use of signs.

Some call them sacraments; but I call them signs, or if you so will, sacramental signs. For Paul calls

Christ himself a sacrament.[112] And if the word sign displeases you, call them σφραγίδες by which term the force of sacraments may be more properly signified. Moreover they are of a credible will who have compared these signs to military signs or tokens, because they were only marks by which it might be known to whom the divine promises pertained. For example, Cornelius was baptized though already justified. This was done that he might be reckoned among the number of those to whom the promise of God's kingdom and eternal life belonged. Now I have pointed out these things about the nature of signs in order to give a proper understanding of the pious use of signs. And, too, I have done so to prevent anyone from following the Sophists who have indeed attributed our justification to signs. They did this however by a horrible error.[113]

In the gospel moreover, Christ has instituted two signs, to wit, baptism and the Table of the Lord.[114] For I judge sacramental signs to be those that have been divinely given as tokens of God's grace. For we

---

[112]Melanchthon means either Col. 1:27 where the Vulgate reads: "Quibus voluit deus notas facere divitias gloriæ sacramenti huius in gentibus, quod est Christus," or I Tim. 3:16 where it reads: "Et manifeste magnum est pietatis sacramentum," etc. Jerome has here translated μυστήριον by the Latin "sacramentum."

[113]Melanchthon already in "Lucubratincula" (C. R. 21:42) and the "propositiones de missa" (C. R. I: 478 ff) had contended against the magical and mechanistic assertions of the Scholastic theologians. With a slight difference he concurs with Luther's opinions expressed in "de captivitate babyl." cf. Lutheri opp. V. arg. V, 64. Also see Luther's famous Sermon on the New Testament, respecting his views of the Roman Catholic Mass. E. A. 27, 148.

[114]Luther in his Babylonian Captivity, speaks of three sacraments, the third being Penance (Busse). Likewise Melanchthon in the Lucubratincula: "Ideoque in novo Testamento: Sacramenta sunt proprie Baptizari, Absolvi et Vesci corpore dominico." C. R. 21:42. On the other hand, in the writing under the name Didymus Faventinus he says: "duo sunt omnino in ecclesia divinæ gratiæ signa, quæ vulgus sacramenta vocat, baptismus et eucharistia, nam poenitentia non est aliud nisi quædam baptismi recordatio." C. R. 1, 350.

men cannot institute a sign of the divine will toward us, nor refer those signs as signifying the divine will, which Scripture has referred to another. I wonder the more, what has entered the minds of the Sophists, especially since they would attribute our justification to signs, to cause them to reckon among signs those things of which the Scripture does not mention even one word. For whence has the priestly order been invented?[115] And too, God never instituted marriage to be a proper sign of grace. The rite of unction is older than the sign of grace. Luther has copiously treated this matter in his "Babylonian Captivity." From it you may seek a more exact discussion of this subject. But this is the sum of the matter: grace is not signified with certainty and indeed properly, except by those signs which have been divinely transmitted. Thus only those which have been added to the divine promises can be rightly called sacramental signs. The ancients were accustomed to say here that sacraments consist of things and words. The thing is the sign, the words the promise of grace.

On Baptism

The Sophists have copiously and superstitiously treated of both the matter and form of the sacraments (so they say) showing however no use for the thing itself. It is a sign to be immersed in water. The minis-

---

[115]Nam unde confictus ordo est?: From this we learn that Melanchthon already taught the universal priesthood; and Luther in December of 1519 in a letter to George Spalatin, distinguishes the priesthood from the laity by calling the former "ministerio, quo sacramenta et verbum ministrantur." He adds: cætera omnia sunt æqualia, si cæremonias et humana stututa demas, et satis miramur, unde ordo nomen sacramenti invenerit. Mira hæc tibi nonne? Sed præsens plura una cum Philippo, quoniam has res et sæpe et acute tractavimus." De Wette I, 378.

ter who immerses signifies a work of God[116] and in addition also signifies that the immersion is a sign of the divine will, when he says he baptizes in the name of the Father and of the Son and of the Holy Spirit, or as the early Apostles in Acts baptized, in the name of Christ. The following is plainly indicated by these words: Behold! because you are immersed you ought receive it as a sure testimony of divine favor toward you, just as if God himself baptizes. Hezekiah considered it a testimony of divine favor because God by a wonderful consequence turned back the shadow of the horologe. The Israelitish people regarded it a testimony of divine favor because the waters in the Arabian Sea opened up to them. In like fashion, you shall consider it (immersion) as a sure pledge of divine grace. For the words: in the name of the Father and of the Son and of the Holy Spirit denote that the Father, Son and Holy Spirit mutually baptize. And he who is baptized should interpret that his sins are remitted unto him by the Father, and the Son, and the Holy Spirit. It is agreed that baptism—for from this its use will be learned—signifies a passing through death unto life, and is a submersion of the Old Adam into death, and an awakening of the New Adam.[117] That is why Paul (Tit. 3:5) calls it the bath of regeneration. This signification will be most easily understood from the use of a type.

---

[116]Significat dei opus: cf. Luther in De Captivitate babylonica," where he uses identical language: "Est enim opus dei, non hominis." opp. V. arg. V, 60.

[117]That Melanchthon is dependent on Luther's ideas in the Babylonian Captivity is noticeable from these not very clear assertions on baptism. Therefore it is instructive to observe how Luther's thoughts are somewhat displaced by Melanchthon so that he does not place the emphasis as does Luther on the word or "promissio gratiæ," but on "mortificatio." For instance compare:—et certam reddit de gratia dei adeoque efficit, ut ne desperemus in mortificatione. Proinde quantisper mortificatio durat, tantisper signi usus est, etc.

Baptism was adumbrated by the children of Israel as they passed through the Arabian Sea. Upon what else did they enter but death when they resigned themselves to the water and waves? They went across by faith through the waters, through death, until they made their escape. In this tradition was performed the very thing that is signified by baptism, that is: the Israelites passed through death unto life. Thus the whole Christian life is a mortification of the flesh, and a renewal of the spirit. That which baptism signifies is carried on until such a time as we forthwith rise from the dead. True penance properly speaking is what is signified by baptism. And besides, baptism is the sacrament of penance, as I shall later say.

Indeed this is the function of the sign: to demonstrate that you pass from death unto life; to witness the fact that your mortification of the flesh is indeed salutary. Sins may terrify, death and other evils of the world may terrify; just trust that since you have received the σφραγίδα of mercy toward you, you will be saved how much soever the very gates of hell may disturb you. Thus you can see that the significance of baptism and the use of the sign endure throughout the whole period of the life of a saint. Nay more I venture to say that no other consolation more salutary can be given to the dying than the mention of this sign, if they should be admonished of their baptism, and that they have received the σφραγίδα of the divine promise for this one purpose: to make them sure of the fact that God will lead them through death unto life.

There would have been no need of this sign if the crossing over could have been made without divine assistance. Therefore the sign was given that they might not despair but be assured that under God's leadership, they would make their escape. If Moses had baptized the Israelites before they entered the sea, ought he not have admonished them in the meantime while they were passing through the same, of the sign that was given in order that they might not in any way doubt but that they would be saved? So it is with the use of baptism in mortification. Wherefore, there is need of this sign so long as mortification lasts. However, mortification is not completed until the Old Adam has become extinct. Wherefore it happens that, in the meantime and forever throughout the entire life, there is need for a sign that will console the conscience in the process of this constant mortification. And it is clear from this that signs are nothing but μνημόσυνα of exercised faith.

Paul (Roms. 6:3) treats of baptism in this manner: "They who are baptized into Christ are baptized into his death." By this he means both that they are mortified as was Christ, and also know (baptism giving warning) that this mortification is a transition unto life. For what he adds in verse 4: "We are buried by baptism," teaches not only that the saints are mortified, but also that during this mortification they rest and make a Sabbath of Christ's burial. The impious are indeed mortified, but because they do not believe that this is a transition unto life through Christ, they forthwith give themselves up to despair and do utterly perish. The pious are mortified, but in such a way that they make Sabbath of Christ's burial. That is, they believe that it is a transition unto life, and they await the consolation through Christ.

In the meantime, according to Paul's saying "we are buried by baptism," baptism is a pledge καὶ μνημόσυνον of this consolation. Faith causes us to sabbatize, to rest, to await the consolation. As to how rich a consolation this use of baptism is to the afflicted conscience or soul, I believe no man can find words to describe justly.

The question is labored as to the institution of baptism and the difference between the baptism of John and of Jesus. Those who have the most correctly perceived about the problem have come to this conclusion: John's baptism is simply a sign of mortification, while the baptism of Jesus is a sign of vivification inasmuch as to the latter baptism has been added the promise of grace or of the forgiveness of sins. And in consequence, John's baptism has been called a baptism unto repentance, Christ's moreover a baptism unto the remission of sins. But John by preaching the law, prepares for Christ consciences acknowledging their sins, and Christ vivifies those whose consciences have been terrified by the law and John's preaching. For the beginning of justification is the knowledge of sin and the fear of divine judgment. The consummation of justification is faith and peace of conscience which the Holy Spirit alone has sown in the heart, as I have said above in the section that deals with the law and the gospel.

It seems to me that these two washings can be more simply distinguished if you accept John's baptism as a sign of grace through Christ to be subsequently declared, and Christ's baptism as a sign of grace already given. Thus both baptisms signify one and the same but with this difference; John's baptism is a sign of grace to come, Christ's a pledge καὶ σφραγὶς of grace already conferred. So both baptisms signify the same: mortification and vivification. For no man is justified save he be first mortified. And to state my opinion, it is as follows: John's office is not only to preach the law, but if you please, also to give a most powerful testimony of Christ and the gospel or the remission of sins.

This latter fact is borne out by John 1:7: "This one came for a witness, that he might bear witness of the light that all might believe through him." And Matt. 11:11: "Among those born of women there has not arisen a greater than John the Baptizer. But he who is least in the kingdom of heaven is greater than he." That means that prior to the revelation of the gospel the office of none excels that of John inasmuch as he is one who not only declares the law as did Moses and the Prophets, but also bears witness of the gospel that was subsequently to be revealed by Christ. Moreover, Christ is greater than John, and therefore the office of the apostles will be greater than the office of John. And because John is a witness of the gospel a sign was instituted by him that was later to be a pledge of the gospel or of grace conferred. Then too, in Luke 3:3: John's baptism is styled "baptism of repentance unto the remission of sins." And John 1:31 most clearly reads: "That it might be manifested in Israel because I come baptizing with water." In Acts 19:4 Paul says: "John baptized the people with the baptism of repentance, saying that they should believe upon him who should come after him," that is on Jesus. In Matt. 3:11, John witnesses that his baptism is a sign of the future baptism by the Holy Spirit when he says: "I baptize you with the Holy Spirit." For he means this: he is not the Christ but only a witness of Christ. And so both baptisms signify one and the same thing but with this difference: John's baptism was a witness of grace still to be declared, while Christ's is a witness of grace already given. I am of the opinion that Christ's disciples baptized none other than as did John, and the more so because Christ was not yet glorified, John

4:1 f. And they who had received John's baptism should have been rebaptized, that they might be made certain that they have now already received the remission of sins which up to that time, they had believed would come.

For signs are to be used for this purpose, to establish the conscience. Neither John's nor Christ's baptism justified (and I speak of the signs as such) but only certified. John's baptism testified that grace was still to come; Christ's baptism testified that grace has come, that it has been conferred, that the promise of grace has been promulgated. In both faith justified. But John baptizes with water because he himself is not the one on whom it is believed that saves. Since Christ is the Savior, he baptizes with the Holy Spirit and with fire. And so they were rebaptized who had already received John's baptism, although they were righteous, in the same manner as the righteous Jews everywhere were baptized who had not received John's baptism. For the baptism of Christ certifies of grace already conferred. Now I do not see what difference there was between the righteous Jews before John and those whom he baptized. For both awaited Christ's coming, except that these latter ones more nearly understood the gospel and the remission of sins.

It is enough to have touched upon these things with a few words, lest I delay one by a longer treatise from reading the Scripture, wherein questions of this nature are to be more diligently examined.

On Penitence

That penitence is not a sign, is by no means obscure. For penitence is the mortification of our age (old man) and a renewal of the spirit. Its sacrament or sign is none other than baptism. And baptism of all things is most correctly called the sacrament of penitence seeing indeed that penitence is our mortification into life, our renewal, which as I have already said, is signified by our baptism. Paul in Roms. 6:3 attests this fact: "We who were baptized into Jesus Christ were baptized into his death." In Titus 3:5, he calls it the bath of regeneration. Mortification is accomplished through the law. For the law terrifies and kills the conscience. Vivification is brought about through the gospel or through absolution. For the gospel is none other thing than absolution itself. When I call "mortification," the Scholastics have chosen to denominate "contrition." Now, I do not at all object to this term provided they do not use it to speak of that "grief" that is feigned by "free will" or by human powers. For human nature cannot hate sin. But it is a divine task to confound and terrify our conscience. I quote Jer. 6:15: "They knew not to be ashamed." And also 17:1: "The sin of Judah is written with an iron pen, with an adamantine finger, written down upon the width of their hearts." Jer. 31:19 says: "After thou didst reveal unto me, I smote upon my thigh," and Christ speaking unto the Pharisees said: "Ye Pharisees make clean the outside of the platter and the dish, but within ye are full of rapine and iniquity." But I spoke more extendedly above when I treated of the comparison between law and gospel. For penitence is none other than our justification. Meanwhile, I warn you to beware of that pest as it were, I mean that scholastic fiction about attritions and that grief feigned by free will. However, your heart will easily judge whether you are truly sorry, or whether you are merely feigning sorrow. But trust not in your sorrow or your grief as though sin will be forgiven simply because there is sorrow. Rather trust in absolution and the word of God, as I shall more fully discuss later on.

Perchance you may grant that baptism is the sign of penitence, that is, of mortification and vivification, provided you persevere. But what is the sign for the fallen that will witness that they are received again? For they have referred the word and sacrament of penitence unto the fallen alone. I answer: just as we who everywhere have fallen have not lost the gospel, so likewise neither have we lost the σφραγίδα of the gospel, I mean baptism. Moreover, it is certain that the gospel, not only once but time and time again, remits sin. Therefore baptism applies to the second no less than to the first forgiveness. For baptism is the earnest or the pledge of the gospel, that is, the remission of sins. Matt. 18:21 records Peter's question as to how many times one must forgive his brother, whereupon the Lord responds: "Seventy times seven." In I John 2:1 f. we read: "But if anyone sin, we have an advocate with the father, Jesus Christ, and he is the propitiation for our sins," etc. and in II Cor. 2:5-8, Paul orders the man guilty of incest to be received back into fellowship. Chrysostom records the tradition that the Apostle John recalled unto repentance a certain young deserter. Clement of Alexandria cites the same incident.[118]

Whereas they have divided penitence into contribution, satisfaction, and confession, I shall briefly state my own view on these matters. Concerning contrition, enough has already been said: that it is the mortification of our age (old man)—so Scripture says—, a kind of sorrow too great for anyone or for that matter even

---

[118]"Ex Clemente . . . ad poenitentiam revocarit. cf. Clement's writing titled τίς ὁ σωζόμενος πλούσιος, , cf. also in Eusebius: Hist. Eccl. III, 23.

human reason, to estimate. So far are we from being consumed and mortified by free will independent of the work of the Holy Spirit! There is one confession by which we confess our sin and condemn ourselves before God. Such confession as this is none other than mortification itself and true contrition, concerning which I was just now speaking. Scripture makes frequent mention of confession. I John 1:9: "If we do confess our sins, he is faithful and just to remit our sins unto us." Pe. 50:5 f.: "For I confess my iniquity and my sin is ever before me: against thee only have I sinned and done evil before thy face, that thou mightest be justified in thy works and overcome when thou judgeth." Likewise Ps. 31:5: "I said: I will confess against myself my unrighteousness unto the Lord and thou forgavest the iniquity of my sin." Without such a confession sin is not forgiven. Upon such a confession on the other hand, sin cannot but be forgiven. For by it we undoubtedly accuse ourselves and condemn ourselves, attributing unto God the glory of truth and righteousness.

Further, there is another confession by which we not only accuse ourselves privately, but also in the presence of others. Once on a time, the following custom prevailed in the church. Whoever might be guilty of offense was first censured by anyone of the brethren, then publicly before the whole church. And there, upon the repentance of the guilty brother, the offense was forgiven. But he who did not heed the church was forthwith expelled from the assembly. You have the form of such a confession in Matt. 16:18: where the use of the keys was given. At the present time there is no example of it in the Church, although there was no more appropriate way of curbing vice than this one. But this was succeeded by that kind of confession wherein the matter was privately discussed in the presence of a few elders. Now between the original confession and that of our day, this difference obtains: the original confession considered only public and open faults, while ours includes also secret faults. It was a custom of long standing for public faults to be reproached before the whole church, and to be absolved upon the votes of the whole church.

This custom long in vogue has now been abrogated, and some one of the elders is designated, before whom the guilty are privately accused although the crimes may be public. The elder so designated, inflicted according to his own will a penalty upon the dissolute before the church. The penalty imposed was in accordance with the public crimes committed. Nor were they admitted to the assembly unless they had paid the penalty for these public crimes.

An example of this custom prevails today in the public penitences of our time; as for instance, when homicides are punished in the church. This form of penitence is described by the author of "Historia Tripartita"[119] (whoever he is, apparently a Greek). He also informs us that it was of long standing in Constantinople, is still the custom in the occidental churches, and is the custom referred to frequently by Cyprian. This speaking of the confession of public crimes indicates that it was made in the presence of a priest rather than before the church at large. If you will, consult his discourse on the fallen. I shall submit the words of the Greek text.

"It seemed best to the ancient pontiffs that the sins of the people be made known openly as it were, before

---

[119]Historiæ auctor: This was the text book of history in the Middle Age. The work is that of Magnus Aurelius Cassiodorus. cf. Ebert: Geschichte der christlich lat. Litteratur." I, S. 384. The section referred to in the Hist. Trip. is IX, 35.

some officer of the church. For this purpose they designated some presbyter of good report who kept his secrecy, and who was a wise man. The fallen had access to him, and to him made a confession of their sins. On the other hand, this presbyter imposed a penalty upon each guilty person. This custom has been diligently preserved in the occidental churches even up to the present moment, especially in the church of Rome where there is even a stated place for penitents, where the guilty stand just as those who are in mourning. Moreover, when the holy celebration has been completed, those who did not receive the communion, prostrate themselves upon the earth with much groaning and lamentation. The bishop then approaches these persons and prostrates himself with tears and groanings of the spirit, while the whole congregation wails. Afterwards, the bishop arises first of all, and raises the other prostrated individuals up from the earth. After a prayer is said for the penitents, they are dismissed by the bishop. In the meantime, they torment themselves with various afflictions according to the judgment or will of the bishop. They await the time for resembling themselves, which time the bishop himself has prescribed. At such a time, just as if a debt had been paid, they participate together in the gathering with the church at large. These things have been observed even up to now by the Roman bishops. But in Constantinople, a presbyter was over the penitents for a long time, until a certain woman of the first nobility, after her confession and doing of penitence in the church several times, committed adultery with a certain deacon. When this was made public, the people rose up against the presbyters because of their profanation of the church. Thereupon Bishop Nectarius expelled the guilty deacon from his office, annulled the old custom of penitence by not appointing any elder for the penitents, and permitted each person to participate in the Lord's Table according to the judgment of his own conscience when he so chose." This is a verbatim quotation from the so-called *Historia Tripartita*.

From these words you can gather that there was a two-fold form of public penitence. The one form was that of the first church where the matter was transacted before the whole church, and either the dissolute who were not willing to repent were ejected from communion with the faithful, or else upon their willingness to repent, were absolved. You have an example of this in I Cor. 5, and II Cor. 2, concerning the man guilty of incest. The other form was that where the penalty is public but not the confession. An example of this is the present day penitence of homicides. Indeed penalties are not due to divine law, but have taken their origin in human traditions, as I shall later say. The ancient canons altogether speak of this kind of penitence. But professors of foolish pontifical law distort this kind of penitence into private.

On Private Confessions

In addition to public penitence there are private confessions. In the first place, there are those private confessions in which we reconcile those whom we have offended. Concerning this kind of confession you have these words in Matt. 5:23 f. If thou offer thy gift on the altar and then remember that thy brother has ought against thee, go reconcile thyself to thy brother." And in James 5:16: "Confess your sins one to the other," that is, one shall intercede for the offense of the other.

Then there are those ecclesiastical confessions whose use is something entirely modern. Apparently these were once of such a nature that those whose consciences were vexed with any matter, might counsel with the saints and those skilled in spiritual things, and could be absolved by them. Mention is made of this by one Basilus (if the title is correct), in his work *De Institutis Monachorum*. This title is thought to have been given in the Latin language by a certain Rufinus. I know so many kinds of confessions until it becomes necessary for me prudently to distinguish them. Especially is this true since some have been given by divine right, and still others are the mere inventions of men.

That that confession which is made unto God has been demanded by divine law is sufficiently established, if you please, by that passage which I quoted above from I John.[120] For sin is not remitted unless we confess unto God, that is unless we condemn ourselves and trust to divine mercy that our guilt is pardoned.

Concerning the public confession before the church of public crimes, where the case is tried before witnesses, what profit is there to dispute? The matter itself forces you to confess not only the divine law, if you have been accused, but likewise the divine law forces you to placate a brother.

The remaining confessions are merely human traditions. For if you voluntarily offer yourself to the church and wish to be absolved, whether you have committed a public or private crime, the divine law does

---

[120] Si quid recensenda confessione . . . In July 1521 Melanchthon wrote a letter to a certain monk touching this very thought: "Von der Beicht habt den Bericht dass ihr nicht schuldig seid zu sagen, was, ihn wollt heimlich haben, wie ihr genugsam werdet finden in dem Buch, so jetzund wird allhie gedrukt von der Beicht. (Luther's writing: von der Beicht, E. A. 27, 318): Dennganz, kein Spruch in der Schrift die Beicht gebeut. Die absolution muessen wir haben, aber sie muessen die Suenden nicht wissen, dieweil die doch auch absolvieren von viel suenden, die uns selbst unwissend Koennen sie von denselben absolvieren, warum auch nicht von allen?"

not demand an enumeration of the facts. In such a manner Christ absolved many; and the disciples in Acts 2:38 f. absolved several thousands, but in no respect did they demand that a catalogue of their sins be given. I have said these things to relieve the weak consciences of those who, if they have left out anything in their recounted confession, may not despair too much.

Private absolution is as necessary as baptism. For although you hear the general preaching of the gospel in the whole church, nevertheless you are not certain that it pertains specifically to yourself until you are privately and individually absolved. He does not thirst for grace who does not desperately desire to hear the divine word concerning him. For it is the word of God, not of man, by which you are absolved, provided of course that you believe the absolution. Just as the woman sinner in Luke 7:47 was certain that her sins had been forgiven when she heard Christ's word: "Thy sins are remitted unto thee," so may you be just as certain also when you are absolved by a brother whoever he may be. Nor are they absolved except those who desire to be and who believe that they are truly absolved.

There is no satisfaction outside the death of Christ, as Isa. 53:11 says: "He hath borne our iniquities." Indeed now, the satisfactions now demanded for penitences are of human origin and take rise in the penitential canons, which have been founded on the onetime public penitences. By this invention of satisfactions, both Christ's satisfaction and faith in the word of absolution have been made singularly extinct. Somewhere in Scripture there are indeed penalties for sins, but not all sins. Therefore no man has correctly called these penalties satisfactions. Out of satisfactions indulgences have grown, that "Roman merchandise" which has remitted these canonic penalties of public penitences. And these indulgences have been instituted for sale by impious men as a substitute for divine forgiveness. The result is that the indulgence is believed rather than the word of God. Moreover, to sum up in one word, there are two parts to penitence, mortification and vivification. The former is done when the conscience is terrified by the law, while the latter is accomplished when one is raised up and confirmed through absolution. For absolution is the gospel, by which Christ forgives you of your faults. The sign of penitence is none other than baptism.

On Participation in the Table of the Lord

Participation in the Lord's Table, that is, the chewing of Christ's body and the drinking of his blood, is a sure sign of grace.[121] Thus Luke 22:20 reads: "This is the cup of the New Testament." And I Cor. 11:25: "As often as ye do it, do it in remembrance of me." That is to say, when ye do it, be reminded of the gospel and of the remission of sins. Therefore it is not a sacrifice, seeing that it has been handed down only as a reminder of the promised gospel. Participation in the Lord's Table does not abolish sin, but faith does. Of

---

[121]Manducare corpus Christi et bibere sanguinem: This phrase is not to be taken as proof that Melanchthon taught the doctrine of the "real presence" at this time. He is simply following the customary phraseology of his time and therefore he exchanges the words Corpus and Panis, cf. C. R. 21:28. At any rate he reflects on the real presence as little as Luther does in this early age. Already in his "Theses of 1519" Melanchthon explained the doctrine of transubstantiation as one that was not obligatory. In other theses (Theses 43, 1. g.) he asserts that mere participation in the Lord's Supper does not justify. He is interested now in the meaning and use of the sacrament. For in 1521 this was the burning interest in Wittenberg. Therefore he published theses on the Mass. cf. C. R. i, 479. The sum of them is expressed in Thesis 43: "Missæ nullus usus est nisi admonere promissæ gratiæ et certificare cor de promissa gratia, de voluntate dei." He denies that the Mass justifies. cf. Theses 44–46 No.

a truth, faith is confirmed by this sign. Just as the mere sight of Christ did not justify the dying Stephen, but only confirmed his faith by which he was justified and vivified, so in like manner mere participation in the table of the Lord does not justify but only confirms faith. Therefore all masses are impious with the exception of those by which consciences are aroused to a confirmed faith. When we offer something to God, it is a sacrifice. But indeed we have not offered Christ. Then rather he has once for all offered up himself. Consequently they who perform masses with a view to doing some good work as it were, or with a view to offering Christ for the living and the dead, thinking thereby that the more often it is repeated the better it is, are in impious error. And these errors for the most part are to be attributed to St. Thomas. For he taught that a mass is beneficial for others beside the one who eats it.

The significance of this sacrament lies in its function of confirming us as often as our consciences do waver, or as often as we doubt God's goodwill toward us. This indeed happens at other times but especially when one comes to die. Hence the dying are to be confirmed by it in an especial manner. For truly the Christian life is but our perpetual death.

Confirmation is (in my opinion) the laying on of hands. I believe unction is what Mark 6:13 notes. But I fail to see wherein these have been given as signs to signify grace for a certainty. There is no reason why any should doubt that matrimony was not instituted to signify grace. And what has come into the minds of those who classify ecclesiastical order (ordination) among the signs of grace, since order is nothing but the selection of those from the church who are to teach, baptize, bless at the table, and to distribute alms to the needy? Nor were there functions so sharply distinguished that it would be peculiar for a deacon to teach, baptize, or bless at the table. Nay, rather these functions belong to all Christians. For the Keys are the possession of all (Matt. 18:18). But the administration of these functions was intrusted to certain ones that there might be some who necessarily know how to manage an ecclesiastical affair and to whom a matter could be referred in case anything should happen.

Incidentally, the word bishop or presbyter or deacon does not agree with the word priest. For in the Scripture a priest is so named by virtue of his making sacrifice and intercession. But all of us who are Christians are priests, because we all offer a sacrifice, to wit, our bodies. Besides this there is no sacrifice in Christianity, and we have the right of interceding with God, nay more of placating him.[122] Peter's words (I Peter 2:9) pertain to this theme. "An holy people, a sacerdotal Kingdom." For we Christians are Kings, because being free through Christ, we rule all creatures life, death, and sin, as I said before. And we are priests because we offer ourselves unto God, and intercede for our own sins. The Epistle to the Hebrews discusses this theme more extensively. Bishops and presbyters, and deacons are none other than they who teach, baptize, and bless at the table, and distribute alms. The mass-priests are prophets of Jezebel, that is, of Rome.

On Love

Thus far on sin, the law, grace, the gospel and in addition, justification. This has been and always shall

---

[122] Et jus habemus interpellandi . . . cf. Thesis 62 and 23: "Omnes enim sacerdotes sumus. Nec est aluid sacerdotium quam jus orandi seu interpellandi deum et offerendi deo." C. R. I, 841.

be a question common to all men: "How can man be justified?" Philosophers and Pharisees have taught that man is justified by his own virtues and attempts. I have taught that man is justified by faith alone, that is, the righteousness of Christ is our righteousness through faith, while our works and our attempts are naught but sin. Who holds these things holds the sum of the Scripture: "They are justified who believe in the mercy of God." Finally, the case demands that I say something about love.

I pointed out above that the love of God is the fruit of faith. For he who comprehends mercy by faith, cannot help but love God in return, and thus love is the fruit of faith. From the love of God arises also the love of one's neighbor when we desire to serve God in all creatures. Indeed, I can give no shorter or more apt rule of such a love than this: "Love thy neighbor as thyself." St. Augustine conceived of an order of things to be loved, namely: we should first love souls, then bodies, first ourselves then others. I always prefer faith to love. And hence, I entirely prefer those things which are of the soul, to the necessities of the body. On the other hand, Christ in Matt. 5:44, and Paul in Roms. 12:17, order that we love others, enemies as well as friends. Your spirit will easily judge to whom you ought to do good, both to friends and to enemies. To be sure, Paul especially wished that regard be had even for domestics. Gal. 6:10 and I Tim. 5:8: For I do not wish the liberty of the spirit to be bound by disputations of this nature, such as those of the "Summularii,"[123] or those of Cicero in Book 3 of

---

[123]Melanchthon refers to the Scholastics as authors of their "Summæ." The "summularii" generally consisted of a number of casuistic questions such as those contained in Cicero, De officiis III:23 where he quotes from the Stoic Hecato of Rhodes. Such a question is: "Si tabulam de naufragio stultus adripuerit, extorquebitne eam sapiens,

his *De Officiis,* where he discourses about the obligations of the man who has arrived ashore on the same plank to which also some wise man has held. Begone such foolish questions as these, the like of which do not easily occur in human affairs!

On Magistrates

It seemed especially necessary for me to submit a topic on magistrates, and for the sake of teaching, I shall follow the customary division. Some magistrates are civil, others are ecclesiastical. A civil magistrate is one who carries the sword and guards the civil peace. Paul proves this in Roms. 13:1 f. The parts of the sword are as follows: civil laws, civil ordinances for forensic judgments and penalties for the guilty. The right of the sword is the administration of the laws against killing, vindication, and the like. Therefore a magistrate piously administers the sword. Likewise lawyers, if they give an opinion about the law or defend the oppressed; although they do especially sin who litigate. Concerning the bearing of the power of the sword, I am of the following opinion.

Firstly, if princes shall have ordered anything that is contrary to God, it is not to be obeyed. Acts 5:29: "It is better to obey God rather than man." You have innumerable examples of this topic, and especially, if you please, that most beautiful passage in Amos 7.

Secondly, if they shall have ordered anything that makes for public weal, it is to be obeyed. Roms. 13:5: "It is to be obeyed not only for wrath's sake, but for

---

si potuerit? Negat, "quia sit injurium." And: "Quid? Si una tabula sit, duo naufragi eique sapientes, sibine uterque rapiat an alter cedat alteri?" "Cedat vero, sed ei, cuius magis interest vel sua vel reipublicæ causa vivere."

conscience's sake." For love binds us to all civil burdens.

Lastly, if they shall have ordered anything that is tyrannical, the magistrate is here also to be suffered for the sake of love, where nothing can be changed without public disturbance and without sedition, Matt. 5:39: "Who smites you on the right cheek, turn the left also."

But if you can escape without offense and public disturbance, do so. For example, if you are cast into prison in no way deserving of evil, and if you can make your escape without creating a public disturbance, then nothing stands in bar of your escaping. I Cor. 7:21: "If you can become free, then use it rather."

I am of the following opinion about ecclesiastical magistrates.

Firstly, if they teach the Scripture, they are to be heard as Christ. Luke 10:16: "Who heareth you, heareth me." Now this pertains to the Scriptures and not to human traditions, as he makes clear with these words: "Whosoever receives a prophet in the name of a prophet," etc. (not a false prophet) Mass. 10:41.

Secondly, if they shall have taught anything contrary to Scripture, they are not to be heard. Acts 5:29: "We ought to obey God rather than man." Also Matt. 15:6: "Ye have made the mandate of God of none effect because of your tradition." Now the Pope at the present time has issued a decree contrary to divine law, in a certain Bull in which he condemns Luther. In this he is by no means to be heard.

Thirdly, if they shall have established anything outside of Scripture with a view to binding consciences, they are not to be heard. For nothing binds the conscience save the divine law. Paul was speaking about this in I Tim. 4:1, when he brands as "doctrines of demons," the law about celibacy and forbidden meats. Although they may not seem averse to Scripture (things which of themselves are not evils), for celibacy as such is not evil; the abstinence from meats of itself is not evil—nevertheless, these are impious things if you think that he has sinned who has not read his Canonic hours, or who has eaten meat on the sixth or seventh day. For no bishop can bind a Christian conscience. II Cor. 13:10 says: "Authority has been given unto us not to destroy but to edify."

Fourthly, if you were not to burden the conscience with an episcopal law, but to interpret it as an external burden as do the spiritually minded and those of understanding, then the conscience can be burdened by no human law. You will judge a bishop's law exactly as you do the tyranny of a magistrate. For whatever bishops order beyond the Scriptures is tyranny. For they have no right to order. You will bear these burdens because of love. (Matt. 5:39: "Who smites you on the right cheek, turn also the left.") Moreover if you could do otherwise without giving offense, nothing prevents your so doing. For instance, if without disturbing the public you could break out of a jail in which you were being held by a tyrant, nothing prevents it according to I Cor. 7:21: "If you can become free use it rather the more." And too, Christ has dispensed with Pharisaic traditions in Matt. 8 and 11. But he has not dispensed with civil laws. And with the Pharisaic laws dispensed with, we enjoy more freedom seeing that these easily ensnare the conscience. Moreover of all human laws, the rules and administration are as follows: faith, love, and in addition, also necessity. This frees us from all traditions, wheresoever either the soul or the physical life has been led into danger by traditions.

On Offense

Moreover, you ask, "how far must the nature of offense be considered?" First of all, I point out what I have said before, that faith and love are the rules of all human functions. But in these faith is the more important.

Offense (scandalum) is that stumbling-block (offensio) by which the faith or for that matter, the love of a neighbor is injured. The faith of a neighbor is offended when for instance something is taught contrary to the sacred letter. The whole Scholastic teaching which, with its approval of satisfactions and the works of free will, has obscured grace, is an offense of this kind. Concerning this kind of offense, Christ has said in Matt. 18:6: "Whoever shall have offended one of these little ones who believe in me, it were better that a mill stone be hung about his neck, and he be submerged in the sea." Love is offended if anyone does not assist a needy brother, or disturbs the public peace. Concerning this kind of offense Christ speaks in Matt. 17:26, about the payment of tribute: "That we might not offend them."

1. In regard to what is demanded by divine law, all must obey without any respect to giving offense. For faith is always to be preferred to love. Here I quote again Acts 5:29: "God ought to be obeyed rather than man." Christ says in Matt. 10:34: "I came not to bring peace but the sword." Thus Daniel did not obey the law concerning the statute that was to be worshiped. Nor let us be submissive to the impious Princes who are this very moment condemning the gospel.

2. With respect to those things which are of human right and indifferent such as celibacy and abstinence from meats, in case of necessity human tradition does not bind one. For Christ, in Matt. 12:1, when his

disciples were plucking the ears of corn, in a case of necessity dispensed with the divine law. How much more then is it permissible to violate human tradition if necessity of life so demands? It is much more permissible to violate them if the soul is in danger. For instance, if a priest burns, as they say. According to II Cor. 13:10: "Authority was given unto us not to destroy, but to edify." And Paul, in Col. II, condemns laws which immoderately burden the body.

3. For the sake of teaching liberty, it is permissible to violate human traditions that the inexperienced may understand, that they have not sinned, even if they commit something contrary to human tradition. Distinctly in such a case, Paul (Gal. 2:2) rebukes Peter because he yielded to the ignorant people foolishly observing law, and not knowing evangelical freedom.

4. In the presence of Pharisees demanding observance of their traditions they are simply violated without any regard to giving offense. Paul did this with the divine law, which he refuses to circumcise Timothy (Gal. 2:3). How much more permissible with the foolish papal laws? And Christ orders those to be endured who were offended, because they were blind and leaders of the blind.

5. In the presence of the weak and those who have not as yet heard the gospel, the obligation of love must be performed, and human traditions regarded, provided of course we admit of nothing contrary to divine law. Thus Paul was shaved (Acts 21:24ss) when in Jerusalem, since in such a multitude there were only a very few who would understand evangelical liberty. Paul prefers also to abstain forever from eating meat, rather than to lose a brother's soul. In Roms. 14:1 he says: "Receive the weak with faith." And although in those times the discussion was about a divine law, since now

merely human traditions are in question, we shall the more freely dispense with them. Nay, it is impious to obey, whenever there are bishops who demand observance of such things, in such a manner that they would wish the conscience to be burdened with sin, if they are violated. For there are some which, when they are demanded, are doctrines of demons. But if they are not demanded, let the rule of Paul obtain: "He does not abound who eats, nor does he want, who does not eat." I Cor. 8:8.

You have the most common topics of theological science. Seek a more exact account from the Scriptures. I am content with having pointed out that which you observe. Moreover, I think I have done well in having treated of such things more sparingly perhaps than I should have, lest I should call anyone from the Scriptures themselves by an unfortunate diligence, unto my own disputations. For I think that human commentaries on sacred things ought to be shunned as though they were a pest; because the teaching of the Spirit cannot be purely drawn from anything save the Scriptures. For who has more appropriately expressed the Spirit of God than He Himself?

οὐχ ἐν λόγῳ ἡ βασιλεία τοῦ Θεοῦ, ἀλλ' ἐν δυνάμει.

BIBLIOGRAPHIA MELANCHTHONIANA

The following list of books dealing with Melanchthon contains, for the most part, only those works which treat of the various matters of interest to hand, i.e., to his theology. It does not purport to be complete. I have submitted only those works which deal specifically with the Loci and with the life and theology of Melanchthon.

The books, dissertations, articles, and learned monographs which discuss phases of his philosophy, have been omitted primarily because they do not have any direct bearing upon the *Loci of 1521*, but also because I propose to publish at a later date, a book which will set forth in an orderly fashion the complete world-view of the Reformer. At such a time I hope to submit an exhaustive bibliography which will cover the entire field of Studia Melanchthoniana from point of view of Melanchthon's philosophical works.

A. Primary Sources

Corpus Reformatorum, Vols. I–XIV, XVI, XX–XXVI, XXVIII. edited by Carol. Gottl. *Bretschneider und Heinrich Ernest Bindseil.* Halle u. Braunschweig, 1834–1860.

Loci Communes Phillipp Melanchthons in ihrer Urgestalt nach Plitt, Von neuem herausgegeben und erlæutert von D. Th. Kolde, 4 Auflage, Erlangen, 1925.

In Ethica Aristotelis commentarius Phillipp Melanchtho. Vuttebergæ, 1529.

Epitome Ethices auctore Phili. Melancht. Pridie nonas Decembres anno XXXII. In: Die ælteste Fassung von Melanch-

thons Ethik. Zum ersten Mal herausgegeben von Hermann
Heineck. Philos. Monatshefte, Berlin, 1893, S. 129 ff.
Melanchthon-Kompendium: Johannes Haussleiter, Greifswald,
1902.
*Aus der Schule Melanchthons. Theologische Disputationen und
Promotionen zu Wittenberg in den Jahren 1546–1560.*
Von Johannes Haussleiter, Greifswald, 1897.
Melanchthoniana aus Brandenburg a. H. und Venedig. von
Nikolaus Mueller. In: Zeitschrift fuer Kirchengeschichte,
Gotha, 1894, S. 133 ff.
De Ecclesiæ Autoritate et de veterum scriptis libellus. Autore
Philip. Melanch. Vitebergæ. Anno MDXXXIX.
Loci Præcipui theologici per Philippum Melanchthonem. Ad
Editionem Lipsiensem A. MDLIX.
*Philippi Melanchthonis Epistolæ, Judicia, Consilia, Testimonia
aliorumque ad eum Epistolæ quæ in Corpore Reformatorum
desiderantur,* von H. E. Bindseil, Halis Saxorum.
MDCCCXXIV.
Supplementa Melanchthoniana: Otto Clemen, Dogmatische
Schriften Philipp Melanchthons. Leipzig, 1910.
*Briefe und Dokumente aus der Zeit der Reformation im 16.
Jahrhundert,* edited by K. and W. Krafft, Elberfeld, 1876.
Philippi Melanchthonis Opera: Caspar Peucer, Wittenberg,
1562–1564.
Epistolarum D. Phil. Mel. Farrago: John Manlius, Basel, 1565.
Epistolarum Phil. Mel. liber quartus: John Saubert, Norimberg, 1640.
Scripta ad vitam et obitum Melanchthonis: In Corpus Reformatorum, Vol. 10, P. 12–316.
Brent, Johannes: Opera Melanchthonis, Tuebingen 1590. Tomi
I–VIII.
Pfaff, Christopher Matthew: Acta et scripta publica Ecclesiæ
Wirtembergicæ. Tuebingen, 1720.
Pipping, Heinrich: Arcana Bibliothecæ Thomanæ Lipsiensis
sacra. Leipzig, 1703.

Francke, Friedrich: Libri symbolici Ecclesiæ Lutheranæ. Leipzig, 1847.
Friedmann: Philippi Melanchthonis prima adumbratio locorum theologicorum, Wittembergæ, 1823.
Twesten, August: Die drey œkumenischen Symbola, die Augsburgische Confession und die repititio confessionis Augustanæ. Kiel, 1816.
Kohl: Gesammelter Briefweschel der Gelehrten auf das Jahr MDCCLI, Hamburg, MDCCLI.

B. SECONDARY SOURCES

Appel: Die Lehre der Scholastiker von der Synteresis, Leipsic, 1891.
August: Phil. Melanchthonis Loci Theol. illust. Leipsic, 1821.
Balthasar: Historia Locorum theologicorum Phil. Melanchthonis, Greifswald, 1892.
Bassermann, H.: Handbuch d. geistl. Beredsamkeit, Stuttgart, 1885.
Baur: Abhandlung ueber das Prinzip des Protestantismus, Tuebingen, 1855.
Baur: Vorlesungen ueber die christliche Dogmengeschichte, Leipsic, 1867.
Baumann: Die Staatslehre des Thomas von Aquino.
Baumgarten: Nachrichten von merkw. Buechern T. VI. 1737.
Baumgarten-Crusius: Lehrbuch der christl. Dogmengeschichte, P. I, S. 444 sqq.
——————: Compendium der chrisl. Dogmengesch. P. I. S. 248.
Camerarius: Vita Melanchthonis, Leipzig, 1556. Edition by Strobel, Halle, 1777.
Cohrs: Philipp Melanchthon, Deutschlands Lehrer, In: Schiften des Vereins fuer Reformationsgeschichte, vol. 14, S. 1–69, Halle, 1897.

Czerwenka: Philipp Melanchthon nach seinem Leben und Wirken, Erlangen, 1860.
Delbrueck: Melanchthon der Glaubenslehrer, Bonn. 1826.
Denifle: Luther und Luthertum, Bd. 2, Mainz, 1909.
Diestelmann: Die letze Unterredung Luthers mit Melanchthon, Gœttingen, 1876.
Doellinger: Die Reformation, Bd. I, S. 649 sqqq. Regensburg, 1846.
Dorner: Zum dreihundertjæhrigen Gedæchtniss des Todes Melanchthons am 19. April, 1860. In: Jahrbuecher fuer deutsche Theologie, Gotha, 1860.
Drews: Humanismus und Reformation, Leipsic, 1887.
Dummler: Auxilius und Vulgaris, Leipsic, 1866.
Durrer: Ethices Christianæ Enchiridion, Altdorf, 1662.
Ellinger: Philipp Melanchthon, Ein Lebensbild, Berlin, 1902.
—————————: Philipp Melanchthon. In: Die Religion in Geschichte und Gegenwart. Handwoerterbuch fuer Theologie und Religionswissenschaft. 2 AUF. Bd. 3, edited by Gunkel and Zscharnack, Tuebingen, 1855.
Engelland: Philipp Melanchthon, Glauben und Handeln, Muenchen, 1931.
Erasmus: Commentary on Thessalonians, 1515.
Feuerlein: Die Sittenlehre des Christenthums in ihrer geschichtlichen Hauptformen. Tuebingen, 1855.
Fischer: Melanchthons Lehre von der Bekerung.
Frank: Die Theologie der Concordienformel.
Funck: Geschichte des kirchl. Zinsverbotes, Tuebingen, 1877.
Galle: Charakteristik Melanchthons, Halle, 1840.
Gass: Die Lehre vom Gewissen, Berlin, 1869.
Georgii: Zur Charakteristik Melanchthons, Tuebingen, 1843.
Gieseler: Lehrbuch der Kichengeschichte, 3 Auf. Bonn, 1853.
Gundert: Gedæchtnissrede auf Melanchthon, Tuebingen, 1816.
Hagen: Melanchthon als Politiker: Prutz, Literarhistor. Taschenbuch III Jhrg. 1845.

Harnack, Adolf: Philipp Melanchthon. Festschrift. Berlin, 1897.
Hartfelder, Karl: Philipp Melanchthon als Præceptor Germaniæ, Berlin, 1889.
Hase, Karl: Kirchengeschichte, I. Vol. Eng. Translation by Blumenthal and Wing, N. Y., 1856.
Haussleiter: Aus der Schule Melanchthons, Greifswald, 1897.
Heerbrand, Jac: Oratio funebris in obitum Melanchthonis, Tuebingen, 1560.
Henke: Das Verhæltniss Luthers und Melanchthons zu einander, Marburg, 1860.
Heppe, H.: Geschichte des deutschen Protestantismus in den Jahren 1555–1581. Bd. I, Marburg, 1852.
——————: Die confessionelle Entwicklung der altprotestantischen Kirche Deutschlands, Marburg, 1854.
——————: Dogmatik des deutschen Protestantismus im sechzehnten Jahrhundert. I–III. Gotha, 1857.
Herrlinger: Die Theologie Melanchthons in ihrer geschichtlichen Entwicklung, Gotha, 1879.
Hildebrant: Melanchthon, sein Leben und Wirken, Stettin, 1839.
Kahnis, Fr. Aug.: Rede zum Gedæchtniss Melanchthons, Leipzig, 1860.
Kauffman, Friedrich: Rede zur Feier Geburstages Melanchthons, Kiel, 1897.
Klix, G. A.: Philipp Melanchthon, der Præceptor Germaniæ, Gross-Glogau, 1860.
Klotsche: An Outline of the History of Doctrines, Burlington, Iowa, 1927.
Loofs, Friedrich: Melanchthon als Humanist und Reformator. Ebenda, 1897.
Lindsay: History of the Reformation, New York, 1928.
Matthes, Carl: Leben und Werke Melanchthons. Altenburg, 1841.

McGiffert, A. C.: Protestant *Thought Before Kant,* New York, 1913.

——————: Martin Luther, the Man and his Work, New York, 1911.

Meuer, Moritz: Melanchthons Leben. Leipzig, 1869.

Mix: Luther und Melanchthon in ihrer gegenseitigen Beuteilung. In: Theologische Studien und Kritiken, Gotha, 1901.

Mosheim: Ecclesiastical History, New York, 1854.

Neander, A.: Charakteristik Melanchthons. In: Piper's Evangelisches Jahrbuch. Berlin, 1851.

Niemeyer, H. A.: Ueber Philipp Melanchthon, Præceptor Germaniæ. Halle, 1817.

Nitzsch: Ueber Philipp Melanchthon, Berlin, 1855.

Planck, Adolf: Melanchthon, Præceptor Germaniæ, Nordlingen, 1860.

Prantl, C.: Geschichte d. Logik im Abend, Bd. III and IV. Leipzig, 1870.

Ritschl, Albrect: Die christliche Lehre von der Rechtfertigung und Versœhnung. 2. Aufl. Bd. I, Bonn, 1882.

Ritter: Philipp Melanchthon, Berlin, 1860.

——————: St. Augustin, Melanchthon, Neander, New York, 1886.

Seckendorf: Commentarius de Lutheranismo, Leipzig, 1694.

Schmidt, Carl: Melanchthons Leben und Wirken, Berlin, 1860.

Sell, Karl: Philipp Melanchthon und die deutsche Reformation bis 1531. In: Schriften des Vereins f. Reformationsgeschichte, Bd. 14, S. 1–118. Halle, 1897.

Spanuth-Poehlde: Philipp Melanchthon und seine Kirksamkeit in der Reformation, Stuttgart, 1897.

Seeberg, R.: Melanchthons Stellung in der Geschichte des Dogmas und der Dogmatik. In: Neue Kirchliche Zeitschrift. Erlangen und Leipzig, 1897, S. 126ff.

Stæudlin: Geschichte der christlichen Moral, Gœttingen, 1808.

Strobel, Georg Theodor: Melanchthoniana, oder Sammlung

einiger Nachrichten zur Erlæuterung der Geschichte Philipp Melanchthons. Altdorf, 1771.

———————: Nachricht von Melanchthons œfterm Aufenthalt und Berrichtungen in Nuernberg. Nuernberg, 1775.

———————: Miscellaneen litterarischen Inhalts, grœssten Theils aus ungedruckten Quellen. 6 Sammlungen, Nuern. 1778–1782.

———————: Beitræge zur Litteratur, besonders des 16th Jahrhunderts. 2 Bænde, Nuern., 1784–1787.

Sohm: Outlines of Church History, London, 1926.

Trœltsch: Vernunft und Offenbarung bei Joh. Gerhard und Melanchthon. Goett. 1891.

Vilmar, A. F. C.: Luther, Melanchthon, Zwingli. Frankfurt A. Main, 1869.

Walter, E.: Erasmus and Melanchthon. Bernbg, 1879.

Zanta: La Renaissance du Stoicisme au XVIe Siécle, Paris, 1914.

Zœckler: Lehrstueck von den sieben Hauptsuenden. Muenchen, 1893.

www.ingramcontent.com/pod-product-compliance
Lightning Source LLC
Chambersburg PA
CBHW051632230426
43669CB00013B/2270